WRITING

A TEXT-BOOK OF STRUCTURE, STYLE, AND USAGE

BY

JOHN C. FRENCH, Ph. D.

ASSOCIATE PROFESSOR OF ENGLISH
THE JOHNS HOPKINS UNIVERSITY

NEW YORK
HARCOURT, BRACE AND COMPANY
1924

PRINTED IN THE U.S.A.

PREFACE

THIS book attempts to supply in one volume material adequate for such a course in English composition as includes the review of elementary principles and the anticipation of mature study in English and other subjects. Consequently it gives much space to rules for correctness and at the same time emphasizes the importance of structure and the search for original material. The plan of finding much of this material in the student's immediate relations with life, particularly in the choice of a vocation, has been found in practice to give a new meaning to the routine of theme-writing.

The author's indebtedness to a rhetorical tradition passed on by Hill, Genung, Wendell, and others will be sufficiently obvious. He acknowledges gratefully the helpfulness of his colleagues and the courtesy of those publishers who have generously permitted the use of copyrighted material.

CONTENTS

PART ONE: STRUCTURE AND STYLE

CHAPTER I:

FRESHMAN THEMES AND THEME–WRITING

CHAPTER II:

STRUCTURE IN THE WHOLE COMPOSITION

CHAPTER III:

STRUCTURE IN THE PARAGRAPH

CHAPTER IV:
STYLE IN SENTENCES

CHAPTER V:
STYLE IN WORDS AND PHRASES

CHAPTER VI:

STRUCTURE AND STYLE IN EXPOSITION

The Nature of Exposition

The Material of Exposition

The Methods of Exposition

CHAPTER VII:

STRUCTURE AND STYLE IN DESCRIPTION

THE NATURE OF DESCRIPTION

THE QUALITIES OF DESCRIPTION

SPECIMENS OF DESCRIPTION

CHAPTER VIII:

STRUCTURE AND STYLE IN NARRATION

NARRATIVE WRITING

THE ELEMENTS OF A NARRATIVE

CHAPTER IX:

STRUCTURE AND STYLE IN ARGUMENTATION

ARGUMENTATIVE WRITING

PROOF

PERSUASION

PART TWO: USAGE

CHAPTER X:

USAGE IN GRAMMAR AND IDIOM

CHAPTER XI:

USAGE IN PUNCTUATION

PUNCTUATION TO ENCLOSE

PUNCTUATION TO SEPARATE

CHAPTER XII:

USAGE IN DICTION

THE LAW OF USAGE

BARBARISMS

IMPROPRIETIES

CHAPTER XIII:
USAGE IN SPELLING

SPELLING AS LITERARY HABIT

CONVENTIONS IN SPELLING

CHAPTER XIV:
USAGE IN LETTERS AND MANUSCRIPTS

THE FORMS OF LETTERS

THE PREPARATION OF MANUSCRIPTS

APPENDIX:

PART ONE

STRUCTURE AND STYLE

CHAPTER I

FRESHMAN THEMES AND THEME–WRITING

Theme Subjects

1. The Purpose of Theme-Writing. The freshman English composition course is designed to serve both as an introduction to college life and as a foundation for all forms of college work. It includes, therefore, counsel on such matters as methods of study, the use of the library, note-taking, the choice and use of books, and the observance of literary ethics. It commonly involves also some necessary review of the principles of grammar and rhetoric. Its main purpose, however, is practice in writing, particularly such systematic and accurate presentation of facts as a student must be capable of if he is really to profit by his studies.

Such practice in writing is especially needed at the beginning of the freshman year. A student's powers of expression should grow with his years, for the ideas with which he must deal become increasingly difficult. Their difficulty is enhanced by the change from high school to college, which brings new methods of study, the use of lectures in place of recitations, lessons that demand the handling of numerous books rather than the persistent study of one, and in general a new self-reliance in intellectual matters. What he is accomplishing in college will be judged chiefly by what he writes — by essays, examination papers, laboratory records, and reports. Later in the year an attempt is made to contribute to the student's general culture and his appreciation of literature. At the beginning of the course, obviously, he needs above everything else correct methods of learning and organizing facts.

These methods are usually studied in the writing and discussion of what are known as weekly themes, a type of literary effort about which many harsh things have been said. It is true, doubtless, that few students ever write them without reluctance, and that nobody reads them quite voluntarily. It is true, also, that they do not ordinarily represent any literary form actually used by mature writers. That the exercises of students of so difficult an art as good writing can escape dullness is, perhaps, too much to expect. Beginners in every art find much of their practice-work uninspiring. It is fair, however, to ask that a course in theme-writing shall come as close as possible to the personal interest of the writers, and that the themes shall approach in character the forms of actual writing.

In the course here proposed, themes will not be disconnected reports of bits of personal experience or opinions on local matters, but will involve a somewhat extended search for facts in a definite and accessible part of the student's world; the use of these facts in a series of related papers; and finally the construction from these or similar materials of a substantial piece of explanatory writing on a scale comparable to that of contemporary magazine articles. Material for such writing will be most easily found in the problems that lie nearest: in the choice of a calling and in the wise preparation for it; in the understanding use of the opportunities of college life; in the essential facts of the larger world of politics and business that lie just beyond college. The topics set forth below are designed to provide related theme-subjects in these fields.

> Yourself and the World's Work.
> Yourself and the College.
> Yourself and the World of Politics.
> Yourself and the World of Business.
> Yourself and the Community.

2. Directions for Theme-Writing. Under each of these topics you will find a series of sub-topics designed to serve as the subjects of weekly themes. Examine these carefully and choose the general subject that seems to you the most interesting and profitable. It is not essential that you should already know much about it, for learning the facts will be an important part of your work. The amount of writing is purposely made small enough to afford time for the careful search for material. Such a search will supply an abundance of matter. Your work will be judged in part by what you leave out. Do not imagine that because this is a course in English composition the form is more important than the material. Write as well as you can, but write primarily to make the facts clear to a reader who does not know them so well as you do. The subject matter is not, however, of such value for itself that it can be presented carelessly. Reserve time for planning a theme and for a careful revision of your first writing.

The first four topics in each group are prescribed. Of these, the first is in each case a brief autobiography, entitled *Myself*. In it write frankly and simply, giving such facts about yourself as the place and date of your birth, the nationality and occupation of your father, the names of schools you have attended, the considerations that have led you to come to college, and the ambitions which will influence your work. Do not be vague, or self-conscious, or facetious. Your theme will not be read aloud in such a way as to identify you as the author of it. Write as clearly and correctly as you can, not less than one page or more than two of the required paper, put your name in the upper right-hand corner, and mark the theme No. 1.

Of the ten topics following the first four, you are to select the five (or such number as your instructor may direct) that seem to you most promising. Number the themes in course, without reference to the numbers which they bear in the printed list. The questions and suggestions supplied for these topics are intended merely to help you begin your work. They are not to determine either your material or your structure. Ignore them if they do not prove useful; but do not wander from the topic or offer your instructor a theme on any subject not in the list. Make your own plan, choose your own title, and write ordinarily not less than four hundred words and not more than eight hundred.

This series of weekly themes is to be followed by an essay of about two thousand words on a subject chosen from the same field. It will be well to have the choice of this subject in mind as you collect material for the themes, so that it will grow naturally out of the experience that you have gained in writing them. A good subject may be found in the combination of several of the assigned topics, in the expansion of one of them, or even in the development of a part of such a topic, if you adapt your material to your scale of treatment. Submit your choice to your instructor for his approval. A week later give him a tentative outline for criticism. The final writing will complete your theme-work for this part of the course.

YOURSELF AND THE WORLD'S WORK

1. *Your Choice of a Calling.* What calling do you now look forward to and why do you propose to enter it? If you are not prepared to decide so important a matter, choose for study in this course the vocation that most interests you at present and that you may most profitably learn more about. Can you discover in yourself, or in your ancestry, any characteristic bent? Are there special opportunities open to you? Have your boyhood aptitudes and hobbies any significance as to your probable fitness for one type of vocation rather than another? Are you prac-

tical or bookish? Do you enjoy collecting objects? Is the work of classifying and arranging such objects a source of pleasure, or does it soon grow irksome? Do you readily subordinate yourself to a team or a captain? Do you need companions in an enterprise or can you enjoy working alone? Take stock of what you really know about the proposed vocation. Is it possible that you are attracted to it by unessentials? Does it require special training, capital, or physical and mental equipment?

2. *An Interview on the Subject.* Report in this theme the result of an interview with somebody who is successfully engaged in your proposed vocation. Decide in advance what things such a person could tell you about it, and be prepared to ask clear and specific questions. Begin your theme by telling whom you talked with and where, and make considerable use of direct quotation. Do not be easily discouraged if at first you have difficulty in securing an interview. The experience will be worth some trouble. If you cannot find a man who is doing precisely what you want to do, interview some person engaged in a vocation of the same general character, or some person of maturity and experience in whose judgment of such matters you have confidence.

3. *A Bibliography of Your Vocation.* This theme is to consist of two parts: a list of books and articles that give information about your proposed calling and a few paragraphs of comment in which you tell how you found them and discuss those of them that you have been able to examine. Look first at the shelf of reserved books; then go to the library catalog, the *Reader's Guide,* and the Encyclopedias. You need not, at present, read all the articles that you list, nor need you list all the works that you find. Your bibliography should be selective, containing the titles that seem to you most important. If you are interested in one of the more specialized callings, you may not find much

that seems to deal with it as a vocation. In such a case be content with fewer titles and give more comment.

4. *Preparation and Apprenticeship.* Remember that you are not required to write on this topic. It may be wise for you now to select the five or more theme-subjects that you wish to use, so that you may save for future papers any information that comes into your possession. For this theme you will gather facts as to the requirements for admission to your calling and as to the experience necessary to make you master of it. Is attendance at a professional school necessary? An examination by a state board? What does preparation cost in money, time, and effort? How does one begin to earn his living in such a calling?

5. *Capital and Equipment.* Some callings require a specific equipment in books or apparatus. Learn what is necessary in yours and get advice as to what is a minimum and what an ample supply. Is capital in money required? What standard of mental and physical efficiency must you meet?

6. *Rewards and Prizes.* What rewards — material and ideal — may be won in your vocation? Begin with money. Find out, if you can, about what income a man may reasonably expect to earn five years after graduation. What other returns can you look for, such as comfort, official position, recognition in the community, personal independence? To what extent does your proposed calling promise to bring you " the durable satisfactions of life "?

7. *The Challenge of the Future.* What opportunities exist in your calling for notable achievements in research, invention, or reform? For example, in medicine certain diseases, such as cancer and influenza, still baffle science. They will be conquered, as small-pox and yellow fever have been conquered. Similarly difficult problems await the engineers, the economists, and the statesmen of the future. Are you entering a vocation that challenges you to employ

your best powers and offers you a share in great achievements?

8. *Your Calling and Society.* In any honorable calling you will contribute more or less to the public welfare. Consider the manner and degree of such contribution. What is the attitude of society toward men in your vocation? Does it give them a title? What does it expect of them in service to the unfortunate or in interest in affairs?

9. *The Ethics of the Craft.* Will your conduct in the practice of your vocation be guided by a definite code of ethics? What are some of the things that a man must do or not do in order to maintain his standing in your calling? How is a violation of the code recognized and punished? Consult *The Annals of the American Academy of Political and Social Science* for May, 1922.

10. *Your Future Fellow Workers.* When you enter upon a specialized calling you become one of a fairly definite class. What are the characteristics of this class? Are there any societies or clubs which you would naturally join? If so, what are their functions?

11. *The Literature of the Craft.* Find out whether there are professional or trade journals devoted to the interests of your calling. If there are, try to examine copies of them. Are there collections of books and pamphlets dealing with your subject? Are these indexed in any special way? Can you learn the names of a few of the men who are writing books and articles in your field?

12. *A Typical Day.* Can you learn by inquiry or observation what would be a typical day's work in your vocation? If you wish, fancy yourself ten or fifteen years from now going through a working day as you like to imagine yourself engaged in your life-work.

13. *Retirement and Old Age.* Find out what happens to men in your calling when they grow too old for active service. Is there a " dead-line " in the vocation? When a

man retires has his work supplied him with interests which
will occupy his leisure?

YOURSELF AND YOUR COLLEGE

1. *What You Expect College to Do for You.* A college
education costs a considerable amount of money and three
or four very valuable years. What do you expect to have
after all those years that you do not now possess? What
do the persons who are most interested in you hope that
you will get out of college? What do you understand by
" a liberal education? " Examine the phrases " the cultural
aim " and " the vocational aim " of education.

2. *What Your College May Expect from You.* Base this
theme on an interview with a college officer or alumnus.
Ask him what your duties and obligations are. The college
is not a business concern capitalized to sell so much education for so much money. It is a community of teachers and
students that has on certain conditions admitted you to
membership. Your education will cost much more than
you pay in fees. Who pays the rest and why?

3. *A Bibliography.* From the library catalog, the
Reader's Guide, and other sources, collect titles of books
and articles dealing with American colleges, with college
life, and with college problems. Choose from them a dozen
or more that seem to you likely to be interesting and helpful. Examine a few of those that are available, but do not
feel obliged to find them all at present or to read them
carefully. List the works that you select, and follow your
bibliography with a few paragraphs of comment in which
you tell how you found them, and why you think them
likely to be of use to you. Prefer works that seem likely
to supply material for the topics in this list; and include
any that deal with your college life.

4. *The History of Your College.* Learn from catalogs

and reports, and by asking questions, something about the founding of your college, its first president, its early years. How did the customs of those days differ from those of the present? How has the college grown and what has it accomplished?

5. *The Home of Your College.* Give an account of the campus and buildings. Get the facts yourself and make them clear, using a simple map of your own construction. Don't overlook trees and shrubbery. What about plans for future buildings?

6. *The Library.* Tell about the college or university library. How many books are there and how are they housed and classified? How does one use the catalogs? Look for yourself and ask questions.

7. *The Organization of the College.* Learn what you can about the plan on which the college has been created. What about the charter, the trustees, the president, deans, and other college officers. How is the faculty organized into departments? Are there any affiliated or subordinate organizations?

8. *Your Fellow Students.* From what sources do they come, with what preparation, and what aims in life? What do they have in common? Can you recognize distinct types among them?

9. *Student Self-Government.* If there is a system of student government, describe it briefly. How are examinations conducted? How does student public opinion assert itself, and what seem to be its standards?

10. *College Sports.* Is there an organization devoted to athletic sports? In what branches of athletics do students take most interest? How are the business details managed? What rules govern participation in athletics? What minor sports are carried on?

11. *College Activities.* What interest besides study and athletics engage the attention of your fellow students?

Do not merely compile a list of clubs and societies but rather discuss such organizations in general, telling of the different types and estimating their value.

12. *College Honors and Distinctions*. What degrees, honors and prizes are awarded by the college faculty? What honorary societies admit students and on what terms? To what offices in the gift of their fellow students do undergraduates aspire? What, in general, are the rewards of scholarship, athletic ability, or social leadership? What honors do alumni seem to think most of?

13. *American Colleges*. The college that you have entered is not an isolated institution but is one of many. Find out something about them — how the oldest and best known came into existence; how they fall into classes; what things they have in common. What is the difference between a university and a college? What is a junior college? a professional school?

YOURSELF AND THE WORLD OF POLITICS

1. *Your Choice of a Political Party*. Affiliation with a political party, though less momentous than the selection of a calling, may prove to be a significant matter. Assuming that you are about to register for the first time as a voter, discuss your preference among the national parties. Ought a citizen to belong to a party? If so what considerations should determine his choice?

2. *An Interview with a Partisan*. Talk with a thoughtful person who avowedly believes in the policies of the party which you have selected. Find out, if you can, the reason for his opinions and, if possible, interview other persons who share his party loyalty.

3. *A Bibliography of Party Doctrines*. Compile a list — not too long — of works that discuss your party and the issues for which it stands. Consult P. O. Ray, *An Intro-*

duction to Political Parties and Practical Politics (Scribner's), for references.

4. *The Origin and History of Your Party.* Be brief. You will find an abundance of material and will be tempted to give too much detail.

5. *The National Party Convention.* Tell how a national convention is organized and conducted and what functions it serves. The bound files of newspapers and weekly periodicals will give accounts of recent conventions.

6. *The Party Platform.* Explain how and with what purpose the platform is framed. Describe a typical platform used recently by your party. You will find it in *The World Almanac* and in the campaign text-book.

7. *The Registration of Voters.* Tell how lists of persons entitled to vote are compiled and corrected. Read the election law for yourself and, if possible, talk with somebody who has served as a judge or a clerk in elections.

8. *The Direct Primary.* Explain briefly the system of nomination by means of primary elections. In what respects is this system superior to nomination by convention?

9. *The Ballot.* How is the official ballot prepared and what is it like? You will find copies in the newspaper files. What is meant by the short ballot?

10. *How an Election is Conducted.* Although material for this theme may be found in text-books of government, you will find it most helpful to interview voters and election officials. Be concrete and omit unnecessary details.

11. *The Party Boss.* What is a boss and what is the source of his power? You will find interesting material in Ford's *The Honorable Peter Stirling*.

12. *The Party Organs.* Discuss the more important newspapers that support your party. What can you learn of the political leanings of the better-known weekly periodicals? What is the attitude of the so-called independent papers?

13. *Political Ideals.* What are some of the things that remain to be done in American politics? Have the old parties outgrown their usefulness? What did Washington say about party spirit in his *Farewell Address?* Were his fears justified? What can a future generation do to improve our political customs and ideals?

YOURSELF AND THE WORLD OF BUSINESS

Every vocation is in some sense a business; and though you may not be destined to buy and sell commodities, you must, in the conduct of your personal affairs and in the practice of your calling, have a place in the world of business. In the following topics you will study some of the matters with which you will be concerned.

1. *Yourself and Your Bank.* What is a bank, and what service does it render to an individual depositor?

2. *Savings.* Base this theme on an interview with a banker or a successful business man. Ask questions about the habit of thrift, the means of safeguarding savings, and wise forms of investment.

3. *A Bibliography of Thrift.* Compile a brief bibliography of books and articles dealing with savings, investment, or insurance. Tell where you found the titles, and discuss such of the works as you have been able to examine.

4. *Insurance.* What is the fundamental principle of insurance? Describe some of the more important kinds of insurance and limit your paper, if you like, to the discussion of a single type.

5. *Taxes on Real Estate.* Explain how a piece of property is assessed for taxation, how the rate is determined, how the taxes are collected. What can one do if his assessment is unjust?

6. *The Federal Income Tax.* Tell briefly how the United States Government taxes incomes. Do not attempt to give

a digest of the income-tax law. Be content with the essential facts. Limit the theme, if you like, to the tax upon relatively small incomes.

7. *The Bonds of the United States.* How does the Government borrow money? Discuss the so-called liberty loans.

8. *A Joint-Stock Company.* Explain the organization of a limited liability corporation created for carrying on a business. What are stockholders? directors? common stock and preferred stock? Use a typical company as an example.

9. *The Bonds of a Corporation.* How does a business corporation borrow large sums of money. Learn something of the different kinds of bonds, and how they are issued, sold to investors, and paid when they fall due.

10. *The Tariff.* Explain the system of duties on imports into the United States. What is a protective tariff? a tariff for revenue? reciprocity? Note the different views on the subject, but do not take sides.

11. *The Cost of Living.* How are variations in the cost of commodities measured by economists? What are some of the causes of the variations? How do you personally know that the cost of living changes? What are some of the remedies proposed?

12. *Public Service Commissions.* Explain the means adopted for the regulation of private corporations that furnish such utilities as street railways, electric lights, gas, and telephone service.

13. *Socialism.* Some persons believe that our present system of private ownership and management of industries should be abandoned. What in general are their reasons for this opinion, and what are some of the plans which they wish to see adopted?

YOURSELF AND THE COMMUNITY

Do not choose this subject unless while engaged upon it you will live in or near the community you propose to study, and will be able to question freely some persons who know it well. Limit your survey to a village or small town or to a homogeneous section of a city. Beware of generalizing from hasty observation or from what you imagine to be the facts. Let some one of your themes take the form of an interview with a member of the community who can speak with authority on the subject. In some other theme endeavor to include a brief bibliography of books and articles that bear upon community activities of the sort you are discussing.

1. *The Community as a Unit.* Fix the limits of the community geographically, tell its approximate population and something of its history, and describe it in general as a chance visitor would see it.

2. *The Citizens.* Discuss the people themselves. What are some of the common interests that make them a community? What in general seems to be their racial and religious heritage, and what social and economic classes among them are sufficiently distinct to be recognizable? Study them until they become interesting.

3. *How the Community is Housed.* What kinds of dwellings and what types of architecture seem to be preferred in the community? By what means are new houses supplied? Do many persons own their homes? On what terms are dwellings rented and at what rates?

4. *Employers and Employed.* What can you learn about employment in the community? The subject is so large that you may wish to limit it to domestic, industrial, or commercial workers. If labor disputes arise, how are they settled?

5. *Amusement and Recreation.* Discuss some of the

ways in which residents of the community use their leisure. Limit the topic, if you choose, to a certain class of the residents, such as the young people, or to a certain type of entertainment.

6. *Churches.* Tell about the churches of the community. How are they equipped and what work do they carry on?

7. *Schools.* Consider the efforts of the community to provide for education, narrowing the topic, if necessary, to public or private schools or to a single aspect of public education.

8. *How the Community is Fed.* From what sources and by what agencies are food supplies brought to the community? What service is rendered by public markets, shops, " chain stores," department stores, and hucksters? If the topic grows too large, limit it to a single staple article of food, such as milk, or to one kind of agency.

9. *Protection from Fire.* How are fires prevented? What provision is made for the prompt control of fires that do occur? Talk with members of the fire department.

10. *The Relief of Want.* Give an account of public and private charity in the community. Note particularly whether there are systematic efforts to find and remove the causes of poverty. Does the community contribute to any national relief organizations?

11. *The Public Health.* What does the community do to help physicians to diagnose disease and combat epidemics? How does it endeavor to remove or prevent causes of disease?

12. *Public Welfare Organizations.* What efforts does the community make to organize for the promotion of causes affecting the public welfare? Are there improvement associations, neighborhood clubs, community centers?

13. *The Community of the Future.* Imagine your community as it would be if all of its residents were far more wise and unselfish and sufficiently prosperous to put their

desire for the public good into effect. Suppose, if you like, that you come back fifty years hence and find greater changes than have taken place during the past half-century. Describe some of them.

READINGS ON THE THEME SUBJECTS

The material for the themes outlined above is to come chiefly from observation, inquiry, and reading for facts. There is another kind of reading which you should do to stimulate your own thinking — to give you ideas about the facts which will enable you to order and interpret them. The following selections are provided both as examples of good writing and as suggestions for your own thought:

THERE'S NO FUN LIKE WORK

The other day I noticed a motto on a teamster's cart in our village: "There's no fun like work." The cart belongs to an original neighbor of mine who thinks himself and sets other people a-thinking; and his motto set me a-thinking. Is it true?

True to my experience, yes. My work has always been my best fun. There is no game that begins to interest me as does my work. I began to wonder whether that was temperamental. Or is it universal? If not, can it be made universal? I reflected that almost every kind of workaday activity is also employed in a more or less modified form as a recreation. I recalled the saying attributed to Phillips Brooks, "It is great fun preaching." I remembered what a very successful and very hard-working business man once said to me, "It is more fun to make money than to have it or to spend it." I recalled the pride and pleasure I had seen all sorts of workmen take in their work: the seamstress in her stitch, the cook in her dishes, the teacher in his pupil, the lawyer in his brief. Surgery would be impossible for me. But I remembered how often I had heard that surgeons speak of "a beautiful operation." To teach an eager pupil would be a joy to me; but to discipline a stubborn or sulky one would be torturesome. But I recalled the teacher who would take in his school only boys whom no one else wanted, and found the joy of his life in developing useful men out of these impossible boys. I began to ask myself whether there is any useful vocation that has not its analogy in some favorite recreation. The railway engineer's is a toilsome occupation; but how many of my friends delight in running their own motors! The driver of the teamster's cart I had thought of as having a dull day of it, until I remembered that driving was my favorite recreation, and recalled the other morning when I saw the teamster's daughter sitting on the wagon seat beside her father, her face beaming with pleasure, and remembered the hour when one of my friends had the time of her life driving a four-in-hand over a mountainous road in California. My father was a teacher and an author; but he had a lathe and a carpenter's shop where he spent many hours for pure recreation. John B. Gough spent his vacation months binding books in a bookbindery which he constructed for that purpose in his country home near Worcester. Farming has always seemed to me a toilsome occupation. But some of my friends find their chief enjoyment in their gardens, and I read only in this morning's paper that Mr. Ryan is anxious to get away from the political convention which he is attending in order that he may go back to his farm. We are all familiar through literature with the privations of a sailor's life. But I find myself every summer looking back with regret upon the three years when I lived a week each summer with a friend in a fisherman's sloop in Penobscot Bay, sleeping on deck under a sail for roof and eating hardtack because good bread we often could not procure.

I hope that my readers will not lay down this article at this point under the impression that I am trying to prove that there is no difference between work and play. Not at all. NOT AT ALL. What I am trying to show is that nearly every activity of mind and body employed in useful work may be made to minister to the pleasure of the worker. The toil of the farmer, of the carpenter, of the railway engineer, of the teamster, of the lawyer, of the teacher, of the surgeon, of the preacher, and whatever other toil there is, may be, and often is, a joy. My epigrammatic friend is right: "There's no fun like work." — LYMAN ABBOTT in *The Outlook*, August 17, 1912. Used by permission.

YOU PAY FOR YOUR MONEY

A wisdom, at least, which professes one set of propositions and yet acts upon another, can be no very entire or rational ground of conduct. Doubtless, there is much in this question of money;

and for my part, I believe no young man ought to be at peace till he is self-supporting, and has an open, clear life of it on his own foundation. But here a consideration occurs to me of, as I must consider, startling originality. It is this: That there are two sides to this question as well as to so many others. Make more? — Aye, or spend less? There is no absolute call upon a man to make any specific income, unless, indeed, he has set his immortal soul on being "One of us."

A thoroughly respectable income is as much as a man spends. A luxurious income, or true opulence, is something more than a man spends. Raise the income, lower the expenditure, and, my dear sir, surprising as it seems, we have the same result. But I hear you remind me, with pursed lips, of privations — of hardships. Alas! sir, there are privations upon either side; the banker has to sit all day in his bank, a serious privation; can you not conceive that the landscape painter, whom I take to be the meanest and most lost among contemporary men, truly and deliberately prefers the privations upon his side — to wear no gloves, to drink beer, to live on chops or even on potatoes, and lastly, not to be "One of us" — truly and deliberately prefers his privations to those of the banker? I can. Yes, sir, I repeat the words; I can. Believe me, there are Rivers in Bohemia! — but there is nothing so hard to get people to understand as this: That they pay for their money; and nothing so difficult to make them remember as this: That money, when they have it, is, for most of them at least, only a cheque to purchase pleasure with. How then if a man gets pleasure in following an art? He might gain more cheques by following another; but then, although there is a difference in cheques, the amount of pleasure is the same. He gets some of his directly; unlike the bank clerk, he is having his fortnight's holiday, and doing what delights him, all the year. — ROBERT LOUIS STEVENSON in *Scribner's Magazine,* Vol. LVII, p. 66. Used by permission.

THE FUTURE OF PREVENTIVE MEDICINE

Preventive medicine was a blundering art until 30 or 40 years ago, when it was made a science by the discovery of the causes of many of the serious epidemic diseases. It is particularly in connection with the great plagues of the world that man's redemption of man may be in the future effected; I say in the future because we have only touched the fringe of the subject. How little do we appreciate what even a generation has done! The man is only just dead (Robert Koch) who gave to his fellow-men the control of cholera. Read the story of yellow fever in Havana and in Brazil if you wish to get an idea of the powers of experimental medicine; there is nothing to match it in the history of human achievement. Before our eyes to-day the most striking experiment ever made in sanitation is in progress. The digging of the Panama Canal was acknowledged to be a question of the health of the workers. For four centuries the Isthmus had been a white man's grave, and at one time during the French control of the Canal the mortality reached the appalling figures of 170 per thousand. Even under the most favorable circumstances it was extraordinarily high. Month by month I get the *Reports* which form by far the most interesting sanitary reading of the present day. Of more than fifty-four thousand employees (about thirteen thousand of whom are white), the death rate per thousand for the month of March was 8.91, a lower percentage, I believe, than in any city in the United Kingdom, and very much lower than in any city in the United States. It has been brought about in great part by researches into the life history of the parasite which produces malaria, and by the effective measures taken for its destruction. Here again is a chapter in human achievement for which it would be hard to find a parallel. But let us not forget that these are but illustrations of widespread possibilities of organization on modern lines. To make these sanitary blessings available in the tropics is the heaviest burden of the white man; how heavy you may know from the startling figures which have just been issued from British India. Exclusive of the native states, for the year 1908 the total deaths from fever and cholera exceeded five millions, out of a population of two hundred twenty-six millions. The bright spot in the picture is the diminution of the mortality from plague — not fewer than a million fatal cases as compared with 1907.

These are brief indications to you of the lines along which effective progress is being made in man's redemption by man. And all this has a direct bearing upon the disease which now remains man's most deadly enemy. Tuberculosis is one of the great infections of the world, and it has been one of the triumphs of our generation to determine its cause. With the improvement of sanitation there has been a reduction in its mortality, amounting since 1850 to above 40 per cent. But it still remains the most formidable single foe, killing a larger number of people than any other disease — some 60,000 in Great Britain and Ireland in 1908, and 589 in London alone. Practically between 10 and 11 per cent. of all deaths are due to it. A plain proposition is before the people. We know the disease, how it is caused, how it is spread, how it should be prevented, how in suitable cases it may be cured. How to make this knowledge effective is the prime thing. It is a campaign for the public; past history shows that it is a campaign of hope. The measures for its stamping out, though simple on paper, present difficulties interwoven with the very fabric of society, but they are not insuperable, and are gradually disappearing. Only prolonged and united efforts carried through several generations can place the disease in the same category with typhus fever, typhoid, and smallpox.

In the comedies and tragedies of life our immutable human nature reacts very much as in the dawn of science, and yet with widening of knowledge the lights and shadows of the landscape have shifted, and the picture is brighter. Much has been taken — nothing can bring back the hour when sin and disease were correlated as surely as night and day; but there has been an enormous gain in a new outlook on the value of life. There are tones in human sentiment to-day which the ancients never heard, which, indeed, our fathers heard but faintly, and did not recognize their significance. The human heart by which we live has been touched as with the wand of Prospero. What has availed the sceptered race, what the glory that was Greece, or the grandeur that was Rome, of what avail even has been the message of the gospel, while the people at large were haunted by fear and care, stricken by the pestilence of the darkness and the sickness of the noonday? The new socialism of science with a definite mission to the individual man cares not a rap for the theories of Karl Marx, of Ferdinand Lassalle, or of Henry George; still less for the dreams of Plato or of Sir Thomas More, only as they help to realize the well-being of the citizen. Nor is there need to fear that in weighing the world in our balance we may drain the sap of its life, so long as we materialize in the service of man those eternal principles on which life rests — moral fervor, liberty, and justice.

The outlook for the world as represented by Mary and John and Jennie and Tom has never been so hopeful. There is no place for despondency or despair. Let the dour dyspeptics in mind and morals who sit idly croaking like ravens come into the arena, and wrestle for their flesh and blood against the principalities and powers represented by bad air and worse houses, by drink and disease, by needless pain, and by the loss annually to the state of thousands of valuable lives — let them fight for the day when a man's life shall be more precious than gold, not as now when the cheapness of life is every day's tragedy.

If in the memorable phrase of the Greek philosopher Prodicus " That which benefits human life is God," we may see in this new gospel a link betwixt us and the crowning race of those who eye to eye shall look on knowledge, and in whose hand nature shall be an open book, an approach to the glorious day of which Shelley sings so gloriously:

> " Happiness
> And Science dawn though late upon the earth;
> Peace cheers the mind, health renovates the frame;
> Disease and pleasure cease to mingle here,
> Reason and passion cease to combat there,
> Whilst mind unfettered o'er the earth extends
> Its all subduing energies, and wields
> The sceptre of a vast dominion there."

— Sir William Osler in " Man's Redemption of Man; A Lay Sermon," New York, 1913. Used by permission of P. B. Hoeber.

An Address to Freshmen

A graduate of Christ Church College, Oxford, recently remarked to me, " One can have such a good time at Oxford that it's a great waste of opportunity to work." The humor of this remark, however, was turned to pathos when his wife told me sadly that, " An Oxford training does not fit a man for anything. There is absolutely nothing my husband can do"; and then I learned that the only thing this thirty-year-old husband and father had ever done was to hold a sinecure political office, which he lost when the Conservative party went out of power; and the only thing he ever expected to do was to loaf about summer resorts in summer, and winter resorts in winter, until his father should die and leave him the estate. Fortunately, American society does not tolerate in its sons so worthless a career; yet the philosophy of college life which was behind that worthlessness, translated into such phrases as " Don't let your studies interfere with your college life," and " C is a gentleman's grade," is coming to prevail in certain academic circles in America.

Put your studies first; and that for three reasons: First, you will have a better time in college. Hard work is a necessary background for the enjoyment of everything else. Second, after the first three months you will stand better with your fellows. At first there will appear cheaper roads to distinction, but their cheapness is soon found out. Scholarship alone will not give you the highest standing with your fellows; but you will not get their highest respect without showing that you can do well something that is intellectually difficult. Third, your future career depends upon it. On a little card, five by eight inches, every grade you get is recorded. Four or eight years hence, when you are looking for business or professional openings, that record will, to some extent, determine your start in life. But you are making a more permanent record than that upon the card; you are writing in the nerve cells and films of your brain habits of accuracy, thoroughness, order, power, or their opposites; and twenty, thirty, forty years hence that record will make or mar your success in whatever you undertake.

Make up your minds, then, to take a rank of *A* in some subject, at least *B* in pretty nearly everything, and nothing lower than *C* in anything. If you ask why I place such stress upon these letters, let me tell you what they mean.

A means that you have grasped a subject; thought about it; reacted upon it; made it your own; so that you can give it out again with the stamp of your individual insight upon it.

B means that you have taken it in, and can give it out again in the same form in which it came to you. In details, what you say and write sounds like what the *A* man says and writes; but the words come from the book or the teacher, not from you. No *B* man can ever make a scholar; he will be a receiver rather than a giver, a creature rather than a creator to the end of his days.

C means the same as *B*, only that your second-hand information is partial and fragmentary, rather than complete.

D means that you have been exposed to a subject often enough and long enough to leave on the plate of your memory a few faint traces which the charity of the examiner is able to identify. Poor and pitiful as such an exhibition is, we allow a limited number of *D's* to count toward a degree.

E means total failure. Two *E's* bring a letter to your parents, stating that if the college were to allow you to remain longer, under the impression that you are getting an education, it would be receiving money under false pretenses.

Please keep these definitions in mind, and send a copy to your parents for reference when the reports come home.

Whatever you do, do not try to cheat in examinations or written work. If you succeed, you write fraud, fraud, fraud, all over your diploma; and if you get caught — there will be no diploma for you.

Your own interests and tastes are so much more important factors than any cut-and-dried scheme of symmetrical development, that we leave you free to choose your studies. At the same time, the subjects open to choice are so limited by conflict of hours, and the requirement of a major and minors, that you can hardly miss the two essentials of wise choice: the consecutive, prolonged, concentrated pursuit of one or two main subjects, and some slight acquaintance with each of the three great human interests — language and literature, mathematics and science, and history, economics, and philosophy.

Having put study first, college life is a close second. College is a world artificially created for the express purpose of your development and enjoyment. You little dream how rich and varied it is. I was myself surprised in looking over the records of the last senior class to find that the members of that class won four hundred and sixty-seven kinds of connection and distinction of sufficient importance to be printed in the official records of college achievement. On the other hand, I was a little disappointed to find that one hundred and forty-two of these distinctions were taken by five men, showing that the law, "to him that hath shall be given," applies in college as well as out of it. Some colleges, like Wellesley, have attempted to limit the number of these non-academic points an individual student may win.

Aim to win some of these distinctions, but not too many. Concentrate on a few for which you care most. Do you ask what they are?

There are eight fraternities, each with its own chapter house and its committees for the control of its own affairs; twelve sectional clubs, covering most of the geographical divisions from which students come; a Christian Association of which a majority of the students, and a much larger majority of the best fellows among them, are members, and which every one of you ought to join, who wants help and support in living the life you know you ought to live, and is willing to give help and support to others in living the Christian life in college. There is the Deutscher Verein, the Rumania, the History Club, the Good Government Club, the Chemical Club, devoted to their special subjects; the Ibis, which represents the combination of high scholarship and good fellowship, and whose members, together with the undergraduate members of Phi Beta Kappa, are ex-officio members of the Faculty Club, a literary club composed of members of the faculty and their families.

There is the Inter-fraternity Council; the Athletic Council; the Debating Council; there is the Glee Club; the Mandolin Club; the Chapel Choir; the College Band; the Dramatic Club; the Press Club; the Republican Club; the Democratic Club. We have three papers — the Quill for literature, the Orient for college news, the Bugle for college records and college humor.

Besides, there are public functions with their management and their subjects: rallies, banquets, assemblies, Ivy Day, Class Day, college teas, fraternity house parties.

Last, but not least, come athletics — baseball, football, track, tennis, hockey, fencing, gymnastics, cross-country running, with first and second teams, captains, managers, and assistant managers.

With all these positions open to you in these four years, every one of you ought to find opportunity for association with your fellows in congenial pursuits, and training in leadership and responsibility in the conduct of affairs.

As I said at the outset, taken apart from study these things are trivial, and absorption in them amounts to little more than mental dissipation; but taken in their proper relation to study, which is your main purpose here, the social experience and capacity for leadership they give are so valuable that if you take no responsible and effective part in them, you miss the pleasantest, and in some respects the most profitable, part of what the college offers you.

I suppose I ought to say a word about college temptations, though the man who enters heartily into his studies and these college activities will not be much troubled by them. That is the case with nine-tenths of the men who come here. But in every class there is a weaker five or ten per cent, and I suppose this class of 1912 is no exception. I suppose there are half a dozen of you who are already addicted to vicious practices, and half a dozen more weak fellows, who are only waiting for some one to show them the ways before they fall into them. I do not know yet who you are; but within three months everybody here will know. Then we shall first do our best to change your plans; and if that fails, we shall promptly ask you to withdraw. You all know what these temptations are: they are the temptations of youth everywhere — smoking, drinking, gambling, and licentiousness.

To begin with the least serious. There is nothing intrinsically evil in the inhalation and exhalation of smoke. Among mature men, some are seriously injured by it; some apparently suffer little harm. Almost all youth of your age are seriously injured by it.

In the first place, it weakens your heart and makes your nerves unsteady. In the second place, it destroys your power of mental concentration and makes you scatter-brained. These evils are generally recognized. The most serious consequence is not so well understood. The habitual smoker tends to become content with himself as he is; he ceases to wrestle earnestly with moral and spiritual problems; falls out of the struggle to be continually rising to heights hitherto unattained. For the man who has attained his moral growth (if such there are) it is not so serious; but for the youth of eighteen or twenty it means arrested spiritual development, and an easy-going compromise instead of the more strenuous ideals. As you go up in a college class the proportion of smokers falls; as you go down it rises. While the college does not make smoking directly a subject of discipline, it is no mere coincidence that nineteen out of every twenty students whom we send away for either low scholarship or bad conduct are inveterate smokers. If you train for an athletic team you have to stop smoking while training; if you are in the most earnest training for life, you will leave it off altogether.

Drinking, however excusable a consolation for hard-worked men of meager mental and social resources, is inexcusable in young men with such a wealth of physical, intellectual, and social stimulus about them as college life affords. All the fraternities, of their own accord, exclude it from their chapter houses. Any student who injures himself or others by this abuse is liable to be requested to leave college in consequence.

Gambling is so utterly inconsistent with the purpose for which you come here, and, when once started, spreads so insidiously, that we always remove a student from college as soon as we discover that he is addicted to the practice.

Licentiousness involves such a hardening of the heart of the offender, such an anti-social attitude toward its victims, and brings such scandal on the institution, that " notorious and evil livers " in this respect are quietly, but firmly, removed at the end of an early year or term.

In dealing with these offenses, we hold no legal trial; we offer no formal proof of specific acts; we do not always succeed in convincing either students or parents of the justice of our action. In a little community like this, where everybody is intensely interested in everybody else, we know with absolute certainty; and, while we cannot always make public the nature and source of our knowledge, we act upon that knowledge. If this seems arbitrary, if any one of you does not wish to take his chance of summary dismissal without formal proof of specific charges, on any of these grounds, he would do well to withdraw voluntarily at the outset. This is our way of dealing with these matters, and you have fair warning in advance.

Such is college work; college life; college temptations. A million dollars in building and equipment; another million of endowment; the services of a score of trained, devoted teachers; the fellowship of hundreds of alumni, fellow-students, and younger brothers who will follow in the years to come; the name and fame, the traditions and influence of this ancient seat of learning; the rich and varied physical, intellectual, and social life among yourselves — all are freely yours on the single condition that you use them for your own good, and to the harm of no one else. — WILLIAM DeWITT HYDE, in *The Independent,* October 1, 1908. Used by permission.

CHAPTER II

STRUCTURE IN THE WHOLE COMPOSITION

THE NATURE OF STRUCTURE

3. The Significance of Structure. Structure is the most important element in good writing. A successful piece of writing is not the accidental assembling of ideas as chance has brought them into the mind of the writer, but the ordering of ideas in accordance with a general design which guides and determines every part of the work. Such a general design, fundamental in every art, is particularly significant in the art of expression in words, for the orderly arrangement of words is necessary to their comprehension. No part of the craftsmanship of writing is more important than the power to recognize the natural divisions of a subject and to set them forth in the most satisfactory order. Good structure in writing is simply clear and orderly arrangement; and such arrangement, more than any other one thing, decrees the quality and success of the writing. What determines the character of a twenty-story sky-scraper? Not the foundation, which is adapted to the weight it has to bear; not the facade, which is merely the style, and is easily varied; the true character of the building lies in the steel frame-work, reared on the foundation before the walls are built and ultimately hidden from view without and within. It is so with a piece of writing. The secret of its success or failure lies first of all in its structure.

For most writers the orderly arrangement of ideas must be thought out in advance. If you do not have predetermined structure you will have accidental structure, and unless you have been schooled by long experience in logical thinking your accidental structure is pretty certain to be faulty. A strawstack has accidental structure; a house has been built in accordance with a general design.

4. Structure and Diction. The arrangement of ideas and the expression of them in words are the products of two very diverse faculties. Structure is the result of an analytic habit of mind — a love of order and a disposition to put things into a one-two-three form, neatly and accurately. It is a matter of forethought, of conscious art. Diction is, to a considerable extent, the result of a pictorial or imaginative habit. It is chiefly a matter of instant execution, and becomes in the hands of a practiced writer instinctive or unconscious art. His choice of words, though subject to painstaking revision, is practically spontaneous. The reader, however, is often more conscious of diction than of structure. His appreciation of the clarity or charm of style sometimes obscures for him the significance of the general design upon which the work has been created. Even in poetry, in which the imagination is expected to predominate, structure is no less important than diction. So romantic a narrative as Longfellow's " Evangeline " is remarkably clear and symmetrical in structure. A careful student of Lowell's " Sir Launfal " will recognize that the great defect of that exuberant poem is a lack of structure. The habit of noting the structure of every piece of writing that one reads — a habit that will help to develop one's power of analysis — will make it clear that really successful writing is always the execution of a carefully framed design.

The following paragraphs from the beginning of an article by Mr. Kenyon Cox make clear the significance of structure in the graphic arts. All that he says of it is equally true of the art of writing:

DESIGN

Whatever else was meant by the assertion that there is now no such thing as composition, it is almost inconceivable that a literal denial of the existence of composition, or design, can have been intended, for that would have been the denial to the arts of the one thing they have in common, of the one great fundamental and unifying principle that makes art art. Design is arrangement, is order, is selection. Design is the thing that makes a work of art a unit, that makes it a whole rather than a hap-hazard collection of unrelated things or a slice of unassimilated nature. It does not merely concern itself with great decorative compositions or arrangements of many figures — it is necessarily present in the simplest problems art can set itself. Suppose you are to paint a portrait head. There will be questions of drawing, of character and expression, of light and shade and color, of the handling of your material, to all of which you must find answers; but before you can consider any of these things, there will be the initial question: where are you to place the head on your canvas? How far from the top and the bottom, how far from the left- or right-hand border? And what is the shape of your canvas to be, rectangular or circular or oval, and what shall be the proportion of height to width? This is the fundamental problem of design, the problem of the division of space. If you are going to do a little more of the figure, other problems will come into play. Shall you include the hands, and, if so, where shall you place them? That is the problem of the balancing of dominant and subordinate masses. What is the general silhouette of your figure, and where shall it cut the borders of your canvas? That is the problem of line. If you do not settle it intentionally and well it will settle itself accidentally, and, in all probability, badly. The problems of design are essentially the same in everything you do; they only become more complicated as the subject becomes more complex.

If you are to paint a still-life it is evident that you must arrange the objects somehow — they will not come together of themselves. You might, conceivably, begin a portrait and wait for a happy accident — a spontaneous pose of the sitter — to give you the arrangement of the hands: you cannot wait for the copper kettle and the dead fish to place themselves agreeably. And still less can nature or accident determine your composition of a number of figures, unless you rely entirely upon snap shots. If you have any intention, any story to tell, any idea to express — if it is no more than the idea of a crowd — you *must* arrange your figures, well or ill. Even in landscape painting of the most naturalistic kind, where it is not uncommon to-day to accept what nature gives, abdicating the right to put in or leave out and retaining only that right of choosing an agreeable view which the photographer exercises equally with the painter — even there, though you may reproduce a natural landscape as literally as you are able, you must determine where to cut it off. You must decide where to make the division between your chosen matter and the rest of nature which you reject, you must think whether your material will go best onto an upright canvas or an oblong one, and what are to be its proportions and dimensions. In that act you are exercising the art of design. You cannot escape from design; you cannot avoid composing. You may compose badly but compose you must. — KENYON COX in *The Classic Point of View*. C. Scribner's Sons, 1911. Used by permission.

THE ELEMENTS OF STRUCTURE

5. The Beginning of Structure. As the surveyor who is about to run the lines for a new building must first have a fixed point from which to begin, the structure of a piece of writing must start from a fundamental idea. This idea is the germ of the general design. Implicit in it are the subject, the purpose, and the point of view of the writing. It may or may not be specifically given to the reader in the title or in the introduction; but it must be clear to the writer before he is prepared to plan the structure of his work. This fundamental idea may exist in his mind as a term to be explained or made concrete, as *The American Commonwealth* or *Civil Government in the United States;* it may be a proposition like *Trust thyself* in Emerson's "Self-Reliance"; it may take the form of a question, as the *What manner of man was he?* in an essay by Lord Bryce on Gladstone. Whatever its form it is the very heart of the matter, the concentrated thought of the whole composition. When one has grasped the fundamental idea he knows what he is writing about. If he is in some degree free to determine his subject, it may be necessary to limit the fundamental idea, to subdivide it for the purpose of writing only about a part of it. For example, a student who has his subject, *My High School,* may on reflection come to realize that a better subject would be, *My High School in its Relation to the Community.* After his practice days, however, the student will probably find that most of his writing will be upon subjects prescribed for him by the circumstances which induce him to write.

6. The Key of Structure. A cardinal rule of literary craftsmanship is, One thing at a time. It is a mere matter of convenience that books are not printed in continuous lines, like the quotations on brokers' tapes or like moving-picture films; the words move in single file from title to conclusion. The first great problem of arrangement, therefore, is the division and sub-division of the fundamental idea so that it may be discussed one part at a time. Upon what principle shall the main divisions of the material be distinguished? They must not be chosen at haphazard, but upon a common basis to be found in the material itself. The discovery of this principle is the key which will unlock the problem of structure. The matter can best be made clear by illustrations.

The fundamental idea of Franklin's little essay on *The Morals of Chess* (see page 57) is obviously that chess, instead of being merely an idle pastime, is a game by which several very valuable qualities of the mind are to be acquired or strengthened. The key is supplied by the term *qualities of the mind,* and we confidently expect the essay to set forth some of these qualities, one after the other. Foresight, circumspection, caution, and resourcefulness rest upon a common basis; they are alike in the respect that they are useful qualities that can be acquired or strengthened by chess. They differ as to their relation to the player and his circumstances. Thus foresight might be defined as a looking ahead, circumspection as looking around, caution as looking carefully, and resourcefulness as looking intently and fruitfully.

The college student who was asked to write on the subject, What the city does for the public health, found the key of his structure in the health department. He had at once two main divisions, the organization of the department and the activities of the department. The activities of the department, tested by their relations to disease, seemed to fall naturally into the two divisions — the combating of actual disease and the prevention of possible disease.

Examples of the careful search for a suitable basis of analysis will be found in good writing everywhere. President Hyde, addressing the freshmen of the year at a first meeting (see page 23), divides his counsel into three parts: college work, college life, and college temptations. President Eliot, making a similar address, talks about the sources of the durable satisfactions of life, which furnish his main divisions as health, intellectual power, and personal honor. Ruskin chooses as the basis for a discussion of war, the purpose for which war is waged. The result is war for exercise or play, war for dominion, and war for conquest. In the introduction of his helpful essay entitled " Self-Cultivation in English," Professor Palmer analyzes the study of English upon the basis of the kinds of mastery aimed at, and chooses from among them the mastery of English as a tool.

THE SOURCES OF STRUCTURE

Good structure is partly inherent in the subject-matter and partly determined by the purpose of the writer. From these two sources come the clues which guide the thought and create out of the central idea a general design for the whole work. As one or the other influence dominates, two general types of structure may be recognized, and, although complete classification is impossible, a study of these types will help to suggest means by which a structure suitable for the development of certain kinds of subjects can be devised.

I. STRUCTURE GUIDED CHIEFLY BY THE MATERIAL

The planes of cleavage along which a subject can be divided are sometimes so natural and so obvious that they can scarcely be ignored, no matter for what readers the writing is intended. The following are examples of such subjects.

7. An Organization. An organized institution has its own structure, devised by those who designed and created it. Such structure is sometimes dictated by a division of responsibility, sometimes by a division of function, sometimes by differences in form or place. However determined, it is likely to be so important that an explanation or a description of the institution will often follow in part, at least, the plan of arrangement thus provided. An account of the government of a city, for example, would naturally proceed by departments. Such institutions as railroads, trust companies, and hospitals supply essay subjects which invite interesting studies in organization. They are illustrations of structure which stands the test of practical use. An example of an author's procedure in the planning of an elaborate work is to be found in the introduction to Bryce's *American Commonwealth:*

There are three things that one wishes to know about a national commonwealth, viz., its framework and constitutional machinery, the methods by which it is worked, the forces which move it and direct its course. It is natural to begin with the first of these. Accordingly I begin with the government; and as the powers of the government are two-fold, being vested partly in the National or Federal authorities and partly in the States, I begin with the National government, whose structure presents less difficulty to

European minds, because it resembles the national governments in each of their own countries.

What "one wishes to know" about an institution may, of course, be something entirely apart from its organic structure. In such a case the discussion will be planned according to aspects of the subject arranged in logical order. An article in a current magazine on an educational institution is a good illustration of such orderly development.

THE UNITED STATES NAVAL ACADEMY

I. Its History
1. Naval instruction before 1845
2. The Academy from 1845 to 1851
3. From 1851 to the present

II. The Reasons for its Success
1. Small sections
2. Military discipline
3. Definiteness of aim
4. Incessant competition

III. The Benefits Gained by its Students
1. The mastery of routine
2. The training of the memory
3. A sense of responsibility
4. Good manners
5. Good physical condition
6. Ideals of
  a. Obedience
  b. Loyalty
  c. Pluck
  d. Honor

IV. Its Importance to the Country as Shown by
1. Its physical growth
2. Its expansion during the war
3. The record of its graduates in the war

(Adapted by permission of the author, from "The United States Naval Academy" by CAROL HOWE FOSTER, in *Scribner's Magazine*, July, 1918.)

8. A Process.   In the explanation of a process or in directions for doing something, the material to be dealt with follows the order of time.   The structure must therefore take some account of chronology, though the time order need not be slavishly followed.   The simplest method is to follow the process through from beginning to end, as for example, a piece of raw material passes through various stages to the finished article.   This method may be modified by varying the order of appliances employed or of parts of an object.   An article on the business of clothing the army uses the following order of topics: (*a*) raw material, (*b*) shirts, (*c*) uniforms, (*d*) shoes.   The author chooses by chance.   He must begin with some article of clothing, and glancing at his own cuff he decides to begin with the making of army shirts.   An explanation of the process of setting up a camp (*The Outlook,* June 9, 1920) has this structure: (1) site, (2) water-supply, (3) fuel supply, (4) sanitation, (5) food supply, (6) structures, (7) equipment.   Here it is obvious that the order of importance has modified the order of time.

9. A General Idea.   The explanation of an idea is more easily molded according to the writer's will than is that of an institution, a concrete object, or a process.   It is curious how readily the material seems to adjust itself to a habit of mind, such, for example, as the traditional division into three heads.   Yet an idea is a concept that has been built up from many generalizations, and any useful discussion of it must depend upon some recognition of the parts of which it is composed.   A clue to this process may be got by examining closely some of the words which writers commonly use in the exposition of an idea.   They speak of *elements,* essential parts not further divided; of *aspects,* appearances seen from differing points of view; of *phases,* changes in the idea itself; of *factors,* things that help to produce it; of *features,* parts of it that stand out prominently.   Use such words accurately in your thinking, and they will often lead the way to useful analysis of your material.

In the exposition of a general term the structure may usually be made logical and the expression of it more or less symmetrical. It will be found helpful to make the heads of a preliminary outline as similar in form as possible, so as to bring out the common basis of analysis, even though in writing the essay it may be well to prevent the symmetry from becoming obtrusive. President Hyde's Address to Freshmen, alluded to above, though obviously planned as (a) *college work*, (b) *college life*, and (c) *college temptations*, does not use those terms until the conclusion, where they appear as summary.

Emerson, whose prose is sometimes regarded as lacking in lucidity of structure, follows in his Phi Beta Kappa address, *The American Scholar*, a plan of the utmost simplicity.

THE AMERICAN SCHOLAR

Introduction: The occasion and the subject. — Man thinking.

I. *The Scholar's Education.* The main influences upon him are:
  1. Nature
  2. The Mind of the Past; i.e. Books
  3. Action

II. *The Scholar's Duties.* They are comprised in Self-Trust.
  1. To guide men according to reason
  2. To resist the popular cry
  3. To be free and brave

III. *The Scholar's Hope* — inspired by auspicious signs; viz.,
  1. The new significance of the commonplace
  2. The new importance of the individual.

II. STRUCTURE GUIDED CHIEFLY BY THE PURPOSE.

Though the material is always influential in determining structure, it is sometimes less significant than the purpose. For what reader is the writing intended and what is it expected to accomplish? What does he already know? What interests or bores him? These are questions that must be answered before you proceed. Regard for the reader may alter structure in various ways: by concealing it to prevent the writing from seeming learned or dry; by borrowing the structure of another type to maintain interest; by making divisions more obvious to aid memory.

10. An Informal Essay. Perhaps the most marked characteristic of the informal essay — a literary form invented in France in the sixteenth century and later developed and perfected — is its avoidance of obvious structure. It is a personal form, seemingly free from the dictation of both material and purpose. Its apparent object is to amuse; its design to instruct is carefully concealed. Yet the familiar essay sometimes has a very definite logical structure. The frame-work of Stevenson's essay, " The Profession of Letters," though not obvious, will be found to be about as follows:

1. The Profession and its Motive
2. Two Reasons for Choosing It
   a. Inbred Taste in the Chooser
   b. High Utility in the Vocation
3. Two Duties of a Writer
   a. Truth to Fact
   b. A Good Spirit in the Treatment of It.

A few of such essays wholly lack a logical plan and seem to be directed merely by the author's whim. It is fair to say, however, that only a rich personality and a brilliant style can succeed with this type. It should not be attempted by a beginner.

11. A Portrayal. The structure of descriptive writing must be determined chiefly with reference to the writer, for it is his task to make others see with his eyes. He must order his material, therefore, with constant regard for his point of view. Impressions gained from the same standpoint will naturally be reported together, and in an elaborate description the major divisions are likely to turn on changes in the point of view. In a description of the coming of spring, such as John Burroughs's "A March Chronicle" (in *A Bunch of Herbs and Other Papers*), it is natural to group the signs of spring in the order of their occurrence to the senses — now as one puts his head out of doors in the morning and again as he takes his afternoon walk. In a description from a fixed physical standpoint, such as a view from a window or scrutiny of an object held in the hand, details are likely to be best arranged when expressed in the order in which they would normally be observed. The mental point of view may similarly determine structure. Newman, in his description of Attica (see page 154), shows us the region from a high point, first with the cool appraisal of a London commercial agent, and then with the sympathy of "a pilgrim student come from a semi-barbarous land."

So difficult is it to give life and movement to portrayal in words that extended descriptions usually lean for their structure upon other forms of discourse. An account of changes in the point of view easily grows into a thread of narrative upon which successive descriptions are strung. Hawthorne's "Sights from a Steeple" (in *Twice-Told Tales*) is descriptive in purpose. The narrative which runs through it is of the slightest, yet without it the picture of the town would be inevitably dull. If mingled with the purpose to portray there is also the intent to explain, the structure of description often follows an outline of exposition. This is likely to be the case when the writer imaginatively transcends the limitations of observation, taking in at one glance the topography of a country or the many rooms of a huge building. Oman, in a description of ancient Greece (in his *History of Greece*), uses the material of description and the order of analysis. From mountains, the most characteristic feature of the country, he passes to the rivers, remarking, " The character of the mountains of a country determines that of its rivers."

12. A Narrative.   The order of narration is substantially the order of occurrence in time. The simplicity of sequence in time is disturbed when it is necessary for the sake of clearness or suspense to reverse the order and when two series of events that happened at the same time must be recounted separately; and problems of structure too complex to be discussed here must be solved by the narrator. It is enough to point out that as exposition is built up of classes of things or of stages in a process, and description, of changes in the point of view, so a story is constructed by successive situations. Thus the structure of Rip Van Winkle may be exhibited as follows: (*a*) Rip's character and home life, (*b*) His trip to the mountain, and his experience with the ghostly crew, (*c*) His return to the village, (*d*) His recognition and his later years.

13. An Argument. An attempt to convince follows much the same method as an explanation. There may be many reasons why something is true. To group these reasons into orderly proof, it is generally wise to look for a common basis upon which the proof may be built up. Macaulay, turning aside in his essay on Warren Hastings to prove that Philip Francis was " Junius," groups his arguments according to the nature of the evidence upon which they rest. His four paragraphs deal successively (*a*) with the external circumstances of the two characters, (*b*) with the internal evidence of their resemblances in style and writing, (*c*) with their likeness in moral character, and (*d*) with the coincidence of their withdrawal from the political struggle. An *Outlook* editorial (in the issue for December 18, 1909) defining a policy for the solution of the American colonial problem first analyzes the possible policies on the basis of the relation of the island possessions to the United States, and then proceeds to test these policies in turn by the question of advantage to both countries.

14. An Appeal. Persuasion, more than any other form of discourse, depends for its structure upon the character of the readers or hearers for whom the writing is intended. Argument may be severely logical, for it is addressed to men's minds; and sane, fair-minded men reason in accordance with the same laws. But persuasion is an appeal to emotions, and men differ widely in taste and feeling. A writer of an appeal for a cause is wise to begin with what will stimulate interest or remove prejudice, to proceed with what enlists feeling, and to end with what will spur his audience into the action that he desires. So Charles Dickens, in a speech in behalf of a children's hospital, first tells about sick children and particularly about a specific case of pitiful suffering, then tells of the work of the hospital designed to relieve such suffering and of its need for funds, and concludes with an appeal for the support of the work.

Whatever the type of material and whatever the purpose of the writer, some structure there must be; and for all but a few gifted persons good structure comes about only as the result of careful forethought. When you have a piece of writing to do, think long, pencil in hand, about the subject-matter as a whole. Jot down topics and outlines, test, and reject until an intelligible framework becomes apparent upon which the work may be constructed. When this has been accomplished, even though your first complete sentence is yet to be written, a large and important part of your task has been performed.

STRUCTURE IN OUTLINE

15. The Form of the Outline.   For indicating the structure of a piece of writing apart from the text or before it is written, the best means is the indented topical outline. Such an outline is an arrangement of the topics that will show both their order and their coördination and subordination.   In making an outline, whether for yourself or for your reader, be exacting as to its neatness and accuracy. Keep all sub-divisions of the same rank evenly indented and clearly marked by symbols.   When, as is frequently the case, three steps in subordination are sufficient, a good order of symbols is I, 1, a.   In a more complex outline these may be conveniently increased to I, *A*, 1, *a*, (1), (*a*); but a high degree of complexity in an outline is not usually desirable.   A topic that runs over the end of the line should be continued by a hanging indention, and not carried back to the margin of the page.   Topics that are not complete sentences need no terminal punctuation.   For example (see page 58 for the full text):

THE DURABLE SATISFACTIONS OF LIFE

   I. *Health* — the foundation for everything else

  II. *Intellectual power* — the main achievement of college life

 III. *Personal Honor:*

      1. What honor requires of a man

      2. How honor comes to a man — from the judgment of his contemporaries

      3. How honor is maintained — by a decent respect for the opinions of mankind

Conclusion: Rules for worthy living.

16. Faults in the Outline.   In making an outline avoid:

1. False coördination and subordination.

A	B
The Industries of My Town	*Insurance*

<table>
<tr><td>

I. Manufacturing

II. The Carpet Factory

III. Commercial Fishing

IV. Canning

</td><td>

I. Life insurance
  1. The principle of insurance
  2. Forms

II. Fire insurance

III. Casualty insurance

IV. Why one should insure

</td></tr>
</table>

In *A* it is clear that II is subordinate to I, even though the carpet factory is by far the most important industry in the town. The outline should read:

> I. Manufactures
>   1. The Carpet Factory
>   2. Other industries

In *B*, on the other hand, the principle of insurance is worthy of higher rank than it receives. A better outline would be:

> I. The principle of insurance
>
> II. The chief types of insurance
>   1. Life insurance
>   2. Fire insurance
>   3. Casualty insurance
>
> III. The importance of insurance

2. Single-topic divisions:

> *Sports at Our School*
>
> I. Autumn sports
>   1. Football
>
> II. Winter sports
>   1. Cross country running
>   2. Skating

The sub-division, 1. Football, is misleading in that it implies the existence of others of the same rank. Write it

I. Autumn sport: football

3. Needless variation in form

Lacrosse as a College Game

I. Value as a sport
  1. Strategy and head-work
  2. Free from professionalism

II. Good exercise

III. Interesting to spectators

From such an outline as this a good theme might possibly be written; but the chances for good work would be much improved if the equality in rank of coördinate heads was marked by similarity of form.

A	or	*B*
I. As a sport		I. Valuable as a sport
1. Strategy and headwork		1. For its strategy
2. Freedom from professionalism		2. For its freedom from professionalism
II. As a form of exercise		II. Good as exercise
III. As an exhibition game		III. Interesting to spectators

INDICATIONS OF STRUCTURE

17. Obvious Structure. It may be assumed that good writing always follows a plan and that the plan followed, whether it has been expressed beforehand or not, is logical and natural. To what extent this plan shall be indicated in the writing and by what devices the reader may most conveniently be made aware of the structure are other and important questions. For the clearness of a piece of writing as a whole depends very largely upon the readiness with which its structure, that is to say, the plan upon which it is constructed, is understood. The dictum of the early rhetoricians in regard to style, namely, that it should be not merely capable of being understood, but so clear that it could not be misunderstood, applies also to structure. In so far as the structure is essential to clearness, it should be more than understandable; it should be obvious.

The structure is obvious when the various units of which it is composed are distinguishable at a glance, and their relation to their context is clearly indicated. In some forms of prose, as, for example, in most fiction, in biography, in artistic description, and in the informal essay, explicit indication of structure, beyond division into chapters, is unnecessary and undesirable. When the matter is complex, however, and the writer's chief purpose is to make it clear, the reading is both easier and pleasanter if the structure is made obvious in some specific way. This may be done by the use of rhetorical means, by mechanical devices, or by both.

18. Forecasts of Structure. The most useful rhetorical means of making structure obvious is to forecast it in an introduction or opening sentence. The reader is thus forewarned and is prepared to take advantage of such hints of transition as may follow when he passes from one division of the work to another. Such deliberate announcement of the plan may at times seem over-formal; but it will be well for students to risk the formality, in order to learn to use the method with skill when it seems applicable. A distinguished college president, at the conclusion of the opening words of his inaugural address, announced the plan of his speech explicitly as follows:

In the consideration of the educational creed of the teacher I will try to give, first, a brief statement of his belief; second, a defense of it against other views of the function of the college;

third, an interpretation of its meaning and significance; fourth, a criticism of what seem to me misunderstandings of their own meaning prevalent among teachers of our day; and, finally, a suggestion of certain changes in policy which must follow if the belief of the teacher is clearly understood and applied in our educational procedure.

Mr. Thomas W. Lamont, in beginning an article on the political problems facing a newly elected president, uses a similar method.

When the editor of *Harper's Magazine* asked me to express my " views on the financial and economic problems which the incoming Administration will have to face," he might as well have invited me to write a third volume to H. G. Wells's history of the world. Each of the party platforms last summer made allusion to most of the problems that are confronting us; but party platforms have the habit of touching only the " high spots." They declare the benevolent intentions of their respective parties, but they can hardly be expected to set forth concrete working programs.   In fact, the field to be surveyed is so large that I shall not attempt at all to touch upon the questions that are pressing for solution in labor, in merchant marine, and in many other matters.   There are, however, three outstanding topics which every citizen ought to study and discuss.   For it is only by reviewing past history that we can gain the data upon which to form sound judgment for future operation.   These three topics — all of which are closely correlated — are those, first, of taxation; second, of the tariff; and third, of foreign trade relations. — *Harper's Magazine*, March, 1921, p. 432. Used by permission.

Such a preliminary statement of the plan of an entire work may be called a major forecast. It is ordinarily carried out by transitions, directive expressions, or symbols which will make clear to the reader the divisions which have been promised him. What may be called a minor forecast foretells in the same way the structure of a part of the whole — a section, a paragraph, or even a few sentences. Examples will be found in the selection cited below from Sir William Osler (page 61), who speaking of overwork, says, " There are dangers, but they may readily be avoided with a little care. I can only mention two, one physical, one mental." As he proceeds later to discuss the mental danger he says, " Of the causes of worry in the student life there are three of prime importance to which I may briefly refer."

In addition to forecasts and transition words, or instead of them, a writer may use to make his plan clear one or another of various mechanical devices. The tendency of modern usage is perhaps towards the more generous use of such devices. Sermons, to be sure, have long tended to fall into carefully marked subdivisions, but the signs of structure in such cases have been intended for the ear rather than for the eye. Without them it would have been impossible to remember the plan of a long discourse. Readers, however, were expected to have ample leisure and unfailing patience. The structure of Milton's " Areopagitica," for example, must be comprehended if at all by a careful reading of the text. That of DeQuincey's " English Mail Coach " is made obvious by subdivisions. A comparison of Blair's lectures on Rhetoric, let us say, with almost any modern text-book of the same subject will illustrate the present tendency to make the reader's path plain before him.

19. Headings. The most explicit sign that can be used to indicate a sub-division of a piece of writing is perhaps a section heading or sub-title; for it not only sets off from the context the element of structure to which it is applied, but also gives a hint as to its content. Such a sub-title, like the title of the whole work, should combine accuracy and attractiveness; but its appeal to the writer is less important than the information which it gives. In form, the heading may appear in the center of the column in smaller capitals than the general title; it may be set into a square space at the left-hand margin, such as is used for an ornamental initial; or — as is the more common usage in text-books — it may be run into the text in bolder type, followed by a period (as at the beginning of this paragraph) or by a period and a dash.

Used in combination, these headings give us a means of indicating subordination in the structure of the full text as accurately as the degrees of indention indicate it in an outline or tabulation. Thus, the small title may cover a division which is itself divided by headings in bold type, and further subdivided by similar heading in italics. In a similar way the run-in headings may be used to indicate subdivisions in structure and the marginal headings to call attention to important topics, serving in this way as a sort of gloss without reference to structure.

20. Symbols. For the more accurate indication of subordinate elements of structure, and particularly to set in order divisions that are of coördinate rank, symbols — numbers, Roman or Arabic, and letters of the alphabet — are available. The designation of books and chapters by Roman numerals and sub-titles is a long established usage. For the indication of divisions between the chapter and the paragraph, units for which we have no rhetorical name, but which may here be termed sections, no such uniform convention exists. Only when there is likely to be need for frequent index reference is it usually necessary to combine numerals and headings for sections. When it is desirable to indicate the subdivisions unobtrusively, a Roman numeral centered in the column is often used, serving equally for literary prose and for text-books. The inaugural address alluded to above was so subdivided in the printed form.

Smaller units are commonly indicated, when indication is needed, by Arabic numbers and by small letters. Paragraphs so numbered of course take the numeral at the beginning of the paragraph. Within the paragraph, numerals or letters, generally enclosed in curves, may indicate divi-

sions of the text, however small, without having any effect
upon the structural punctuation. The following is an example of the use of such symbols to indicate the parts of
a definition:

> If we accept as our definition of an Epic: (*a*) A long poem,
> (*b*) of an interest not less than national, describing (*c*) in noble
> language (*d*) a series of naturally and organically connected actions
> (*e*) of heroic actors, we shall find that, while we must deny the
> name to some so-called epics, we have to thank the spirit, the
> imagination, the genius of the Middle Ages for two great epics. —
> A. S. WAY, Preface to "The Lay of the Niebelungen Lied."

THE TITLE

21. The Purpose of the Title. The title of a piece of
writing, though not a part of its structure, is an essential
adjunct serving an important special purpose. This purpose is more than merely to provide a convenient designation, as do the names of boats and sleeping cars; the title
must be, in some degree at least, descriptive of the work,
giving the reader his first hint of the fundamental idea.
Descriptiveness was once regarded as the main consideration in the phrasing of a title. So Captain John Smith's
first work dealing with America bore the accurate though
clumsy title, " A True Relation of such Occurrences and
Accidents of Note as hath hapned in Virginia since the first
planting of that Collony, which is now resident in the South
part thereof, till the last return from thence." Informing
as this description of Smith's work is, it is unsatisfactory
as a title, for it is both inconvenient and unattractive.

In modern writing the title is brief, for convenience in
printing and in references, and, further, it should be neatly
and effectively phrased. The title of a work is an adver-
tisement of it as well as a name. It is the first point of
contact with a reader, and must necessarily be read by many
more persons than will ever read a table of contents or an

introduction, to say nothing of reading the work itself. It is therefore part of the purpose of the title to attract the attention of readers. Like other advertising, the title should be true; for a reader who is misled by the title of a work into thinking it something other than it is, is rarely satisfied. The title is a writer's promise to his readers, a promise that must be faithfully kept.

22. The Form of the Title. The title, then, is the name of the piece of writing, as descriptive of its contents as the brief, compact form permits, and as pleasing and striking in phraseology as truth permits. How both these considerations have influenced the form of the title of a later work on a subject similar to Smith's may be seen in Fiske's "Old Virginia and her Neighbors," and still better, perhaps, in the name of another work by a countryman of Smith's, namely, "The American Commonwealth."

Though every piece of writing is the better for a happily phrased title, it is evident that an exposition, a history, or an argument has particular need to be named accurately, whereas a piece of fiction or a descriptive sketch must depend far more upon the appeal of the title. For writing of the first kind, the shortest way to a good title is, perhaps, to express the theme of the work in as compact a sentence as possible, and then to try to put into the still more compact title the main idea of the theme. An examination of the titles of all the text-books easily within reach will be likely to prove instructive; for it will be apparent that the authors, while striving to avoid titles already preëmpted, have been at pains to express the main idea of the book. One will find the synonyms, "Essentials of," "Elements of," "Principles of," "Introduction to," and the like almost inevitable in the titles of books that begin the study of a subject. There is wisdom in such adherence to terms which accurately designate the nature and purpose of the writing. Sketches of travel usually combine in the title accuracy and attractiveness with an even hand. It is essential to show where and how the traveling was done, yet a striking phrase is important. " Views Afoot," " Innocents Abroad," " A Bicycle of Cathay " are examples of such a compromise. The title of a work of fiction, since it need give the reader only a hint as to the character of the narrative, may be chosen with considerable freedom. It gives free rein to the author's ingenuity, and demands the skilful use of all the resources of style.

23. The Titles of Themes. Every theme written for practice should have a title, if the writing pretends at all to completeness. It will ordinarily be best, too, to choose the title first; for with the title before him the writer always knows what he has promised his readers. The result of keeping the title constantly in mind is likely to be a unified paper. It is possible to write the theme and then think of the title, but it is not always easy to find any but a very long and awkward phrase that will really fit a completed theme.

EXERCISES IN THE CHOICE OF TITLES

I

Mosses from an Old Manse. Beside the Bonnie Brier Bush. The Rise of Silas Lapham. Puck of Pook's Hill. Paradise of Dainty Devices. The Red Rover. The Trail of the Lonesome Pine. The American Commonwealth. The Changing Chinese. The Wept of the Wish-ton-wish. Helen with the High Hand. When a Man Marries. Harnessing Heredity. Incense and Iconoclasm.

Study these titles as to their reliance upon alliteration, tone-color, and meter for attractiveness in phrasing. Do any of them overdo the matter?

II

Far from the Madding Crowd. The Undiscovered Country. Under the Greenwood Tree. Opening the Oyster (A story of

travel and adventure). A Spinner in the Sun. Sesame and Lilies.
The Way of an Eagle. The Street Called Straight. Vanity Fair.
The House of Mirth. A Far Country.

Trace, so far as you can, the sources of the allusions made
use of in these titles. What is the value of such allusions?

III

It Never Can Happen Again. Alice-for-Short. How to Live on
Twenty-four Hours a Day. V.V.'s Eyes. An Inland Voyage. Sartor Resartus. The Man Who Rocked the World.

Discuss the devices used in these titles to pique curiosity
and to demand attention. What works thus named should
you be most likely to wish to read?

IV

The Art of Rendering (A work on Elocution). The Standard
English Speech (A history of the development of the East Mid-
land dialect into Modern English). Conversion and Redemption
(A study in public finance). The Lesson of the Master (Not a
religious work!). What May be Secured by a Liberal Education.
Making People Happy (A novel). The Underlying Principles of
Modern Legislation.

Apply to these titles the tests of accuracy and attractiveness.

V

Ruskin is said to have rejected in turn each of the following names as title for a published collection of his
letters:

Public Letters	Totus in Illis
Spare Minutes	Here and There
Spent Shot	To-day
Surdis Auribus	Signals on the Old Road
A Quiver of Arrows	The Faggot

It is obvious that the subject-matter of the letters themselves, being diverse, did not give a ready clue to a good

title. The two considerations most significant were probably the fact that they were a collection, and the fact that they had already served their first purpose and were being used again.

Arrange the titles in groups according as they express one or the other of these characteristics. The title finally chosen was "Arrows of the Chase." Note how well this title represents both, and how attractively phrased it is.

VI

Phrase appropriate titles for themes to be written on the following subjects:

1. My high school considered in its relation to the community which supports it by taxation.
2. The question whether horses are destined to disappear entirely from cities.
3. An explanation of the various problems involved in managing a school paper.
4. Some of the ways by which students earn their way through college.
5. How my home town endeavors to prevent loss by fires.
6. The various services performed by a policeman in a city.
7. The different ways by which dwelling houses may be heated and the advantages of each.
8. A detective story, the clue of which is furnished by an irregular button of some striking color.
9. The story of an episode on a bicycle trip in which a kindness that you did caused you immediate loss and inconvenience, and ultimately brought you a great and wholly unexpected advantage.
10. An argument to prove that it would be wise to exempt from final examinations students whose standing in class-room work has been high.

THE INTRODUCTION AND THE CONCLUSION

The time-honored advice that a piece of writing should have a beginning, a middle, and an end has fallen into some disrepute; but it is by no means obsolete. Unnecessary delay in coming to the point is bad, and there should be no formal flourish in one's approach to the main issue. But the beginning and the end of a piece of writing stand in a special relation to the structure; and whether such a division is apparent to the reader or not, the writer will do well to conceive any work of more than a thousand words as composed of three parts — the introduction, the body, and the conclusion.

24. The Function of the Introduction.   The chief purpose of the introduction is to make explicit the hint of the subject and the point of view given by the title. Of these matters it can treat as fully as may be desirable, preparing either directly or indirectly for the unfolding of the fundamental idea.

The introduction that leads directly into the subject may define and limit the fundamental idea, as Professor Palmer does when he explains that English may be studied from four different points of view, only one of which he means to consider. It may, as has already been explained, give a forecast of the plan. Or it may frankly discuss the relation of the author to his work or the bearing of the work itself and its importance to the reader. A good illustration of the direct introduction is the following paragraph beginning the explanation of the steam engine (GEORGE V. HOLMES, *The Steam Engine*, Chapter I, cited in Lamont, *Specimens of Exposition*).

A complete knowledge of the steam engine involves an acquaintance with the sciences of physics, of chemistry, of pure and applied mathematics, as well as with the theory of mechanism and the strength of materials. My plan, however, is to begin by showing in a very simple case how steam can do work, and then to explain an actual steam engine of the most modern construction, but at the same time remarkably free from complexity.

The indirect introduction serves the same purpose connotatively, that is, by suggestion rather than by explicit statement. An anecdote, a bit of description, a literary or historical allusion may, like an attractive title, interest the reader and at the same time prepare perfectly for the discussion of the subject. President Hyde (see page 23) introduces his address to freshmen by the story of an English student whom college life seemed to have unfitted for any practical work in the world. George W. Curtis began one of his most effective addresses by the description of a fanciful painting in which an aged couple meet their own younger selves. It is futile to give directions for the writing of this type of introduction. Success in the use of it is the result of literary tact, best acquired by observant reading.

25. The Qualities of the Introduction. A good introduction will be apposite, because the reader expects it to fit its context perfectly, to lead into the subject and not to exist for itself. It must be lucid, because the beginning bears the first test of criticism; and the critical judgment is not yet softened by interest. Fresh attention and unwearied eyesight bring the introduction under a keener scrutiny than is given to any other part of the work. It should, if possible, be attractive and interesting; for the writing is still in some degree on trial, and the reader needs to be tempted to go on. It is for this quality that practiced writers so often use the indirect introduction, preferring to begin the explanation of an abstract matter with something concrete. Huxley's *The Physical Basis of Life,* a popular presentation of a scientific subject, begins with a detailed illustration of the outward dissimilarity of natural objects which at the same time makes clear and invests with interest the assertion that all these diverse objects are alike in substance.

26. The Conclusion. Most writing is intent on getting on; it is like walking, which has been described as a process of continually falling forward. The conclusion is free from such intent. It looks back, not forward, and its function is to say the appropriate last word, the word that shall linger in the mind. This last word will not be a new idea, which would require development, not something foreign to the thought, which would violate its unity, nor even a conclusion for the last division of the subject. It will recur either directly or indirectly to the fundamental idea. It may do this by a recapitulation, a going over the heads of the structure in a brief restatement, or by a summary, a gathering up of the whole into a significant condensed statement. The recurrence to the main idea may be indirect, a matter of spirit rather than of form, but it is essential.

In style the conclusion should observe the law of climax. What comes last should be most impressive. Consequently it must be brief and to the point, free from useless lumber, unnecessary moralizing, weak repetition. Here, if anywhere in the work, is the place for a touch of connotation, for figurative language which is capable of expressing the spirit of an idea in a compact form and with telling force.

SPECIMENS OF STRUCTURE

I

THE MORALS OF CHESS

The game of chess is not merely an idle amusement. Several very valuable qualities of the mind useful in the course of human life are to be acquired or strengthened by it, so as to become habits, ready on all occasions. For life is a kind of chess, in which we have points to gain, and competitors or adversaries to contend with, and in which there is a vast variety of good and ill events that are in some degree the effects of prudence or the want of it. By playing chess, then, we learn:

First, Foresight, which looks a little into futurity, and considers the consequences that may attend an action; for it is continually occurring to the player, If I move this piece what will be the advantage to my new situation? What use can my adversary make of it to annoy me? What other moves can I make to support it and to defend myself from his attacks?

Second, Circumspection, which surveys the whole chessboard or scene of action — the relations of the several pieces and situations, the dangers they are respectively opposed to, the several possibilities of their aiding each other, the probabilities that the adversary may make this or that move and attack this or that piece, what different means can be used to avoid this stroke or turn its consequences against him.

Third, Caution, not to make our moves too hastily. This habit is best acquired by observing strictly the laws of the game, such as, If you touch a piece you must move it somewhere; if you set it down you must let it stand. It is best that these rules should be observed, as the game thereby becomes more the image of human life, and particularly of war, in which if you have incautiously put yourself into a bad and dangerous position, you cannot obtain your enemy's leave to withdraw your troops and place them more securely, but you must abide all the consequences of your rashness.

And lastly, we learn by chess the habit of not being discouraged by present bad appearance in the state of our affairs, the habit of hoping for a favorable change, and that of persevering in the search of resources. The game is so full of events, there is such a variety of turns in it, the fortunes of it are so subject to sudden vicissitudes, and one so frequently after long contemplation discovers the means of extricating oneself from a supposed insurmountable difficulty that one is encouraged to continue the contest to the last in the hope of a victory by our own skill or at least of getting a stalemate by the negligence of our adversary. And whoever considers, what in chess he often sees instances of, that particular pieces of success are apt to produce presumption and its consequent inattention, will learn not to be too much discouraged by the present success of his adversary, nor to despair of final good fortune upon every little check he receives in the pursuit of it.

— BENJAMIN FRANKLIN.

II

THE DURABLE SATISFACTIONS OF LIFE

For educated men what are the sources of the solid and durable satisfactions of life? I hope you are all aiming at the solid, durable satisfactions of life, not primarily the gratifications of this moment or of to-morrow, but the satisfactions that are going to last and grow. So far as I have seen, there is one indispensable foundation for the satisfactions of life — health. A young man ought to be a clean, wholesome, vigorous animal. That is the foundation for everything else, and I hope you will all be that if you are nothing more. We have to build everything in this world of domestic joy and professional success, everything of a useful, honorable career on bodily wholesomeness and vitality.

This being a clean, wholesome, vigorous animal involves a good deal. It involves not condescending to the ordinary barbaric vices. One must avoid drunkenness, gluttony, licentiousness, and getting into dirt of any kind, in order to be a clean, wholesome, vigorous animal. Still, none of you would be content with this achievement as the total outcome of our lives. It is a happy thing to have in youth what are called animal spirits — a very descriptive phrase; but animal spirits do not last even in animals; they belong to the kitten or puppy stage. It is a wholesome thing to enjoy for a time, or for a time each day through life, sports and active bodily exercise. These are legitimate enjoyments, but, if made the main object of life, they tire. They cease to be a source of durable satisfaction. Play must be incidental in a satisfactory life.

What is the next thing, then, that we want in order to make sure of durable satisfactions in life? We need a strong mental grip, a wholesome capacity for hard work. It is intellectual power and aims that we need. In all the professions — learned, scientific, or industrial — large mental enjoyments should come to educated men. The great distinction between the privileged class to which you belong, the class that has opportunity for prolonged education, and the much larger class that has not that opportunity, is that the educated class lives mainly by the exercise of intellectual powers and gets therefore much greater enjoyment out of life than the much larger class that earns a livelihood chiefly by the exercise of bodily powers. You ought to obtain here, therefore, the trained capacity for mental labor, rapid, intense, and sustained. That is the great thing to get in college, long before the professional school is entered. Get it now. Get it in the years of college life. It is the main achievement of college life to win this mental force, this capacity for keen observation, just inference, and sustained thought, for everything that we mean by the reasoning power of man. That capacity will be the main source of intellectual joys and of happiness and content throughout a long and busy life.

But there is something more, something beyond this acquired power of intellectual labor. As Shakespeare puts it, " The purest treasure mortal times afford is spotless reputation." How is that, treasure won? It comes by living with honor, on honor. Most of you have already begun to live honorably, and honored; for the life of honor begins early. Some things the honorable man cannot do, never does. He never wrongs or degrades a woman. He never oppresses or cheats a person weaker or poorer than himself. He never betrays a trust. He is honest, sincere, candid, and generous. It is not enough to be honest. An honorable man must be generous, and I do not mean generous with money only, I mean generous in his judgments of men and women, and of the nature and prospects of mankind. Such generosity is a beautiful attribute of the man of honor.

How does honor come to a man? What is the evidence of the honorable life? What is the tribunal which declares at last, " This was an honorable man " ? You look now for this favorable judgment of your elders, — of parents and teachers and older students; but these elders will not be your final judges, and you had better get ready now in college to appear before the ultimate tribunal, the tribunal of your contemporaries and the younger generations. It is the judgment of your contemporaries that is most important to you; and you will find that the judgment of your contemporaries is made up alarmingly early, — it may be made up this year in a way that sometimes lasts for life and beyond. It is made up in part by persons to whom you have never spoken, by persons who in your view do not know you, and who get only a general impression of you; but always it is contemporaries whose judgment is formidable and unavoidable. Live now in the fear of that tribunal, — not an abject fear, because independence is an indispensable quality in the honorable man. There is an admirable phrase in the Declaration of Independence, a document which it was the good fashion of my time for boys to commit to memory. I doubt if that fashion still obtains. Some of our public actions look as if it did not. " When, in the course of human events, it becomes necessary for one people to dissolve the political bands which have connected them with another, and to assume among the powers of the earth the separate and equal station to which the laws of Nature and Nature's God entitle them, a decent respect to the opinions of mankind requires that they should declare the causes which impel them to the separation." That phrase " a decent respect " — is a very happy one. Cherish " a decent respect to the opinions of mankind," but never let that interfere with your personal declaration of independence. Begin now to prepare for the judgment of the ultimate human tribunal. Look forward to the important crises of your life. They are nearer than you are apt to imagine. It is a very safe protective rule to live to-day as if you were going to marry a pure woman within a month. That rule you will find a safeguard for worthy living. It is a good rule to endeavor hour by hour and week after week to learn to work hard. It is not well to take four years to do what you can perfectly accomplish in three. It is well to learn to work intensely. You will hear a good deal of advice about letting your soul grow and breathing in without effort the atmosphere of a learned society or place of learning. Well, you cannot help breathing and you cannot help growing; these processes will take care of themselves. The question for you from day to day is how to learn to work to advantage, and college is the place and now is the time to win mental power. And, lastly, live to-day and every day like a man of honor. — CHARLES W. ELIOT. An address given to new students at Harvard University, on October 3, 1905, in " The Durable Satisfactions of Life." Thomas Y. Crowell Company. Used by permission.

III

WORK THE MASTER-WORD

It seems a bounden duty on such an occasion to be honest and frank; so I propose to tell you the secret of life as I have seen the game played, and as I have tried to play it myself. You remember in one of the Jungle Stories that when Mowgli wished to be avenged on the villagers he could only get the help of Hathi and his sons by sending them the master-word. This I propose to give you in the hope, yes, in the full assurance, that some of you at least, will lay hold upon it to your profit. Though a little one, the master-word looms large in meaning. It is the open sesame to every portal, the great equalizer in the world, the true philosopher's stone, which transmutes all the base metal of humanity into gold. The stupid man among you it will make bright, the bright man brilliant, and the brilliant student steady. With the magic word in your heart all things are possible, and without it all study is vanity and vexation. The miracles of life are performed with it; the blind see by touch, the deaf hear with eyes, the dumb speak with fingers. To the youth it brings hope, to the middle-aged confidence, to the aged repose. True balm of hurt minds, in its presence the heart of the sorrowful is lightened and consoled. It is directly responsible for all advances in medicine during the past twenty-five centuries. Laying hold upon it Hippocrates made observation and science the warp and woof of our art. Galen so read its meaning that fifteen centuries stopped thinking, and slept until awakened by the *De Fabrica* of Vesalius, which is the very incarnation of the master-word. With its inspiration Harvey gave an impulse to a larger circulation than he wot of, an impulse which we feel to-day. Hunter sounded all its heights and depths, and stands out in history as one of the great exemplars of its virtue. With it Virchow smote the rock, and the waters of progress gushed out; while in the hands of Pasteur it proved a very talisman to open to us a new heaven in medicine and a new earth in surgery. Not only has it been the touchstone of progress, but it is the measure of success in every-day life. Not a man before you but is beholden to it for his position here, while he who addresses you has that honor directly in consequence of having had it graven on his heart when he was as you are to-day. And the master-word is *work,* a little one, as I have said, but fraught with momentous sequences if you can but write it on the tablets of your hearts, and bind it upon your foreheads. But there is a serious difficulty in getting you to understand the paramount importance of the work-habit as part of your organization. You are not far from the Tom Sawyer stage with its philosophy " that work consists of whatever a body is obliged to do," and " that play consists of whatever a body is not obliged to do."

A great many hard things may be said of the work-habit. For most of us it means a hard battle; the few take to it naturally; the many prefer idleness and never learn to love labor. Listen to this: " Look at one of your industrious fellows for a moment, I beseech you," says Robert Louis Stevenson. " He sows hurry and reaps indigestion; he puts a vast deal of activity out to interest, and receives a large measure of nervous derangement in return. Either he absents himself entirely from all fellowship, and lives a recluse in a garret with carpet slippers and a leaden inkpot, or he comes among people swiftly and bitterly, in a contraction of his whole nervous system to discharge some temper before he returns to work. I do not care how much or how well he works, this fellow is an evil feature in other people's lives." These are the sentiments of an over-worked, dejected man; let me quote the motto of his saner moments: " To travel hopefully is better than to arrive, and the true success is in labour." If you wish to learn of the miseries of scholars in order to avoid them, read Part I, Section 2, Member 3, Subsection XV, of that immortal work, the

Anatomy of Melancholy; but I am here to warn you against these evils, and to entreat you to form good habits in your student days.

At the outset appreciate clearly the aims and objects each one of you should have in view — a knowledge of disease and its cure, and a knowledge of yourself. The one, special education, will make you a practitioner of medicine; the other, an inner education may make you a truly good man, four square and without a flaw. The one is extrinsic and is largely accomplished by teacher and tutor, by text and by tongue; the other is intrinsic and is the mental salvation to be wrought out by each one for himself. The first may be had without the second; any one of you may become an active practitioner, without ever having had sense enough to realize that through life you have been a fool; or you may have the second without the first, and, without knowing much of the art, you may have the endowments of head and heart that make the little you do possess go very far in the community. What I hope to infect you with is a desire to have a due proportion of each.

So far as your professional education is concerned, what I shall say may make for each one of you an easy path easier. The multiplicity of the subjects to be studied is a difficulty, and it is hard for teacher and student to get a due sense of proportion in the work. We are in a transition stage in our methods of teaching, and have not everywhere got away from the idea of the examination as the " be-all and end-all "; so that the student has constantly before his eyes the magical letters of the degree he seeks. And this is well, perhaps, if you will remember that having, in the old phrase, commenced Bachelor of Medicine, you have only reached a point from which you can begin a life-long process of education.

So many and varied are the aspects presented by this theme that I can only lay stress upon a few of the more essential. The first step towards success in any occupation is to become interested in it. Locke put this in a very happy way when he said, give a pupil " a relish of knowledge " and you put life into his work. And there is nothing more certain than that you cannot study well if you are not interested in your profession. Your presence here is a warrant that in some way you have become attracted to the study of medicine, but the speculative possibilities so warmly cherished at the outset are apt to cool when in contact with the stern realities of the class-room. Most of you have already experienced the all-absorbing attraction of the scientific branches, and nowadays the practical method of presentation has given a zest which was usually lacking in the old theoretical teaching. The life has become more serious in consequence, and medical students have put away many of the childish tricks with which we used to keep up their bad name. Compare the picture of the " sawbones " of 1842, as given in the recent biography of Sir Henry Acland, with the representatives to-day, and it is evident a great revolution has been effected, and very largely by the salutary influences of improved methods of education. It is possible now to fill out a day with practical work, varied enough to prevent monotony, and so arranged that the knowledge is picked out by the student himself, and not thrust into him willy-nilly, at the point of the tongue. He exercises his wits and is no longer a passive Strasbourg goose, tied up and stuffed to repletion.

How can you take the greatest possible advantage of your capacities with the least possible strain? By cultivating system. I say cultivating advisedly, since some of you will find the acquisition of systematic habits very hard. There are minds congenitally systematic; others have a life-long fight against an inherited tendency to diffuseness and carelessness in work. A few brilliant fellows try to dispense with it altogether, but they are a burden to their brethren and a sore trial to their intimates. I have heard it remarked that order is the badge of an ordinary mind. So it may be, but as practitioners of medicine we have to be thankful to get into that useful class. Let me entreat those of you who have had to fight a hard battle, and not always a successful one, for the little order he has had in his life; take away with you a profound conviction of the value of system in your work. I appeal to the freshmen especially, because you to-day make a beginning, and your future career depends very much upon the habits you will form during this session. To follow the routine of the classes is easy enough, but to take routine into every part of your daily life is a hard task. Some of you will start out joyfully as did Christian and Hopeful, and for many days will journey safely towards the Delectable Mountains, dreaming of them and not thinking of disaster, until you find yourselves in the strong captivity of Doubt and under the grinding tyranny of Despair. You have been over confident. Begin again and more cautiously. No student escapes wholly from these perils and trials; be not disheartened, expect them. Let each hour of the day have its allotted duty, and cultivate that power of concentration which grows with its exercise, so that the attention neither flags nor wavers, but settles with a bull-dog tenacity on the subject before you. Constant repetition makes a good habit fit easily into your mind, and by the end of the session you may have gained that most precious of all knowledge — the power to work. Do not underestimate the difficulty you will have in wringing from your reluctant selves the stern determination to exact the uttermost minute on your schedule. Do not get too interested in one study at the expense of another, but so map out your day that due allowance is given to each. Only in this way can the average student get the best that he can out of his capacities. And it is worth all the pains and trouble he can possibly take for the ultimate gain — if he can reach his doctorate with system so ingrained that it has become an integral part of his being. The artistic sense of perfection in work is another much-to-be-desired quality to be cultivated. No matter how trifling the matter on hand, do it with a feeling that it demands the best that is in you, and when done look it over with a critical eye, not sparing a strict judgment of yourself. This it is that makes anatomy a student's touchstone. Take the man who does his " part " to perfection, who has got out all there is in it, who labors over the tags of connective tissue and who demonstrates Meckel's ganglion in his part — this is the fellow in after years who is apt in emergencies, who saves a leg badly smashed in a railway accident, or fights out to the finish, never knowing when he is beaten, in a case of typhoid fever.

Learn to love the freedom of the student life, only too quickly to pass away; the absence of the coarser cares of after days, the joy in comradeship, the delight in new work, the happiness in knowing that you are making progress. Once only can you enjoy these pleasures. The seclusion of the student life is not always good for a man, particularly for those of you who will afterwards engage in general practice, since you will miss that facility of intercourse upon which often the doctor's success depends. On the other hand sequestration is essential for those of you with high ambitions proportionate to your capacity. It was for such that St. Chrysostom gave his famous counsel, " Depart from the highways and transplant thyself into some enclosed ground, for it is hard for a tree that stands by the wayside to keep its fruit till it be ripe."

Has work no dangers connected with it? What of this bogie of overwork of which we hear so much? There are dangers, but they may readily be avoided with a little care. I can only mention two, one physical, one mental. The very best students are often not the strongest. Ill-health, the bridle of Theages, as Plato called it in the case of one of his friends whose mind had thriven at the expense of his body, may have been the diverting influence towards books or the profession. Among the good men who have studied with me there stands out in my remembrance many a young Lycidas, "dead ere his prime," sacrificed to carelessness in habits of living and neglect of ordinary sanitary laws. Medical students are much exposed to infection of all sorts, to combat which the body must be kept in first-class condition. Grosseteste, the great Bishop of Lincoln, remarked that there were three things necessary for temporal salvation — food, sleep, and a cheerful disposition. Add to these suitable exercise and you have the means by which good health may be maintained. Not that health is to be a matter of perpetual solicitation, but habits which favor the *corpus sanum* foster the *mens sana,* in which the joy of living and the joy of working are blended in one harmony. Let me read you a quotation from old Burton, the great authority on *morbi eruditorum.* There are "many reasons why students dote more often than others. The first is their negligence; other men look to their tools, a painter will wash his pencils, a smith will look to his hammer, anvil, forge; a husbandman will mend his plough-irons, and grind his hatchet, if it be dull; a falconer or huntsman will have an especial care of his hawks, hounds, horses, dogs, etc.; a musician will string and unstring his lute, etc.; only scholars neglect that instrument, their brain and spirits (I mean) which they daily use."

Much study is not only believed to be a weariness of the flesh, but also an active cause of ill-health of mind, in all grades and phases. I deny that work, legitimate work, has anything to do with this. It is that foul fiend Worry who is responsible for a large majority of the cases. The more carefully one looks into the causes of nervous break-down in students, the less important is work *per se* as a factor. There are a few cases of genuine over-work, but they are not common. Of the causes of worry in the student life there are three of prime importance to which I may briefly refer.

An anticipatory attitude of mind, a perpetual forecasting, disturbs the even tenor of his way and leads to disaster. Years ago a sentence in one of Carlyle's essays made a lasting impression on me: "Our duty is not to *see* what lies dimly at a distance, but to *do* what lies clearly at hand." I have long maintained that the best motto for a student is, "Take no thought for the morrow. Let the day's work suffice; live for it, regardless of what the future has in store, believing that to-morrow should take thought for the things of itself." There is no such safeguard against the morbid apprehensions about the future, the dread of examinations and the doubt of the ultimate success. Nor is there any risk that such an attitude may breed carelessness. On the contrary, the absorption in the duty of the hour is in itself the best guarantee of ultimate success. "He that observeth the wind shall not sow, and he that regardeth the clouds shall not reap," which means you cannot work profitably with your mind set upon the future.

Another potent cause of worry is an idolatry by which many of you will be sore let and hindered. The mistress of your studies should be the heavenly Aphrodite, the motherless daughter of Uranus. Give her your whole heart, and she will be your protectress and friend. A jealous creature, brooking no second, if she finds you trifling and coquetting with her rival, the younger, earthly Aphrodite, daughter of Zeus and Dione, she will whistle you off and let you down the wind to be a prey, perhaps to the examiners, certainly to the worm regret. In plainer language, put your affections in cold storage for a few years, and you will take them out ripened, perhaps a bit mellow, but certainly less subject to those frequent changes which perplex so many young men. Only a grand passion, and all-absorbing devotion to the elder goddess can save the man with a congenital tendency to philandering, the flighty Lydgate who sports with Celia and Dorothea, and upon whom the judgment ultimately falls in a basil-plant of a wife like Rosamond.

And thirdly, one and all of you will have to face the ordeal of every student in this generation who sooner or later tries to mix the waters of science with the oil of faith. You can have a great deal of both if you only keep them separate. The worry comes from the attempt at mixture. As general practitioners you will need all the faith you can carry, and while it may not always be of the conventional pattern, when expressed in your lives rather than on your lips, the variety is not a bad one from the standpoint of St. James; and may help to counteract the common scandal alluded to in the celebrated diary of that gossipy old pastor-doctor, the Rev. John Ward: "One told the Bishop of Gloucester that he imagined physicians of all other men the most competent judges of all other affairs of religion — and his reason was because they were wholly unconcerned with it." — WILLIAM OSLER. From *Aequanimitas, with Other Addresses to Medical Students, Nurses, and Practitioners of Medicine.* P. Blakiston's Sons and Co. Reprinted by permission.

IV

What the City Does for the Public Health

Of the many duties of the government of a large city, none is more important in its results than the preservation of the public health. The size and manifold complexity of the task are hardly appreciated at first glance. Much of the work is done behind the scenes, without the glamour of the limelight in which the men of the fire department play their part, or the glory of the uniforms which seem to make such heroes of the overconspicuous policemen. Consequently it is work with which the average citizen is not very familiar. In fact, if the municipal department should cease its activities to-day, most of us would notice little difference. We should get along about as before, without realizing that our lives had suddenly been shortened. Only when the yearly mortality tables were made out would the difference be apparent. Surely, a department that adds to the years of human life is well worth study.

In an unattractive neighborhood in the older part of the city a narrow alleyway leads back between dingy buildings to a dilapidated courtyard, ugly and uninviting. Across the entrance to this alley an old sign may be seen bearing in faded gold letters the inscription, "City Hall Annex." Here, tucked away in this time-worn corner, may be found the man who has the final responsibility for the health of the city. He is Health Commissioner, James Bosley. Under him are an Assistant Commissioner and twenty-four Health Wardens, one for each ward of the city. These wardens are physicians who supervise the work of the department in their several wards. The actual labor is performed by a force of inspectors, chemists, clerks, and other employees.

The equipment of the department consists principally of the offices and laboratories at the City Hall Annex and the quarantine station in the harbor. The headquarters of the department will repay a visit and will afford a revelation to many who have no idea of their size and importance. On the two lower floors are the offices and clerical department. One of the most interesting features here is the system of indexing all cases of contagious and infectious diseases as they are reported. Above are the two laboratories, chemical and bacteriological, and the stock rooms. Here we are in the real work-shop of our health authorities. Especially in the bacteriological laboratory is one impressed by the wonderful aid science has furnished in the fight against disease. Interesting as it might be, however, a description of these laboratories would swell this paper far beyond its reasonable length. Their value will be shown later.

Let us consider, for example, the work of the health department when a case of typhoid fever, or tuberculosis, or one of the contagious diseases like diphtheria is reported. A complete record of all the important facts is kept in a large card index used for that purpose. Thus the officials have always at their finger tips the latest information as to the state of the city's health, and can act intelligently in accordance with their knowledge. But in many cases the physician may be in doubt as to the exact nature of the disease he is endeavoring to treat. Here the bacteriological laboratory comes to his relief. At various convenient supply centers throughout the city, the health department distributes to the doctors what are known as culture sets. These are convenient receptacles for material which the physician inoculates with the germ of the suspected disease and sends to the bacteriological laboratory. Here a careful examination is made, and he is informed, usually within a few hours, of the result. That the medical men appreciate the value of this service is shown by the fact that in 1907 nearly three thousand such examinations were made to determine the presence of diphtheria alone.

Nor does the work of the department stop with the diagnosis of the disease. When the patient is too poor to pay for treatment, he is supplied without charge with antitoxin or vaccine virus. In contagious diseases, too, the health authorities see to the establishment of a quarantine. The lack of a suitable " pest-house " hampers this work. In this connection it may be well to mention the work of the ship quarantine to show what might be accomplished if this crying need were filled. This is the only port in the United States which has a municipal ship quarantine. The United States Government has charge of all the others. Yet a " clear bill " for a ship from Baltimore is accepted at any other port more readily than any other certificate.

The final and not least important service of the department in the matter of disease is the compiling, from the records I have mentioned and from the death reports, of the large volume of statistics issued at the close of each year. The information thus made available in the shape of tables, maps, and diagrams is important to the public and invaluable to the health authorities themselves. Only the intelligent study of these figures can show the points at which the brunt of the attack upon disease must be delivered. Without this knowledge the fight would be in the dark.

So far we have considered the work of the health department in curing disease only, but a large part of its work is directed toward the prevention of sickness. The food and water supply of the city must be healthful, or all else will be in vain. Especially must we have pure milk, for much of the illness in our cities the doctors attribute to impure milk. The work of the health department in this matter consists chiefly in enforcing the city ordinances. These prescribe in detail the conditions under which the cows shall be kept, the milking done, and the product handled and sold. Not only is all dilution or adulteration prohibited, but the exact minimum percentage of solids and butter fats is carefully prescribed. To enforce these provisions the health department employs a number of inspectors, whose energy is attested by the official statement that in a single year they inspected over two million gallons of milk. In this work of securing pure milk, both laboratories have their part. Seven thousand chemical analyses a year are required for the enforcement of the law requiring a given percentage of butter fats, while frequent bacteriological examinations reveal the causes of many typhoid cases.

But these energetic inspectors deal with many problems besides that of milk. Bakeries, shops, markets, and slaughterhouses all come under their watchful eye; and woe betide the unlucky butcher whose meat is tainted, or the baker who thinks more of his own pocket than of his customer's stomach. To the thousands of gallons of milk that failed to satisfy the legal requirements are to be added tons of bread, meat, and vegetables destroyed on account of some impurity.

Equally important with the food supply is the purity of the water. Here Baltimore faces a problem to the solution of which the health department can furnish little but information. Frequent analyses of the water show the city what it is drinking, even though the health authorities have no power to do more than recommend improvements.

Finally, the department performs a valuable service, even though a most thankless one, in the abatement of nuisances. Probably no public officer wins more cordial hatred than the man who, in the name of the law, interferes with a person's constitutional right to make himself obnoxious and dangerous to the community. The variety of forms in which this right is exercised is too great to catalogue here. Every one is familiar with many of them.

The official report shows clearly that the department has been of great service in doing away with these nuisances, yet they need not seek just yet for other worlds to conquer. The city is still able to furnish them with ample opportunities for more work of the same kind. As a whole, however, her health department and its work may rightly be to the city a source of pride. (Student Theme.)

EXERCISES IN STRUCTURE

Practice the analysis of topics by applying to them one key after another and noting the value of the resulting structure for use in oral or written discussion. For example:

Idea	Key	Divisions
My future fellow-workers	Their relation to me	1. As friends and comrades 2. As competitors 3. As helpers 4. As judges of my worth
	Their activities as a group	1. In professional societies 2. In social clubs 3. In the maintenance of standards 4. In publications 5. In the collection of books
My future vocation	Its significance	1. As a business 2. As a daily occupation 3. As a service of society 4. As a source of pleasure and interest

Analyze in this way: Moving Pictures; The Airplane in Peace; Sources of Mechanical Power; The Value of

Courtesy; Good Roads; Student Self-Government; College Athletics; Postal Savings; The Cost of Living; Poetry.

REFERENCES

1. To discussions of the principles of structure. *English Composition* by Barrett Wendell (Scribners); *The Working Principles of Rhetoric* by J. F. Genung (Ginn); *English Composition in Theory and Practice* by H. S. Canby (Macmillan); *English Composition* by Greenough and Hersey (Macmillan); *Studies in Structure and Style* by W. T. Brewster (Macmillan).

2. To selections for analysis as to structure. *Self-Cultivation in English* by G. H. Palmer (Houghton Mifflin); *The Physical Basis of Life* by T. H. Huxley in *Methods and Results* (Appleton); *The Old Manse* by Nathaniel Hawthorne in *Mosses from an Old Manse; Farewell Address* by George Washington; *The Formation of Good Habits* by William James in *The Principles of Psychology,* Volume I, Chapter IV; *An Adventurer in a Velvet Jacket* by Henry Van Dyke, *Scribner's Magazine,* August, 1922; *The Great Stupidity* by William Archer, *The Atlantic Monthly,* June, 1921; *What England Thinks of America* by Sir Philip Gibbs, *Harper's Magazine,* June, 1920; *Civilization and Oil* by Leo Pasvolsky, *The Atlantic Monthly,* February, 1923; *The Call of the Job* by R. C. Cabot, *The Atlantic Monthly,* November, 1913; *Gladstone the Man* by James Bryce, *The Outlook,* February 12, 1910.

CHAPTER III

STRUCTURE IN THE PARAGRAPH

DIVISION INTO PARAGRAPHS

27. The Nature of the Paragraph. Division into paragraphs may be taken as typical of the simplest and most-used of all mechanical devices for making written speech understandable, namely, the separation of units by blank spaces. A glance at a printed book will show how variously useful this device is. Words, which in the old manuscripts were run into each other with no separation at all and had to be puzzled out by the reader, are made distinct from each other by spaces. Sentences are separated by a wider space than is thought necessary between words — a refinement that may well be imitated in handwriting. Each paragraph begins on a new line indented one or two " ems " from the left margin. Each chapter is distinguished from its context by beginning on a new page with ample space left blank at the top.

The rhetorical unit set off by paragraph division has tended in modern usage to receive more and more attention. From being regarded as a mere convention not important enough to be discussed in lectures on rhetoric, it has come to be treated as an extremely significant unit of structure. Boys and girls are told to " think in paragraphs," the unity, coherence, and emphasis of paragraphs are familiar terms in text-books of rhetoric, and the development of " topic sentences " is a routine method of teaching the art of writing. One who obeys modern rhetorical doctrine will use the paragraph as a unit of construction, just as he uses the sentence as a unit of style. Sentences will form themselves almost automatically as the thought unfolds; paragraphs will be foreseen and will ordinarily grow out of topic sentences, expressed or implied, that bear to the paragraph much the same relation as the central idea bears to a whole composition.

28. Types of Paragraphing. Usage in paragraph division differs markedly in different forms of writing. In explanation and argument the paragraph is a grouping of ideas, serving as an extremely useful device for carrying out the general design. The discussion of paragraph structure which follows in this chapter refers to units of this type. In portrayal a paragraph is usually a grouping of impressions rather than of ideas; consequently its unity is less exacting and it has less to do with the general plan. In narration paragraphs serve two distinct purposes: in dialogue they indicate every change of speaker; in prolonged speeches, as in portrayal, they are merely convenient groupings of sentences which may be shaped according to the taste and judgment of the author. The paragraphing of business letters and advertising is still more free from the conventions of unity and emphasis observed by careful writers of exposition and argument.

29. The Length of the Paragraph. The length of the paragraph is, to a certain extent, conventional, and the trend of usage has been, until recently, toward shorter paragraphs. This tendency has reached its limit in the paragraphing of certain newspapers, especially in the editorial column, in which almost every sentence is indented and a paragraph of more than two or three sentences is unusual. Such so-called paragraphs are really sentences written large. However useful they may be for strident emphasis in a column that might otherwise be neglected in favor of more sensational reading matter, they are not to be imitated in other kinds of writing. Although paragraphs of a thousand words or more, once not uncommon, are now rare, a paragraph of less than one hundred words is still noticeably short.

The length of a given paragraph is to be determined by two considerations — convenience and proportion. Convenience requires that the paragraph, no matter how well unified, shall not be longer than can be readily grasped by the reader with a single mental effort. If a topic designed as the subject of a single paragraph requires seven or eight hundred words for its development, the writer may well ask himself if it does not naturally fall into two or more sub-topics, each of which may be developed in a single paragraph. Proportion requires, on the other hand, that no topic shall be given the distinction of treatment in a separate paragraph which does not deserve such prominence. Paragraphs naturally vary in length, for there is more to be said on some topics than there is on others; but a relatively long paragraph must be clear in substance and structure if it is to bear the test of convenience, and a relatively short paragraph must convey matter of high significance if it is to escape the violation of proportion.

How these principles are observed in practice may be learned by an examination of the paragraph division of President Hadley's speech of welcome (see page 100). The first of the five paragraphs is merely directive; it does not develop the thought expressed in it, but gives direction to the thought of the context. Such a paragraph is normally much shorter than the usual connected paragraph. It may consist of only one sentence, and may serve to introduce a series of paragraphs or to link two parts of a discourse. The remaining four paragraphs range from 126 to 207 words. Each fulfils a part of the forecast made by the last sentence of the directive paragraph, and each develops the thought stated in its own opening sentence. The paragraph division thus cuts the speech into convenient lengths representing natural divisions of the thought. Had proportion required that the thought expressed by the four paragraphs be reduced in importance, the idea that the brotherhood of learning transcends bounds would have been developed in a single paragraph of, say, three hundred words. Had the subject-matter deserved fuller treatment, the second paragraph would probably have been expanded into two paragraphs, one devoted to the hosts and one to the guests. The third paragraph would perhaps have been expanded into two paragraphs, in one of which the absence of natural limits and in the other the lack of artificial limits of place would be discussed. Thus division into paragraphs adjusts itself to the convenience of the reader, to the scale of treatment, and to the natural divisions of the thought.

THE CONSTRUCTION OF PARAGRAPHS

The break between two paragraphs is a stopping-place where the writer may fix his attention anew upon the plan of his work. One unit of construction has been completed; another is about to be undertaken. A new paragraph is foreseen much as one who takes a walk across country looks ahead to the next fence or to the brow of a hill. The walker's glance includes neither the separate steps, which will adjust themselves to the footing, nor the ultimate goal of his outing, which has already determined his general direction, but only the stretch of field before him. The paragraph is thus the smallest unit of prevision, a practical device the general use of which is a characteristic of modern literary method. To take advantage of it, the beginner should learn to build up his thought one paragraph at a time.

30. The Paragraph Idea. The first essential in the construction of a good paragraph is to know definitely what idea you want it to express. Time spent in thinking between paragraphs is usually time well spent. The paragraph idea may be foreseen as a sub-division in your plan; it may be only a part of such a sub-division; it may as you turn it over in your mind appear to be the proper subject for two distinct paragraphs; but it must be distinct in your mind before you are ready to write effectively.

31. The Topic Sentence. Though the subject of a paragraph should be foreseen, its structure is not usually thought out in advance. Knowing what idea you wish the paragraph to express, write as fluently and freely as you can. While you write, and in revision, you may make the structure of your paragraph good by having in mind two simple devices: the use of a topic sentence and care for the coherent sequence of sentences.

The topic sentence is some one sentence in the paragraph which expresses the paragraph idea explicitly, as the title of a chapter expresses the fundamental idea of that chapter. Good paragraphs can be written without the use of a topic sentence; but the employment of such a sentence is so useful a device that it is the routine method of many careful writers. It is used in a variety of ways.

1. As a first sentence generalizing the paragraph idea. Study the following examples.

What we need is a genuine enthusiasm for criticism. We need young men as avid for criticism as the poets are for poetry. We need a school which shall be at once learned and supple — a school whose devotees will look forward to perfecting their art through their whole lives. It is not criticism to say that you like a thing, nor is it criticism to be unwilling to examine a thing. Criticism is the art of finding out what a man is trying to do and then, through knowledge and understanding, seeing if he has done it. If a man makes a chair half our criticism is occupied in regretting that he has not made a saddle and criticizing the chair for its inadequacies in regard to horseback-riding; while the other half cheerfully declares, either " I do like chairs " or " I don't like chairs." But the school some one must come and found will do neither of these things. It will spend itself in learning all there is to know about all sorts of chairs, and all sorts of saddles, and all the sorts of things which men make, so that when it is confronted with any of them it will recognize at once that particular kind of thing and be, at least in a measure, qualified to pronounce upon how good a thing of its kind it is. — AMY LOWELL, " On Criticism." *The Literary Review,* December 3, 1921. Used by permission.

As a nation, we are commonly accused by unsympathetic Europeans of being excessively practical. We are supposed to specialize in practicality. Thus, when England wants a railroad system reorganized she looks to America for a manager; and when Germany wants to make a better record in the Olympic games she sends to America for a trainer. There is less demand in Europe for American poets and musical composers, and, I regret to say, for American philosophers. Now we may believe that this reputation is not deserved, or we may glory in it. But in either case we can afford at least to see just what it means. Consider for a moment the verdict of one of our harshest critics, Mr. Lowes Dickinson of Cambridge University. " I am inclined to think," he says, " that the real end which Americans set before themselves is Acceleration. To be always moving, and always moving faster, that they think is the beatific life; and with their happy detachment from philosophy and speculation, they are not troubled by the question, Whither? If they are asked by Europeans, as they sometimes are, what is the point of going so fast? their only feeling is one of genuine astonishment. Why, they reply, you go fast! And what more can be said? " — R. B. PERRY in " The Useless Virtues." *The Atlantic Monthly,* September, 1914. Used by permission.

The effect of historical reading is analogous, in many respects, to that produced by foreign travel. The student, like the tourist, is transported into a new state of society. He sees new fashions. He hears new modes of expression. His mind is enlarged by contemplating the wide diversities of laws, of morals, and of manners. But men may travel far, and return with minds as contracted as if they had never stirred from their own market town. In the same way, men may know the dates of many battles and the genealogies of many royal houses, and yet be no wiser. Most people look at past times as princes look at foreign countries.

More than one illustrious stranger has landed on our island amidst the shouts of a mob, has dined with the king, has hunted with the master of the stag-hounds, has seen the Guards reviewed, and a Knight of the Garter installed, has cantered along Regent Street, has visited St. Paul's, and noted down its dimensions; and has then departed, thinking that he has seen England. He has, in fact, seen a few public buildings, public men, and public ceremonies. But of the vast and complex system of society, of the fine shades of national character, of the practical operation of government and laws, he knows nothing. He who would understand these things rightly must not confine his observations to palaces and solemn days. He must see ordinary men as they appear in their ordinary business and in their ordinary pleasures. He must mingle in the crowds of the exchange and the coffee-house. He must obtain admittance to the convivial table and the domestic hearth. He must bear with vulgar expressions. He must not shrink from exploring even the retreats of misery. He who wishes to understand the condition of mankind in former ages must proceed on the same principle. If he attends only to public transactions, to wars, congresses, and debates, his studies will be as unprofitable as the travels of those imperial, royal, and serene sovereigns who form their judgment of our island from having gone in state to a few fine sights, and from having held formal conferences with a few great officers. — MACAULAY in *History*.

2. As a first or second sentence forecasting the paragraph idea and the structure of the paragraph.

Two kinds of expository writing are natural for Americans. The first is a hard-hitting statement, straight out of intense feeling or labored thought. That was Emerson's way (in spite of his expansiveness), and Thoreau's also. You read them by pithy sentences, not paragraphs. They assail you by ideas, not by insidious structures of thought. The second is an easy-going comment on life, often slangy or colloquial and frequently so undignified as not to seem literature. Mark Twain and Josh Billings wrote that way; Ring Lardner writes so to-day. — HENRY S. CANBY in *The Literary Review*, November 19, 1921. Used by permission.

Of gifts, which are essential in courtship, I would say only two things, the second being very English. One is that they should be varied, just as pleasures should be varied. Two pounds of chocolate every Tuesday afternoon punctually is very nice, but it cloys. Occasionally substitute peppermints. The second and English suggestion is: don't overdo it. Excessive gifts create an unfortunate precedent in the married state; also, fulfillment feeds desire in these things, and he who begins in silver may end in platinum. Lastly, frequent gifts blunt surprise; gifts are made rare mainly by their rarity. — W. L. GEORGE in " The Art of Courtship," *Harper's Magazine,* January, 1922. Used by permission.

3. As a question. The answer to the question constitutes the paragraph. Sometimes, as in the paragraph by Mr. Colton cited below, the question topic is the subject of more than one paragraph. Notice that the paragraph idea is not expressed by the topic sentence. The answer to the question, Wherein lies the magic of narrative? is found specifically in the next to the last sentence of the second of the two paragraphs.

Wherein lies the magic of narrative? There are other magics in literature — the magic of rhythm and melodious words; the magic of vivid description, of felicitous phrases, of images that give a sudden sense of expansion, or are like the explosion and glare of a flashlight; the magic even of concision, logic, and clarity. But there is no spell or enchantment that on the whole strikes as surely and quickly as narrative. A something to the mind's eye is visible and in motion, and because it is like the something in ourselves that moves forward from hour to hour, from memory to hope — out of that resemblance comes a merging and blending, and we " forget ourselves to marble." We have crossed a misty threshold into another room. Alice through the looking glass is an allegory of the fiction process, as it appears to the reader. She looked into the Looking Glass Room, and then, suddenly and somehow, she was through the glass, and the wooden chess men were all alive.

Story writing is imagining persons and setting them in action. It is the kind of literary creation that most resembles the creation of life, and the quick grip of narrative comes probably from this. We blend and lose ourselves in a story more readily and completely because it is more like us. Hence the rule: " Make it visible and make it move "; and do so from the start, because its peculiar spell does not begin to work until the visible motion begins. Make it visible and make it move; other things being equal, it should begin to move as soon as it is visible; which means, in application, never begin with discussion, and as a rule begin with incident rather than description; for even description, before the narrative picks it up, is something of a dead weight. The main magic and kindling spark is in the motion of the story. The motion once started will give life and heat to the comment it carries, but the spell does not begin until the movement begins. — ARTHUR COLTON in " The Short Story." *The Literary Review,* October 1, 1921. Used by permission.

What is, after all, the aim of education? I suppose it is two-fold: firstly, to make of the mind a bright, keen, and effective in-strument, capable of seeing a point, of grappling with a difficulty, of presenting facts or thoughts with clearness and precision. A young man properly educated should be able to detect a fallacy, to correct by acquired clearsightedness a false logical position. He should not be at the mercy of any new theory which may be pre-sented to him in a specious and attractive shape. That is, I sup-pose, the negative side. Then secondly, he should have a cultivated taste for intellectual things, a power of enjoyment; he should not bow meekly to authority in the matter of literature, and force him-self into the admiration of what is prescribed, but he should be possest of a dignified and wholesome originality, he should have his own taste clearly defined. If his bent is historical, he should be eagerly interested in any new masterly presentation of historical theory, whether new or old; if philosophical, he should keep abreast of modern speculation; if purely literary, he should be able to return hour after hour to masterpieces that breathe and burn. — A. C. BENSON in *The House of Quiet.* By permission of E. P. Dutton and Co.

4. As a summary final sentence.

The wild things are creatures of the moment. They live ex-clusively in the present. For them there is neither past nor future, and so there can be no regret for what has happened or foreboding of what may some time come to pass. There is present pain, of course, and there is present fear; but both are evanescent. When the immediate cause is removed, they vanish and there is no realization that they may return. It is true that the wild things live in constant danger, but it is not true that they live in constant terror. The operation of those unchanging natural laws which science writes out with her cold deliberate finger cannot be denied, nor can it be maintained that they are not as cruel as death itself. We cannot blind ourselves to the slaughter which results from the struggle for existence. But the great truth is that, in spite of all the slaughter and of all the pain through which nature works to some far-off and undiscoverable end, the living creatures of the earth — helpless though they be in the grip of immutable law — are happy. — H. R. SASS in "A Suit against Science." *The Atlantic Monthly,* May, 1914. Used by permission.

Any definition is the clearer for examples. To make sure of ours, then, we may well recall a few names which undoubtedly illustrate it. The Psalms are literature, so is the Iliad, so are the Epistles of Saint Paul, so is the Æneid, and the Divine Comedy, and Don Quixote, and Hamlet. These few names are enough to remind us not only of what literature is, but also of the fact which most distinguishes it from other arts of expression. The lines and colors which embody architecture, sculpture, and painting, can be understood by anybody with eyes. Though to people like ourselves, who have grown up amid the plastic traditions of classical antiquity and the Italian Renaissance, an Egyptian painting or a Japanese print looks odd, it remains, even to us, comprehensible. The Psalms, on the other hand, were written in Hebrew, the Iliad and the Epistles in dialects of Greek, the Æneid was written in Latin, the Divine Comedy in Italian, Don Quixote in Spanish, and Hamlet in Elizabethan English; except through the unsatisfactory medium of translation one and all must be sealed books to those who do not know the languages native to the men who phrased them. World-old legends, after all, are the wisest; the men who fled from Babel could each see in the deserted tower a monument of impious aspiration, but this thought of each was sealed from the rest by the confusion of tongues. So to this day literature is of all fine arts the most ineradicably national. — BARRETT WENDELL in *The Literary History of America.* Used by permission of Charles Scribner's Sons.

32. The Sentence Sequence. The paragraph idea unfolds in a series of sentences which must come to the reader in single file. Each of these sentences is to be understood in relation to its context, and that relation must be unmistakable. These are some of the devices by means of which the logical connection of successive sentences is made easily apparent.

1. The Closeness of the Thought.

The only large values are those in which our ancestors participated. The oldest of wonders is the greatest — life. An ironclad, as such, is a commonplace beside a ship, and society merely as society is a more stupendous fact than Rome or England. The Iliad is less remarkable than speech, and the aeroplane is only a mote in the sky. Landscape, the family, the nation, religion — their origins are lost in the silence of a gray antiquity. The Now — the present — is indeed sacred; but its sacredness is inappreciable to those who are circumscribed by its limits; it is reserved for minds that escape its bounds. — R. B. PERRY in " The Useless Virtues." *The Atlantic Monthly,* September, 1914. Used by permission.

2. Parallel or Antithetical Sentence Structure. Such parallelism gives the thought a recognizable pattern.

Before proceeding let me say that I think I have no prejudice against the Southern people. They are just what we would be in their situation. If slavery did not now exist among them, they would not introduce it. If it did now exist among us, we should not instantly give it up. This I believe of the masses North and South. Doubtless there are individuals on both sides who would not hold slaves under any circumstances, and others who would gladly introduce slavery anew if it were out of existence. We know that some Southern men do free their slaves, go North and become tip-top Abolitionists, while some Northern ones go South and become most cruel slave-masters. — ABRAHAM LINCOLN in a speech at Peoria, Illinois, October 16, 1854.

3. Connective Words. Such words, both conjunctions and pronouns, give the thought a close texture.

Among the innumerable victims of the Great War there is one unwept, unhonored, almost unnoted — and that is British Liberalism. By that is not meant, here, the Liberal Party, which, indeed, still pretends to exist, although it is divided against itself. What for the time being has disappeared is something profounder and more important than that — the spirit of Liberalism. The characters of that spirit may be indicated by recalling two great names: John Milton and John Stuart Mill; and two masterpieces: the *Areopagitica*, and the *Essay on Liberty*. From those men and in those works the spirit breathes. It is a spirit of individualism, of moral courage, of free speech and free thought, with a faith that, in a fair and open contest, truth will win the day. This account does not indeed define the political programme of Liberalism. But the programme grew out of the spirit. For freedom of thought, freedom of speech, freedom of trade, freedom of nationality, political freedom of every kind, spring from, and are directed to, freedom of soul. — G. LOWES DICKINSON in " The Future of British Liberalism." *The Atlantic Monthly,* April, 1920. Used by permission.

4. Directive Expressions. Such expressions guide the thought. They make the structure formal but very clear. The directive words in the following paragraph could be omitted without destroying the integrity of the thought.

In short, we may say, and that without hesitation, that the community of mankind could not be formed out of such men as now exist anywhere on the earth. The human material for such a community is lacking. In the first place, neither our intellect nor our knowledge is equal to drawing up a code of laws which would be universally applicable to all mankind — we should lack the legislators. Secondly, even if the legislators were forthcoming, the task of administering the laws with a just regard to the interests of the whole human race is far beyond any powers we at present possess. Thirdly, even if we had both competent legislators and competent administrators, it is doubtful if we could find anywhere, at present, a race or a nation which could be trusted to *submit* to universal legislation, when this required it to sacrifice its own interests to the interests of mankind at large. To this may be added a fourth inability, which is not strictly in line with the other three but which illustrates them all, namely, that no means exists of coping with the widespread disobedience that would unquestionably arise if the attempt were made to impose universal legislation on the many immature nations which now exist on the earth. — L. P.

JACKS in "The International Mind." *The Atlantic Monthly,* March, 1920. Used by permission.

33. Emphasis in the Paragraph. We use the paragraph as a means of unfolding an idea — of developing it into its parts. All the things that we have to say in it are subordinate to the paragraph idea and all are related to each other. But not all are of the same importance. Some deserve more of the reader's attention than do others. One of the sentences of which a paragraph is composed may be entitled to prominence because it generalizes the others, because it is more forcibly expressed, or because it summarizes the thought of the whole. First, then, determine what parts of a paragraph are entitled to prominent places.

1. Position. Next, consider what are the prominent places. In a two-dimension composition these would be in the foreground and the eye would be led toward them. In the single file of sentences the places of prominence are next to spaces — at the beginning and the end.

The beginning and the end, though alike in claiming attention, differ as to the use that can be made of them for emphasis. A guiding principle may be found in this rule, Begin with what is significant and end with what is impressive. The beginning should be significant. It looks forward; it may perhaps not be the topic-sentence but it should give some clue to what the paragraph is about. The ending should be impressive. It exists to clinch what has gone before, to stamp upon the mind the thought of the whole paragraph. This amounts to saying that the opening sentence has particular need to be clear and the closing sentence to be forcible. The first is more likely to be general and literal; the last, to be specific and imaginative. A comparison of the opening and closing sentences of the following paragraph will sufficiently illustrate the principle.

Among the peculiarly beautiful effects that America produces the sky signs must be counted high. I had seen some when in San Francisco against the deep Californian sky, and they captivated the startled vision; but the reckless profusion and movement of the great white way, as I turned out of Forty-second Street, on my first night in New York, came as something more than a surprise — a revelation of willful gayety. We have normally nothing in England to compare with it. Nor can we have even our summer exhibition imitations of it so long as coal is so rare and costly. But though we have the driving power for the electricity we could never get such brilliance, for the clear American atmosphere is an essential ally. In our humid airs all the diamond glints would be blurred. For the purest beauty of traceries of white light against a blue background one must go, however, not to Broadway, which is too bizarre, but to Luna Park on Coney Island. Odd that it should be there, in that bewildering medley of sound and restlessness, that one extreme of loveliness should be found; but I maintain that it is so, that nothing more strangely and voluptuously beautiful could be seen than all those minarets and domes, those lines and curves formed of myriad lamps, turning the night into an ocean of velvet blue mysterious and soft and profound. — E. V. Lucas in "From an American Note-Book." *The Outlook,* September 15, 1920. Used by permission.

Whoever has made a voyage up the Hudson, must remember the Kaatskill Mountains. They are a dismembered branch of the great Appalachian family, and are seen away to the west of the river, swelling up to a noble height, and lording it over the surrounding country. Every change of season, every change of weather, indeed every hour of the day, produces some change in the magical hues and shapes of these mountains, and they are regarded by all the good wives, far and near, as perfect barometers. When the weather is fair and settled, they are clothed in blue and purple, and print their bold outlines on the clear evening sky; but sometimes when the rest of the landscape is cloudless, they will gather a hood of gray vapors about their summits which, in the last rays of the setting sun, will glow and light up like a crown of glory.

At the foot of these fairy mountains the voyager may have descried the light smoke curling up from a village, whose shingle roofs gleam among the trees, just where the blue tints of the upland melt away into the fresh green of the nearer landscape. It is a little village of great antiquity, having been founded by some of the Dutch colonists in the early times of the province, just about the beginning of the government of the good Peter Stuyvesant (may he rest in peace!) and there were some of the houses of the original settlers standing within a few years, built of small yellow bricks brought from Holland, having latticed windows and gable fronts, surmounted with weathercocks.

In that same village and in one of these very houses (which, to tell the precise truth, was sadly time-worn and weather-beaten), there lived many years since, while the country was yet a province of Great Britain, a simple good-natured fellow, of the name of Rip Van Winkle. He was a descendant of the Van Winkles who figured so gallantly in the chivalrous days of Peter Stuyvesant, and accompanied him to the siege of Fort Christina. He inherited, however, but little of the martial character of his ancestors. I have observed that he was a simple good-natured man; he was, moreover, a kind neighbor, and an obedient, hen-pecked husband. Indeed, to the latter circumstance might be owing that meekness of spirit which gained him such universal popularity; for those men are most apt to be obsequious and conciliating abroad, who are under the discipline of shrews at home. Their tempers, doubtless, are rendered pliant and malleable in the fiery furnace of domestic tribulation, and a curtain lecture is worth all the sermons in the world for teaching the virtues of patience and long-suffering. A termagant wife may, therefore, in some respects, be considered a tolerable blessing; and, if so, Rip Van Winkle was thrice blessed.
— IRVING in *Rip Van Winkle.*

2. Climax. The prominence of the end of a paragraph is greatly heightened if it is reached by a series of upward steps constituting a climax. Do not merely close with what is impressive. Arrange your material so that your sentences will gain in power as they approach the close.

Having, then, resolved that you will not waste recklessly, but earnestly use, these early days of yours, remember that all the duties of her children to England may be summed in two words — industry, and honor. I say, first, industry, for it is in this that soldier youth are especially tempted to fail. Yet, surely, there is no reason, because your life may possibly or probably be shorter than other men's, that you should therefore waste more recklessly the portion of it that is granted you; neither do the duties of your profession, which require you to keep your bodies strong, in any wise involve the keeping of your minds weak. So far from that, the experience, the hardship, and the activity of a soldier's life render his powers of thought more accurate than those of other men; and while, for others, all knowledge is often little more than a means of amusement, there is no form of science which a soldier may not at some time or other find bearing on business of life and death. A young mathematician may be excused for languor in studying curves to be described only with a pencil; but not in tracing those which are to be described with a rocket. Your knowledge of a wholesome herb may involve the feeding of an army; and acquaintance with an obscure point of geography, the success of a campaign. Never waste an instant's time, therefore: the sin of idleness is a thousand-fold greater in you than in other youths; for the fates of those who will one day be under your command hang upon your knowledge; lost moments now will be lost lives then, and every instant which you carelessly take for play, you buy with blood. — RUSKIN in *The Crown of Wild Olive*.

To an Englishman who is not entirely devoid of imagination, America brings a sense of incalculable enlargement of the powers and privileges conferred upon him by the accident of birth. His mother-tongue has made him free of this gigantic, this illimitable civilization, with all its stupendous achievements and its fabulous potentialities. He is akin by blood to the people who remain, in spite of all admixture, the leading factors in that civilization; and he has no doubt that the non-English elements — all but one — will mean ultimate enrichment of the composite stock. For the calamitous presence of the African element he ought to feel co-responsible, since it is largely due to the sins of his forefathers. America, to put it at the very lowest, is a product, an extension of English history. It is born of the follies of English kings, the bigotry of English prelates, the greatness and the littleness of English statesmen, the indomitable tenacity of British pioneers, the liberal conservatism of British nation-builders, and the magnanimity of two world-heroes who, though they never saw the shores of Britain, were none the less of the purest British blood. An Anglo-Saxon nation it certainly is not; but a creation of the Anglo-Saxon spirit it as certainly is. The Englishman is either an ignoramus or a fool who does not recognize in his kinship to America an inestimable enhancement of his birthright. — WILLIAM ARCHER in "The Great Stupidity." *The Atlantic Monthly*, June, 1921. Used by permission.

3. Contrast. Emphasis in a paragraph, as in other units both larger and smaller, is gained by contrast. If your subject-matter includes ideas that are distinctly opposites, arrange them so as to bring out their opposition.

People often ask why the practical Americans use four syllables to designate an appliance which we denote by the single syllable — lift. This is at first sight paradoxical; but after a few days in America, you realize that the two words are admirably appropriate to two very different things. The American elevator exhilaratingly elevates, the British lift laboriously lifts. I confess to taking great delight in the swift, sensitive machines that rush you up in the twinkling of an eye to the twentieth floor of a great hotel or business building. They are to the crawling, doddering British lift as a race-horse to a pack-mule. The tone of mind that professes to shrink in horror from such achievements of "mechanical civilization" is one of the innumerable phases of the Great Stupidity. — WILLIAM ARCHER in "The Great Stupidity." *The Atlantic Monthly*, June, 1921. Used by permission.

The Puritan was made up of two different men, the one all self-abasement, penitence, gratitude, passion; the other proud, calm, inflexible, sagacious. He prostrated himself in the dust before his Maker; but he set his foot on the neck of his king. In his devotional retirement he prayed with convulsions, and groans, and tears. He was half-maddened by glorious or terrible illusions. He heard the lyres of angels or the tempting whispers of fiends. He caught a gleam of the Beatific Vision, or woke screaming from dreams of everlasting fire. But when he took his seat in the council, or girt on his sword for war, these tempestuous workings of the soul had left no perceptible trace behind them. People who saw nothing of the godly but their uncouth visages, and heard nothing from them but their groans and their whining hymns, might laugh at them. But those had little reason to laugh who encountered them in the hall of debate or on the field of battle. These fanatics brought to civil and military affairs a coolness of judgment and an immutability of purpose which some writers have thought inconsistent with their religious zeal, but which were in fact the necessary effects of it. The intensity of their feelings on one subject made them tranquil on every other. One overpowering sentiment had subjected to itself pity and hatred, ambition and fear. Death had lost its terrors and pleasure its charms. They had their smiles and their tears, their raptures and their sorrows, but not for the things of this world. Enthusiasm had made them Stoics, had cleared their minds from every vulgar passion and prejudice, and raised them above the influence of danger and of corruption. It sometimes might lead them to pursue unwise ends, but never to choose unwise means. They went through the world, like Sir Artegal's iron man Talus with his flail, crushing and trampling down oppressors, mingling with human beings, but having neither part nor lot in human infirmities, insensible to fatigue, to pleasure, and to pain, not to be pierced by any weapon, not to be withstood by any barrier. — MACAULAY in *Milton*.

4. Repetition. Emphasis in a paragraph is secured also by repetition. A phrase that is skilfully echoed and re-echoed acquires a momentum that drives it home and makes it unforgettable.

Mr. President, I know how imperfectly I have stated this argument. I know how feeble is a single voice amid this din and tempest, this delirium of empire. It may be that the battle for this day is lost. But I have an assured faith in the future. I have an assured faith in justice and the love of liberty of the American people. The stars in their courses fight for freedom. The Ruler of the heavens is on that side. If the battle to-day go against it, I appeal to another day, not distant and sure to come. I appeal from the clapping of hands and the stamping of feet and the brawling and the shouting to the quiet chamber where the Fathers gathered in Philadelphia. I appeal from the spirit of trade to the spirit of liberty. I appeal from the Empire to the Republic. I appeal from the millionaire, and the boss, and the wire-puller, and the manager, to the statesman of the elder time, in whose eyes a guinea never glistened, who lived and died poor, and who left to his children and to his countrymen a good name, far better than riches. I appeal from the Present, bloated with material prosperity, drunk with the lust of empire, to another and a better age. I appeal from the Present to the Future and to the Past. — GEORGE F. HOAR in a speech in the United States Senate, April 17, 1900.

So downe he fell, and forth his life did breath,
That vanisht into smoke and cloudes swift;
So downe he fell, that th' earth him underneath
Did grone, as feeble so great load to lift;
So downe he fell, as an huge rocky clift,
Whose false foundacion waves have washt away,
With dreadfull poyse is from the mayneland rift,
And rolling downe great Neptune doth dismay:
So downe he fell, and like an heaped mountaine lay.
— SPENSER, *The Faerie Queene*, I, 2, stanza liv.

34. The Thought of the Paragraph. How does a paragraph idea grow into a paragraph? There is no question that an inexperienced writer would rather hear answered. Good writing reads so easily that it seems there must be magic in the flow of the thought, yet the beginner often finds it hard to discover anything to say. Good writing is not really easy writing; it is most often the writing of somebody who has thought and felt so much about his subject that ideas seem to come of themselves. For such a person the suggestions that follow are unnecessary. For a student who has to write a theme or a mature writer whose subject has not yet unfolded itself in his mind it may be profitable to consider ways of discovering something to say about a paragraph topic that seems to belong in his plan.

1. How to start the development of an idea.

First, phrase the paragraph idea for yourself — not necessarily for a reader — and look closely at the main words. Examine the subject of your sentence as if that word stood by itself and you had not thought about it before. Do the same thing with the predicate. If you have expressed your idea clearly the chief words of your tentative sentence will prove to be fuller of meaning than you had at first imagined. Next, think of synonyms and concrete equivalents for these main words. The comparison of two words which mean pretty nearly the same thing will help you to find out what you really do mean. Finally, if necessary, try to image your idea, or the thought expressed by one of your capital words, either literally or figuratively.

2. *How to carry on the development of an idea.*

If you have thought earnestly about your paragraph idea, you are ready to experiment with its development in your first draft. Try to unfold it for your reader by using one or more of these devices.

(*a*) By particularization. Turn your general terms into less general terms. If you are to discuss the value of good temper in a man's college life and you have got to the point of showing that it is one of the traits of character that most influence a man's friendships, offer us some of the particular qualities in an even-tempered man — his ability to remain cheerful in defeat, to conceal disappointment, to see another's good fortune without envy, to ignore petty irritations, to keep silent under taunts, let us say — which make him an agreeable companion. The simplest and often the most useful means of analyzing an idea is to set forth its component parts.

Meditation has an advantage over discussion. It takes two to carry on a discussion, whereas any one who is so disposed can meditate. Moreover in a discussion we are limited. We cannot contemplate the whole subject, but we must take one side while our opponent takes the other. We cannot look at the facts as they go about their ordinary business in the actual workaday world. They must be mobilized. They leave their peaceful avocations, hurriedly put on a uniform, and flock to the colors. When we review them we think of nothing but their fighting value. — S. M. CROTHERS in " Meditations on Votes for Women." *The Atlantic Monthly*, October, 1914. Used by permission.

(*b*) By exemplification. Cite examples of a class of persons or things or instances of the working of a principle. Perhaps you can recall a student whose equanimity carried him successfully through severe trials. Telling about him will make concrete your idea of the worth of good temper.

Now we live in an age in which the possibilities of change have suddenly been greatly enhanced; in which the old moral and religious restraints have been greatly relaxed; in which routine and habit are violently disturbed. Modern means of communication alone have opened up such possibilities of varied human intercourse that it seems slavery to be forced to continue to act on the former incapacities of mankind. We can move about four or five times as fast as our ancestors; all parts of the world are relatively accessible with a fair degree of comfort; we can send word to our fellow beings in various speedy, informal, and inexpensive ways. We are moreover relieved from many of the detailed labors once necessary to supply our daily needs. A hundred years ago a country family had to spend several hours looking after its own milk supply; days would be consumed in preparing food material, garments, candles, or soap, now to be bought in a few hours by an excursion in a Ford to the nearest store. The hours of labor are being steadily reduced and new problems of free time emerge. All these things combine to stir new forms of restlessness — a consciousness of unrealized possibilities and new resentments against boredom and routine. — JAMES HARVEY ROBINSON in " Freedom Reconsidered." *Harper's Magazine,* November, 1923. Used by permission.

(c) By proof. If your paragraph topic is an assertion that may be challenged, think of reasons why it is true. What would convince a reader that you are right?

A steadfast concert for peace can never be maintained except by a partnership of democratic nations. No autocratic government could be trusted to keep faith within it or observe its covenants. It must be a league of honor, a partnership of opinion. Intrigue would eat its vitals away; the plottings of inner circles who could plan what they would and render account to no one would be a corruption seated at its very heart. Only free peoples can hold their purpose and their honor steady to a common end and prefer the interests of mankind to any narrow interest of their own. — WOODROW WILSON. *Message to Congress,* April 2, 1917.

(d) By obverse statement. Tell what a thing is not and we may be better able to understand what it is.

Theology is not religion. Theology is what men think about religion, and that changes. Ritual is not religion. Ritual is the way in which men give emotional expression to their devotional life, and that changes. Ecclesiasticism is not religion. Ecclesiasticism is the form of organization which men adopt for the purpose of promoting religion in themselves or in others, and that changes. But religion does not change, except as the life of faith and hope and love is developed by the developing of manhood. The relation of the creed to religion is the relation of botany to flowers, astronomy to stars, grammar to language. The flowers precede the botany, the stars precede the astronomy, language precedes grammar. So religion precedes theology. Theology affects religion, because the life of men is affected by what they think about it. Liturgy affects religion, because life is influenced by the methods which men take to express it. Ecclesiasticism affects religion, because life is affected by the organizations which men frame to promote it. But religion, the life of God in the soul of man, the life of faith and hope and love, the life that seeks justice and mercy and humility and reverence, the life that strives after self-mastery and beneficent action and reverent loyalty and hopeful progress, is always essentially the same. — Editorial in *The Outlook,* November 3, 1906. Used by permission.

(*e*) By definition. If you have used terms that may not be instantly understood, define them. Making quite clear what you mean may be all that is required to get your contention accepted as true.

Our reconsideration of Freedom has brought up many matters which could merely be suggested and not discussed. Freedom is a mood, a frame of mind, and if our mood or frame of mind have a fair correspondence with our circumstances, then we are Free!
— JAMES HARVEY ROBINSON, *loc. cit.*

(*f*) By illustration, analogy, or fancy. Let your mind play with your idea. Ask yourself what it is like. Don't suppress your own whims. They may not belong in your finished draft but they may lead you to ideas that will be of use.

Style is the dress of thoughts; and let them be ever so just, if your style is homely, coarse, and vulgar, they will appear to as much disadvantage, and be as ill received as your person, though ever so well proportioned, would, if dressed in rags, dirt, and tatters. It is not every understanding that can judge of matter; but every ear can and does judge more or less of style; and were I either to speak, or write to the public, I should prefer moderate matter, adorned with all the beauties and elegancies of style, to the strongest matter in the world, ill-worded and ill-delivered. Your business is Negotiation abroad and Oratory in the House of Commons at home. What figure can you make in either case if your style is inelegant, I do not say bad? Imagine yourself writing an office-letter to a Secretary of State, which letter is to be read by the whole Cabinet Council, and very possibly afterwards laid before Parliament; any one barbarism, solecism, or vulgarism in it would, in a very few days, circulate through the whole kingdom to your disgrace and ridicule. — LORD CHESTERFIELD, *in a letter* (1748) *to his son.*

35. The Sequence of Paragraphs. If we express a single clearly conceived idea in each paragraph and then separate the successive paragraphs by spacing, we emphasize their distinction. Now it is entirely possible to get the parts of a whole too distinct. That is our objection to the very short paragraphs used by a few writers; they indicate a degree of distinction that doesn't really exist and make the thought asthmatic and broken. Properly constructed paragraphs need to be kept apart but they also need to be bound together, to follow each other in a connected sequence. From distinct paragraphs it is but a step to wholly unrelated paragraphs, such as are used in the first editorial column of certain newspapers. These are separate brief editorials linked only by the fact that they are all concerned with the news of the day. No such distinction may be permitted to the paragraphs in connected writing. Each of these has two duties — to express its own single idea and to carry forward the general idea so as to produce a continuous effect.

How can this continuous effect be maintained? First of all, of course, by the unity of the general design, which was clear to the writer as he made his plan and which has been hinted to the reader in the title if it is not clearly announced in a forecast. It may be made still more clear by obvious structure throughout the writing. Besides this general unity the following specific devices are employed by practiced writers to link paragraph to paragraph.

1. Echo Words. When a significant word in the last sentence of one paragraph is caught up in the first sentence of the paragraph that follows, the thought is carried forward by one of the easiest of transitions. Note the effectiveness of this device as a means of linking the paragraphs of Eliot's " The Durable Satisfactions of Life," quoted among the specimens of structure (page 58).

2. Reference Words. The reference words best suited to bridging the break between two paragraphs are demonstratives. Personal pronouns also serve but they reach back somewhat less firmly, and it is often better to repeat the antecedent in the first sentence of a paragraph.

3. Connective Words. Do not hesitate to link two paragraphs by a conjunction when close connection between them seems desirable. Connectives which, like *however, moreover, therefore,* easily bury themselves in the sentence and permit the opening phrase to be made up of more important words, are particularly useful.

4. Directive Expressions. Guiding phrases, such as *indeed, for example, to recur to the main issue,* since they relate the thought of a paragraph to the general idea, are effective devices to promote continuity of effect.

How all the methods described above are used by a careful writer will be evident from a glance at the openings of successive paragraphs from Irving's *English Writers on America,* the sixth essay in *The Sketch Book.*

English travelers are the best and the worst in the world . . . .
Hence, their travels are the more honest . . . .
It has *also* been the peculiar lot of our . . . .
That *such* men should give prejudicial accounts . . . .
They may, perhaps, have been disappointed . . . .
Perhaps . . . *they* may have been treated . . . .
One would suppose, *however,* that information . . . .
I shall not, *however,* dwell on this . . . . topic . . . .
All the writers of England . . . .
But why are we so exquisitely alive to . . . .
For ourselves, *therefore,* it is comparatively of but little impor-
tance . . . .
I am not laying too much stress . . . .
There is a general impression in England . . . .
Is all this to be at an end? . . . .
Short-sighted and injudicious, *however,* as . . . .
The members of a republic . . . .
Opening, *too,* as we do an asylum for strangers . . . .
What have we to do with national prejudices?
But *above all* let us not be influenced
Let it be the pride of our writers, *therefore,* discarding . . . .

Specimens of Paragraph Structure

I

Washington and Lincoln

As a people we are indeed beyond measure fortunate in the characters of the two greatest of our public men, Washington and Lincoln. Widely though they differed in externals, the Virginia landed gentleman and the Kentucky backwoodsman, they were alike in essentials, they were alike in the great qualities which made each able to do service to his nation and to all mankind such as no other man of his generation could or did render. Each had lofty ideals, but each in striving to attain these lofty ideals was guided by the soundest common sense. Each possessed inflexible courage in adversity, and a soul wholly unspoiled by prosperity. Each possessed all the gentler virtues commonly exhibited by good men who lack rugged strength of character. Each possessed also all the strong qualities commonly exhibited by those towering masters of mankind who have too often shown themselves devoid of so much as the understanding of the words by which we signify the qualities of duty, of mercy, of devotion to the right, of lofty disinterestedness in battling for the good of others. — THEODORE ROOSEVELT in *Abraham Lincoln*, a speech delivered at Lincoln's birthplace, Hodgenville, Kentucky, February 12, 1909.

II

THE SOURCES OF NEW WORDS

Where do all our new words come from, both the feeble vocables destined to an early death and the verbal entities lively enough to force themselves into the vocabulary? Who makes them? How are they made? These are questions to which it is often difficult to find an answer. Sometimes we know who made a word, why he made it, where he made it, and when he made it. Huxley manufactured *agnostic,* from a Greek root, intending it to be a more accurate description of his own attitude toward inherited religious belief than *positivist;* it was aptly and correctly formed; it was needed; it was immediately adopted both by his friends and his foes; and from English it has made its way into most modern languages.

But where did *jazz* come from? Who was responsible for this fit name for misfit music? And when was it that some person or persons to us unknown had a happy inspiration and described syncopated measures as *rag-time?* We can make a guess that *pep* is a curtailing of *pepper* and that *boob* is only a shortened *booby;* but why is a recently invented combination of ice-cream and fruit syrup known as a *sundae?* And why is this name not more simply spelled either *sunday* or *sundy?* Why was the armored tractor which helped powerfully to win the war entitled a *tank?* Here indeed is an instance of the way in which an old word is sometimes applied to a new thing in spite of the fact that it is not at all a good name for this invention. There is no likeness at all between a receptacle for liquids (which was the only meaning of *tank* five years ago) and a caterpillar tractor, steel-clad and bristling with guns (which is what *tank* means to-day even though it retains also its earlier significance). — BRANDER MATTHEWS in " The Latest Novelties in Language." *Harper's Magazine,* June, 1920, p. 83. Used by permission.

III

METHODS OF CALLING BIRDS

If one wishes merely to discover what birds are living in the vicinity, if he is primarily interested in seeing the birds so as to identify them, there is a very simple way of calling together all of the birds of the neighborhood. It consists merely in imitating the distress call of a wounded or young bird, which is very similar for all species of birds, and which seems to be recognized by them indiscriminately. The sound is best made by moistening the lips and kissing the back of the hand or the knuckle of the bent forefinger very lightly so that a shrill, distressing sort of a squeak is produced. It usually requires some practice before the sound is made perfectly, but many birds, like the robins and the catbirds, respond to even the crudest imitations. If one selects an inconspicuous place to sit and remains quiet while he is " squeaking," the birds will come very close in an endeavor to discover the trouble. On one occasion the writer had thirty different kinds of birds in view at one time and some of them within three or four feet of him. The " squeak," however, is a good deal like the cry, " Wolf! wolf! " and its virtue wears off if it is too frequently used.

Another method of calling birds, but one which requires more skill, is that of imitating their songs. The songs of most birds are very difficult to imitate, but some, like those of the chickadee, wood pewee, Baltimore oriole, white-throated sparrow, and fieldsparrow, are remarkably clear whistles, and can be imitated closely by any one who will practice sufficiently. Song seems to stimulate song, and one may often, for example, start the whole woods to ringing with the notes of the whitethroat by imitating their song, even when they have been quiet for some time. Again, when there is but a single bird about, or if one has approached the spot from which some male has determined to drive away all other males because he is wooing a mate, the answering bird will approach very closely. Indeed, on several occasions a little chickadee, answering the writer's call, has flown down to his cap and then, hovering in front of his pursed lips, has peered into the little round hole as though searching for the other bird. — A. A. ALLEN in " Bird Hunting with Field Glass and Camera," *The Outlook*, June 9, 1920. Used by permission.

IV

THE BROTHERHOOD OF LEARNING

Of all the pleasures and the duties which a birthday brings with it, the most welcome duty and the most exalted pleasure are found in the opportunity which it affords for seeing, united under one roof, the fellow-members of a family who are often far separated. On this two-hundredth birthday of Yale University, it is our chief pride to have with us the representatives of that brotherhood of learning which knows no bounds of time or place, of profession or creed.

It knows no bounds of age, either among the hosts or among the guests. The Yale that welcomes you here includes in its membership all parts of the collegiate body, from the youngest student to the oldest professor. It includes all those who, coming here without officially recognized connection with the University itself, bear to it such relationship that they partake in its spirit, and feel themselves sharers of its glories and its duties. Nor is it the living alone that welcome you. Present with us in spirit are men who have recently gone from us, like Phelps and Dana and Whitney. Present is a long line of great dead who have devoted their services to Yale, and who, being dead, yet speak. Present are those givers of books who, two hundred years ago, out of their poverty founded that college of Connecticut which to-day welcomes brothers, younger and older, to its anniversary. Representatives of colleges whose birth we have watched and in whose growth we can claim an almost paternal interest stand here side by side with delegates from those institutions, whether in the New World or the Old, which can point to a longer past than ours, and with whose achievements the centuries have rung.

Our brotherhood knows no bounds of place, no limits, natural or artificial. Characteristic of university learning from the very beginning was its cosmopolitan spirit. While States and cities dwelt in self-centered isolation, the universities of the Middle Ages established the first post-office by which intelligence could be interchanged and nations grow by one another's intellectual work. That community of thought which the members of the brotherhood of learning have thus pursued from the outset has been in recent days helped beyond anticipation by those modern inventions which have annihilated space, and have made it possible to have with us representatives, not only from the North and the South, from the Mississippi and from the Pacific, but from Stockholm and St. Petersburg, from Japan and from Australasia.

Our brotherhood knows no bounds of occupation. The day is past when people thought of the learned professions as something set apart from all others, the exclusive property of a privileged few. Opinions may differ as to the achievement of democracy; but none can fail to value that growing democracy of letters which makes of every calling a learned and noble profession, when it is pursued with the clearness of vision which is furnished by science or by history and with the disinterested devotion to the public welfare which true learning inspires. We are proud to have with us not only the theologian or the jurist or the physician; not merely the historical investigator or the scientific discoverer; but the men of every name who, by arms or by arts, in letters or in commerce, have contributed to bring all callings equally within the scope of university life.

Nor does our brotherhood know any bounds of creed. Even those institutions of learning which at some period in their history have had a more or less sectarian character tend to grow as the world grows — making their theology no longer a trammel but an inspiration, and welcoming as friends all who contribute to that inspiration, whether under the same forms or under others. Our common religion, so fundamental that we can all unite therein, teaches us broad lessons of reverence, of tolerance, and of earnestness. Ours be the reverence of those who have learned silence from the stars above and the graves beneath; ours the tolerance which can " see a good in evil and a hope in ill-success "; ours the earnestness which would waste no time in the discussion of differences of standpoint, but would unite us as leaders in the world's great movement toward higher standards in science and in business, in thought and in life. — ARTHUR T. HADLEY. An address delivered at the Bicentennial of Yale University, 1901. Used by permission.

EXERCISES IN PARAGRAPH CONSTRUCTION

Recast this paragraph for emphasis. Note particularly the weak ending.

If a man is a " poor loser," his friends grow to despise him; but, to be a " good loser " he must school himself to a calm indifference toward the depletion of his own resources. In the case of a student, his " resources " are mostly achieved through somebody else's perspiration, and have been entrusted to him for quite another purpose than the hazards of the game. Somewhat bluntly stated, he is misappropriating funds. Just when this ceases to be a "mere youthful misdemeanor" and becomes "embezzlement" is a very fine point. But the student who gambles with money furnished by parents who are under the impression that he is using it to defray legitimate college expenses, should not be sensitive about the word "embezzlement." It is an admittedly ugly word, however.

The following selections are the beginnings of themes. Revise them so as to make one suitable opening paragraph for each theme.

Pigeon Raising

In the lives of most people, more especially during boyhood and girlhood, there is a time when they have a fancy which resolves itself into a hobby. With boys pigeon raising is a hobby most common. A hobby is educational and it will keep a boy off the streets, for if he hadn't a hobby the street is where he would spend his spare time.

Pigeon raising is a pleasant pastime for a boy for he gets great pleasure in seeing the young pigeons hatched from the eggs, and after a time flying about his home. You can change pigeon raising from a pastime to a profit if skilfully managed.

An Ideal Boys' Camp

The location that we chose for our camp is one of the largest lakes in the county of Lunenburg, Nova Scotia, and is about seventeen miles north of Chester, the main summer resort of the province, thus putting us within easy reach of supplies.

The lake itself is a beautiful expanse of water about five or six miles long and a mile and a half wide, full of huge trout in the spring of the year, and in the fall the surrounding woods abound with both large and small game, such as ruffed grouse, woodcock, and moose.

Use these sentences for development in paragraphs.

1. Good manners react upon character.
2. The city is recruited from the country.

3. Good roads are beneficial to all classes of citizens.

4. For many reasons the celebration of Washington's Birthday is desirable.

5. Example is more efficacious than precept.

6. Religion is more than the observance of rites.

7. The love of beauty is mainly the love of measure or proportion.

8. Better fifty years of Europe than a cycle of Cathay.

9. A cultivated man should express himself by tongue or pen with accuracy and elegance.

10. Life is not so short but that there is always time for courtesy.

11. In college a man has unusual opportunities for making friends.

12. College friendships are likely to be lasting and valuable.

13. Education should enable a man to play a solid part in practical life and to use his leisure hours with intellectual zest.

14. In college one ought to acquire the habit of seeking the truth and liking it for its own sake in a disinterested way.

15. The world must be kept safe for democracy.

16. No right anywhere exists to hand people about from sovereignty to sovereignty as if they were property.

17. Our generation cannot escape history; we shall be remembered in spite of ourselves.

18. Many persons think of the government as something entirely apart from themselves.

19. In the long run every government is the exact symbol of its people, with their wisdom and unwisdom.

20. The most satisfactory thing in all this earthly life is to be able to serve our fellow-beings (first those who are bound to us by ties of love, then the wider circle of fellow-townsmen, fellow-countrymen, or fellow-men).

21. Out of his college course a student should get some knowledge, some skill, and some cultivation of his taste. (Develop this topic in three paragraphs.)

22. The strength and the weakness of the moving picture drama are obvious. (Develop the topic in two connected paragraphs.)

23. The popularization of the automobile has had several important effects. (Three paragraphs.)

24. What are the sources of self-respect in a young man?

REFERENCES

1. To works on paragraph structure: *The History of the English Paragraph* by E. H. Lewis (Chicago Press); *English Composition* by Barrett Wendell (Scribner); *Paragraph-Writing* by Scott and Denny (Allyn and Bacon); *Model Paragraphs* by L. N. Broughton (Harcourt Brace); *A Study of the Paragraph* by Helen Thomas (American Book Co.); *The Working Principles of Rhetoric* by J. F. Genung, Chapter XI.

2. To selections for study and analysis: *Essay on Milton* by Macaulay; *Culture and Anarchy* by Arnold, Chapter I (Macmillan); *Sartor Resartus* by Carlyle; *The American Commonwealth* by James Bryce (Macmillan).

CHAPTER IV

STYLE IN SENTENCES

THE STUDY OF STYLE

36.. The Mastery of Style. The term style is not easy to define. Writers of essays on style find in it subtleties which they do not entirely succeed in making clear and they are not wholly agreed as to what style is. The distinction between style and structure, however, is plain enough. Structure is concerned with the ordering of thought; style with the manner of its expression. Structure is a new problem with each piece of writing, now easier and now more difficult; style is much the same problem in every page that one writes. Structure can be translated from one language to another, can be borrowed without plagiarism, and can be imitated. Style is untranslatable, is an individual possession, and in its essential quality is inimitable. The mastery of style, therefore, requires more than insight into one's material and acute realization of the reader; it requires the slow acquisition of skill in one of the most individual of arts, the art of expression in words.

A serviceable style is acquired, as mastery of any art is acquired, by practice and self-discipline. For style is not a dress of thought, an added finish put on by fastidious writers only, but the very essence of expression. Everybody who writes uses some style — unformed, clumsy, absurdly ineffective, perhaps, like a child's first attempts at walking, but still his own style, capable of being matured and improved by intelligent practice. One who writes well has so perfected his style that it has become a transparent medium for the expression of his thought and feeling, as characteristic of him as his manner of walking or the tones of his voice.

Improvement in style depends on two things — practice and self-criticism. Either alone is inadequate, for aimless practice merely perpetuates errors and unapplied criticism discourages. The first draft of a piece of writing should not, however, be hampered by much thought about the manner in which it is being done. Write as freely and as readily as possible. Then rewrite with close attention to the manner, trying to detect faults and to discover improvements. You will find it possible, not merely to recognize violations of usage that escaped you in the haste of the first writing, but also to think of resources of expression that did not at first occur to you. To a practical writer these resources are easy and natural. When he has an idea to express, several different ways of saying it will readily offer themselves. The beginner thinks of but one, and having used it can see no other way of phrasing the same thought.

To criticize your own work, read it from more than one point of view. The following methods of doing this may prove helpful. (1) Read it aloud to yourself by paragraphs, pausing at the close of each paragraph to summarize the thought. (2) Hear it read aloud by somebody else. (3) See some of your work in a different form, typewritten or printed. Type is so much more compact than handwriting that larger units may be grasped by a single mental effort. (4) Read a selection for sentences only. (5) Read for words, trying to interpret them as if they had been used by somebody else. (6) Compare different parts of your writing to see whether you habitually overuse any particular forms of expression.

37. The Sentence as a Unit of Style. The study of style

is best approached through the sentence. A competent writer foresees his task as a whole and by paragraphs; he executes it by sentences. The form of the sentence is not a matter of forethought or even of conscious thought at the moment of writing. Sentences attract as little attention to themselves as the steps with which we walk on a good path with a definite purpose. It is only when the walking is bad that we think about each step as we take it. A reader makes use of the sentences in much the same way. He grasps the thought sentence by sentence and is not ordinarily conscious of the steps by which he proceeds. The sentence, then, is for the writer a unit of execution, for the reader a unit of apprehension.

How long or short this unit shall be is determined chiefly by the convenience of both. Whether a given body of thought shall be expressed in a few sentences or in more is a matter in which the writer is free to choose. If he is skilful he is not influenced primarily by clearness; he can make his thought clear in either way. Shorter sentences will give greater distinction to the separate elements of his thought. Longer sentences will indicate more definitely the relation of part to part and their relative significance. Macaulay writes:

The spirits of Milton are unlike those of almost all other writers. His fiends in particular are wonderful creations. They are not metaphysical abstractions. They are not wicked men. They are not ugly beasts. They have no horns, no tail, none of the fee-faw-fum of Tasso and Klopstock. They have just enough with human nature to be intelligible to human beings.

In about sixty words he has made seven sentences. Yet entirely satisfactory sentences sometimes run to several times sixty words. It is quite conceivable that another writer might have chosen to make one sentence of Macaulay's seven. For example:

The spirits of Milton are unlike those of almost all other writers, and his fiends in particular are wonderful creations; for they are not metaphysical abstractions, nor ugly beasts, nor wicked men, nor have they horns, or tail, or any of the fee-faw-fum of Tasso and Klopstock; they have, indeed, just enough with human nature to make them intelligible to human beings.

The difference between these two versions is not wholly a matter of emphaiss. It is a difference of mental habit. The short sentences are positive, unqualified, challenging. The long sentence is deliberate and analytic. Of course, Macaulay's sentences in this passage are exceptionally short, considerably below his average sentence-length. They serve, however, to illustrate the value of short sentences and their defects. In general short sentences have greater force and pictorial power and are more easily grasped. Long sentences — of thirty words or more, let us say — can better indicate the precise relation between ideas, their coördination or subordination, their uniformity or diversity, their mutual dependence.

The inexperienced writer is not so likely to make his sentences too long or too short as he is to make them too much alike both in form and in length. Close examination of a successful piece of writing will show that the sentences seem naturally adjusted to the thought, and that much of the charm of an attractive passage lies in the skilful use of variety.

The Arrangement of Words

In the arrangement of words and phrases in a sentence two considerations are of particular importance — coherence and effectiveness. Coherence is the result of such ordering of the parts of the sentence as makes clear the relation of each part to its context. A coherent sentence is understandable. Effectiveness is an added quality. It is the result of such ordering of words as will bring out their relative importance and convey their meaning with force or charm. A sentence may be coherent and yet ineffective.

38. The Resources of Coherence. Three devices for making a sentence coherent may be worthy of special study. These are (1) Proximity, the nearness of related parts; (2) Uniformity, the likeness of related parts; (3) Articulation, the linking of part to part by connective words.

39. Proximity. The principle of proximity, as usually stated, is very simple. Place related parts as near each other as possible. The rule is subject to some qualifications, however. Colloquial style, having the help of inflection of the voice and emphasis, often prefers an unstudied arrangement. For example:

I received an interesting letter from Mr. Brown yesterday which I wish to read to you, is acceptable arrangement in oral speech. Written style would place related words next to each other: I received yesterday from Mr. Brown an interesting letter which I wish to read to you.

Another qualification is that adverbial modifiers are often more effective at the beginning of the sentence than next to the predicate, to which they grammatically belong. In general, however, regard for proximity will promote coherence and will prevent constructions that make the meaning obscure or ridiculous.

Faulty: (1) The groom concealed the fact that he was a divorced man from the clergyman.

(2) Plans are being made for the movement of the supplies recently purchased by the government from the interior to the seaboard.

(3) She wore an antique comb in her hair which had been given to her by her aunt.

(4) The bill makes it a crime to accept a pass by any citizen of Nevada with certain exceptions.

(5) It is against the law for any state official to ride on a rail-

road pass or to accept reduced rates for transportation from a common carrier.

(6) Members of the recruiting office are today distributing 10,000 highly colored handbills telling of the advantages of army life among the automobile factories of the city with a view to inducing mechanics to enlist.

(7) Away in the ages 250 B.C. it is now certain that this same comet was visiting the earth.

(8) Patrolman Hanson, while returning home from duty, slipped on a treacherous pavement at Lambert Street and Pennsylvania Avenue and strained his back this morning.

Note the importance of the placing of adverbs.

At least we have had a pleasant evening (whatever else happened to us).

We at least have had a pleasant evening (whatever the others have had).

Many men are not satisfied (many are dissatisfied).

Not many men are satisfied (most are dissatisfied).

Incorrect: (1) The Indians chiefly subsisted by hunting and fishing.

(2) I only wanted one but I received several. (This position for *only* is almost idiomatic in colloquial use. In writing and in formal speech say, I wanted only one, or I wanted one only.)

(3) There was not much that I could do; I even could not harness the horse.

Place correlatives — either, or; not only, but also; both, and; and the like — next to corresponding parts of speech.

Correct: You must either go or stay.

Incorrect: (1) She was not only happy over his victory but also over the defeat of his rival.

(2) I neither trusted him nor his brother.

(3) Not only resemblances exist in things whose analogy is obvious but also in objects wherein there is great superficial unlikeness.

Of more than one possible opening choose that which conforms to the point of view of the sentence and its place in the paragraph.

At last, to their surprise, they were admitted by special order to the ambassador's train (the point of view is the attitude of the persons admitted).

By special order, they were to their surprise admitted at last to the ambassador's train (the point of view is the difficulty of being admitted).

Emerson wrote Nature while he was living at Concord (the preceding sentences led up to the subject of writing).

While he was living at Concord Emerson wrote Nature (the preceding sentences had to do with Concord).

40. Uniformity. Words and phrases uniform in structure are readily assumed to be similar in significance, or at least to stand in the same relation to their context. Parallel structure is therefore likely to be clear. A very long sentence will seem unified if it is sufficiently parallel in form; a sprawling long sentence is likely to be incoherent.

Coördinate, if possible, words with words, phrases with phrases.

Faulty: (1) The notes are arranged with care and accurately.

(2) Military training teaches a man obedience, to think quickly, and how to command others.

Coördinate clauses with clauses.

Faulty: (1) When I saw him wavering and that his skate was loose, I knew he would fall.

(2) These banks have two departments of accounts — one that of savings and the other is subject to check.

(3) We could see the lake through the woods and how the river makes a sharp turn southward.

Coördinate active voice with active, passive voice with passive.

Faulty: (1) The company then went to the dining room and a delicious luncheon was enjoyed.

(2) We read Caesar and Livy during the first term and the last term Horace was begun.

(3) A series of ventilators keeps the car cool during the summer months while in winter it is warmed by electric heaters.

Coördinate concrete with concrete, abstract with abstract. Avoid unequal yokefellows.

I like Whittier for his undaunted courage and scenes of home life.

Express the signs of parallel structure, unless they are quite unnecessary.

They try to win and keep those who fall into their hands and make them as bad as their master. (The author means they try to win and to make.)

41. Articulation. Nearness in place and similarity in form are convenient devices sometimes available for making the logical relation of the parts of a sentence more obvious. To make this relation explicit we must use connective words. Such words articulate the thought by joining part to part, very much as the proper linking of sound to sound articulates speech. Only the simplest concrete ideas, such as those used by children or savages, can be made intelligible without articulation. Coherence has been said to be the secret of clearness in style. The exact use of connective words is the secret of coherence.

The classification of connectives and the study of their use are topics that belong to grammar. For a discussion of them see the section on Usage. A few general faults of style resulting from careless articulation are described below.

1. The And-Habit. Untrained or careless writers frequently use *and* or *but* when the relation which they wish to express is really not coördination. To link clause after clause by *and* is a juvenile habit.

Faulty: Yesterday's snowstorm was the heaviest March storm in this section for fifteen years *and* by night nearly seven inches had fallen. A great deal of it melted during the day *and* had the mercury been two degrees higher we should have had rain instead of snow. Yesterday was a typical winter day *and* in the parks the scene was beautiful. The snow began to melt as soon as it came down *but* enough fell to make a good covering *and* there were many sleighs on the street.

2. The So-Habit. Do not overwork *so* as a means of adding causal clauses. Such use is often due to a failure to think the sentence out before beginning to write it. Sometimes prefer *as, since,* or *because,* and put the subordinate clause first. Remember that a so-clause should be set off by a semicolon.

Bad: The hall was crowded when we arrived, so we came home. The task is difficult for me, so I crave your indulgence.
Better: As the task is difficult for me, I crave your indulgence.

3. The As-Habit. Avoid much use of the trailing as-clause to express causal relations. Such clauses easily and naturally precede the main clause. They should sometimes give way to clauses introduced by *for, since,* or *because,* or should be reduced to participial phrases.

Faulty: The chain should be cleaned frequently, as if this is not done the machine will work badly.
The matter of collecting fares and ringing them up is important, as a slight mistake on the part of a new conductor might cost him his job, as there are men hired by the company known as spotters whose duty it is to report all inaccuracies in handling the fares.

42. The Resources of Effectiveness. In the arrangement of words in a sentence, or in a succession of sentences, coherence is fundamental. But coherent sentences may yet be ill-proportioned, monotonous, uninteresting. A good style should do more than convey the denotation of the words — the bare meaning, capable of expression in more than one way or of translation into another tongue; it

should add to lucidity so much as is possible of those
qualities which rhetoricians have called by various names
— force, interest, vigor, energy, ease, and the like — and
which may be summed up in the single term effectiveness.
Four devices, among others, used by skilled writers to
make arrangement effective are (1) Prominence, (2) Symmetry, (3) Climax, (4) Suspense.

43. Prominence.   The more important words or phrases
in a sentence should receive a greater share of the reader's
attention.   They may be made prominent in various ways.

1. By position.

(*a*) At the beginning.

Faulty: 1. A man to be a good lacrosse player must possess
coolness and agility.

2. I suspect that this subject if properly handled will be very
interesting.

3. Indeed, his plans were so cunning that at the outset not the
least suspicion fell on him.

Note that the relative importance of the beginning may
be determined by the context.   Contrast:

They at last gave up and retired.

For twenty-four hours the British vessels lay out of range and
bombarded the fort.   At last they gave up and retired, leaving
Baltimore still in American hands.

(*b*) At the end.

Faulty: 1. We cannot hope to succeed if we do not start in
the right way.

2. The princess had been told of woman's slavery to man in
her childhood.

3. We close at 5 P.M. during July and August.

4. The most complete veterinary college in the world will be
founded in Chicago under the auspices of the University of Illinois
in the near future.

5. Be sure to end your sentences with words that deserve the
distinction that you give them.   (Cited by Professor Barrett Wen-

dell from his first writing.   On revision he wrote " End with words
that deserve distinction.")

(*c*) At the unexpected place; *i.e.,* by inversion.   For
example:

To grave and fundamental distinctions of national character and
life, commonly correspond similar distinctions in religious belief.
    Silver and gold have I none, but such as I have give I thee.
(Acts III, 6.)
    He saved others; himself he cannot save. — Authorized version
(Matthew 27, 42).
    He saved others, but he cannot save himself. — Twentieth
Century Testament.

(*d*) Isolated; *i.e.,* set off by punctuation or put into a
separate sentence.   For example:

1. He has been a national benefactor and to-day we are all
speaking kindly of him — sorrowfully.   Note the difference in
effect of We are all speaking kindly and sorrowfully of him.
2. It seems not credible that respectable married people, with
umbrellas, should find appetite for a bit of supper within quite a
long distance of a fiery mountain. — STEVENSON.
3. Such a method of attack is not war.   It is murder.

2. By the Use of Demonstrative Words.

(*a*) Demonstratives may be used to anticipate the word
that is to be made prominent.   For example:

1. There is one broad proposition on which I stand.   It is *this:*
That no American citizen shall with my consent be subjected to
the infamous punishment of the lash.
2. The two ways in which you can prove your right to leadership are *these:* By good judgment or by heroism.

(*b*) In a similar way demonstratives summarize and
point back to the prominent words.   For example:

1. Religion and education, love of God and regard for man, —
this is the secret of New England's strength in the nation.
2. To be or not to be — *that* is the question.

3. By Mechanical Devices.

(*a*) Heightened punctuation.

They were unaware of Indians, nor recked they anything of bisons or of pirates (with pistols!), though the whole place swarmed with such portents.

(*b*) Italics. The use of italics for routine emphasis has gone out of fashion. They are still available, however, to give special prominence to particular words and phrases.

(*c*) Capital letters. Words repeatedly used, like the names of subjects of study in a college catalog, are sometimes capitalized to give them prominence.

4. By Repetition.

1. All his books are written in a learned language; in a language which nobody hears from his mother or his nurse; in a language in which nobody ever quarrels or drives bargains or makes love; in a language in which nobody ever thinks. — MACAULAY.

2. Men of great place are thrice servants: Servants of the sovereign or state; servants of fame; and servants of business. — BACON.

44. Symmetry. The effectiveness of symmetry — the correspondence of part with part — is attested by its use in poetry, in which line is symmetrical with line, stanza with stanza. In prose such regularity of form must be only incidental; otherwise it may become a disagreeable mannerism. Used with skill, however, uniformity — already mentioned as a resource of coherence — is one of the most serviceable devices for making prose effective.

1. The Balanced Sentence. For example:

1. This fate which you ordain for the wretched you believe to be all their inheritance; you may crush them, before the moth, and they will never rise to rebuke you. — RUSKIN.

2. It is generally better to deal by speech than by letter; and by the mediation of a third than by a man's self. — BACON.

3. Intreat me not to leave thee, or to return from following after thee: For whither thou goest, I will go; and where thou lodgest, I will lodge; thy people shall be my people, and thy God my God: Where thou diest, will I die, and there will I be buried: The Lord do so to me, and more also, if aught but death part thee and me. — Ruth I, 16.

2. Antithesis.

1. Words are the counters of wise men and the money of fools.
2. Wilful waste makes woeful want.

Note the almost universal dependence of proverbs upon symmetrical form. In many cases, as in this, the uniformity is increased by alliterations.

3. Chiasmus; i.e., an inverted antithesis — the most artificial form of symmetry in prose.

1. The Lord is the peasant that was.
        The peasant the Lord that shall be. — EMERSON.
2. It hath been an opinion that the French are wiser than they seem, and the Spaniards seem wiser than they are. — BACON.

4. Parallelism; i.e., uniformity carried on through more than two similar parts.

Some mysterious fascination fixes the gaze and stills the hearts of the wanderers, and their amazement deepens into awe as they gradually recognize themselves as once they were; the soft bloom of youth upon their rounded cheeks, the dewy light of hope in their trusting eyes, exulting confidence in their springing step, themselves blithe and radiant with the glory of the dawn. — G. W. CURTIS in *The Leadership of Educated Men.*

45. Climax. That a series will be more effective if its members grow in significance, interest, or intensity to the end is a fundamental principle in all forms of expression. In the ordering of the parts of a sentence this principle should be followed whenever climax is possible. For example:

1. "I know it," I replied, — "I concede it, I confess it, I proclaim it." — HOLMES.

2. Abiit, excessit, evasit, erupit.

3. Nothing can be better for your people than that you should value, respect, honor your universities as I see you do. — BRYCE.

4. What a piece of work is man! How noble in reason! how infinite in faculty! in form and moving how express and admirable! in action, how like an angel, in apprehension how like a god!

Anti-Climax: Faulty, as in these examples, except when used for humor or irony.

1. Honor, life, liberty, property — all are at stake.

2. The soldiers suffered, some from King's evil, some from ague, some from toothache.

3. I am astonished to hear such principles avowed in this house or in this country: principles equally unconstitutional, inhuman, and unchristian.

Negative Climax (Note that it properly goes in the opposite direction):

1. I did not strike the defendant, I did not call him names, I did not even look at him.

2. Your investment is still secure; your credit is unimpaired; you will not lose a cent.

46. Suspense. A sentence is made up of successive parts, grasped and held by the mind until the thought is complete at the end. If qualifying or subsidiary parts are put first, they can give no complete impression of any sort until the main idea is added. This is the order of suspense. If the main idea precedes, a complete impression is possible at once, though this impression is added to or altered by the parts that follow. This is the loose or unperiodic order. In an unstudied arrangement, as in conversation, the loose order is likely to prevail. Such an arrangement is not in itself undesirable, for it gives naturalness and simplicity. It is so, for the most part, that one thinks. Yet some sentences are much more effective if the thought is suspended, and style is improved by a judicious variation of the two types of arrangement.

According to the usual text-book definition of the periodic sentence — a sentence in which no grammatically satisfactory stop can be made before the end — the distinction between these types is easily made. All such sentences are periodic; all others are loose. But this distinction is of little value, and statistics as to the proportion of periodic sentences in a given style are practically worthless unless various other considerations are taken into account. Though technically loose, a sentence may be markedly periodic in effect. The question really is to what extent in clause and sentence the order of suspense is used. For example:

1. At the foot of these fairy mountains, the voyager may have descried the light smoke curling up from a village, whose shingle roofs gleam among the trees, just where the blue tints of the upland melt away into the fresh green of the nearer landscape.

2. In that same village and in one of these very houses, (which, to tell the precise truth, was sadly time-worn and weather-beaten,) there lived many years since, while the country was yet a province of Great Britain, a simple good-natured fellow, of the name of Rip Van Winkle.

The first of these two sentences from Irving is technically loose; the second is periodic; yet both admirably illustrate the use of suspense. In the first the suspense culminates on the phrase *from a village,* giving to those words an emphasis which they obviously deserve. In the second the name of Rip Van Winkle is introduced for the first time in the tale, and is very appropriately put at the end of a long and skilfully ordered sentence. For an example of the equally skilful use of unperiodic arrangement see the context of these two sentences in the second and third paragraphs of *Rip Van Winkle.*

47. The Value of Suspense. The most obvious effect of suspense is, as these sentences show, to focus attention upon the significant element that is put at the end. It gives also the variety of a movement different from that of colloquial style. Suspense carried to the close of a very long sentence puts a burden upon the attention. In a very short sentence the effect is neutral; such a sentence is as likely to be periodic as not. The periodic structure is most useful in longer simple sentences, such, for example, as double the subject or the predicate or heap up modifiers, and in longer complex or compound sentences. In such sentences suspense is not likely to come about by chance. One who wishes to improve his style will do well to look, in revising his work, for sentences in which the periodic order will be an improvement.

Effective suspense may be produced in various ways. Inversion has already been illustrated. Correlatives hold the sense incomplete until the second member of the correlation is expressed. Restrictive clauses and anticipating words produce a similar result. For example:

1. He was not only industrious and faithful but also unusually efficient.

2. He was so industrious and faithful that he won prompt promotion.

3. His work was done with the fidelity that wins promotion (instead of, with fidelity, which wins promotion).

4. His rise to success was due to these two qualities — industry and fidelity to the interests of his employers.

EXERCISES IN SENTENCE STRUCTURE

Rewrite the following sentences, improving them in every way possible.

1. In order to place you on the same basis with a purchaser in the city, we will agree to deliver any article you may purchase by freight.

2. Modern inventions are reducing the cost of manufacturing electricity to a great extent.

3. I want you to take lunch with me and meet my cousin who is spending her Christmas vacation with us at the Dutch Tea Room.

4. High winds prevailed, thus making the day very uncomfortable.

5. Besides being a scenic spectacle you can here enjoy a unique outing.

6. The long climb tired us, so we stopped and had the lunch under the trees that Mary had put up.

7. By reporting a change of address it will not be necessary to miss any copies of the paper.

8. A single brass bedstead stood in the corner and was surrounded by a large canopy.

9. The exercise keeps you in condition and a fellow can study better.

10. Two things are necessary to a successful track man; endurance to enable him to stand the strain and pluck carries him through to the end.

11. There are to be better accommodations for spectators when the new gymnasium is built I hear.

12. A sudden harsh clatter of a bell disturbed my mind concentrated on my book one morning.

13. The machine must be kept dry, clean, and must be frequently oiled.

14. All men are not happy and all men are not contented.

15. By parcel post from Greensburg is the best way you get fancy groceries.

16. All the property was bequeathed to the widow during her life and then to go to his heirs.

17. They have a plan for profit sharing with their employees of an original character.

18. This process is only profitable in a large modern factory.

19. The reason why I like him is on account of his thoughtfulness.

20. Satan's character is much more imaginatively drawn than Lucifer's.

CHAPTER V

STYLE IN WORDS AND PHRASES

ENGLISH WORDS

48. The Word-Hoard. Style is ultimately dependent upon diction — the choice of words and phrases. To write English one must have a share in that general stock of English words which Anglo-Saxon poetry picturesquely called the word-hoard. This word-hoard is an inheritance, age-old and precious. It has come down to us from ancestors so remote that, except for the words which they have transmitted to us, we should not know they had ever existed. It is so necessary to our life that no human device or invention could be less easily spared. Our inheritance does not diminish with use, but grows steadily, so that we now have more words than our grandfathers possessed and many times more than belonged to our Anglo-Saxon ancestors.

The growth of our stock of words has come about chiefly by borrowing. Some words are gained by invention, some by the multiplication of meanings assigned to old words, some by the making of compounds; but many more have been imported into English from the speech of other peoples. The result is that English is a composite speech. Of English words in use to-day not more than one quarter are of native origin and considerably more than one half come directly or indirectly from Latin. This does not imply that our language has lost its English character. The grammar of our speech is native, and the words of native stock are those that are most frequently used. Counting every word on a page, you will find that ninety per cent of the printed words in Shakespeare are native, and that even Dr.

Johnson's learned style employs only about one word of foreign origin to three of English stock.

49. Strata in words. The English vocabulary is a composite also from the point of view of use. Though a language does not ordinarily preserve two words that mean precisely the same thing, English speech is rich enough to enable us to express the same idea by a number of words which differ subtly in effect. There are thus strata of the English vocabulary which correspond to distinct levels of usage. Some words, like *father* or *good,* are appropriate on any of these levels; others are instantly recognized as belonging on but one.

Common use	*father*	*good*	*good society*
Archaic	sire	goodly	the gentles
Foreign	pater	bravo!	the élite
Literary	parent	admirable	the aristocracy
Colloquial	daddy	fine	nice people
Dialect	pap	goot	de quality
Slang	the old man	bully	the swells

By a somewhat broader distinction our words may be divided into two classes: those that come to us chiefly from talk, sometimes called popular words, and those that we acquire from books and bookish speech, known as learned words. Study the difference in effect between the corresponding terms in this table.

Popular	*Learned*
break	fracture
busy	industrious
fat	corpulent
lazy	indolent
letter	epistle
pay	compensate
poor	impecunious
stingy	parsimonious
sweat	perspiration
teach	inculcate

For the same general idea we have often three terms —
a word in common use, another restricted to scientific or
technical use, and a less familiar literary or poetic word.

Common	Scientific or Technical	Literary
cold (noun)	coryza	rheum
deadly	lethal	mortal
death	decease	demise
glassy	vitreous	crystalline
home	domicile	residence
joint	mortise	juncture
name	alias	cognomen
pay	indemnify	remunerate
sleep	coma	slumber
tear	lacerate	rend

50. The Acquisition of Words. Precious as our inheritance of English is, it is ours individually only as we exert
ourselves to possess it. The infant with no language but
a cry begins a life-long task of accumulating words. From
his mother or his nurse he so rapidly acquires simple words
that a child of three is able to use a thousand different
terms. School adds a whole new vocabulary. Ability to
read emphasizes the distinction between words that are
used — the active or dynamic vocabulary — and words
that are understood when seen or heard — the passive or
latent vocabulary. The reading habit tremendously increases the latent vocabulary. Hobbies, travel, and various
special interests constantly promote words from this latent
vocabulary to the smaller group available for instant use.
One's trade, business, or profession demands the possession
and constant use of a considerable capital of words and
fixes the character of one's thought and speech.

The accumulation of words is thus a natural result of
experience. The mastery of words, the last step in their
acquisition, comes only from practice in speaking and writ-

ing. Really to possess a word is to have it spring readily to expression when it is needed. To further such acquisition of words, various special devices have been used:

1. Word-Study. The memorizing of lists of words, the study of the dictionary, and the study of etymology are all of some value. Dictionaries have grown too large, however, to be serviceable as text-books, and word-study can be only incidentally helpful.

2. Reproduction. Franklin's method of using the *Spectator,* described in his *Autobiography,* is well-known. A similar plan is sometimes helpful in teaching. In general, however, the reproduction of another's thought in the same language is a dull and laborious process.

3. Translation. Translation into English is helpful, particularly if one is exacting as to the precise expression of the thought. Slovenly use of what has been called translation-English does more harm than good.

4. Scribbling. Stevenson has described in detail (in *A College Magazine*) his method of assiduous practice and imitation. Writing for practice, in one form or another, is really the only way in which most of us can become exact in the use of words.

5. Speaking. "Look well to your speech," says Professor Palmer in his *Self-Cultivation in English.* Care to make one's intimate English correct and effective is a good way to improve one's written English. Speaking in public is so severe a test of the mastery of words that the opportunity to speak should be regarded as valuable.

6. Word-Weighing. An exacting habit of mind that demands the right shade of meaning constantly adds useful words. Cultivate a feeling for synonyms.

7. The Dictionary-Habit. The office of the dictionary is to make words accessible. Men of wide learning and experience need it only occasionally. Students need it so much and so often that the possession of a good dictionary and willingness to consult it frequently should be matters of course. Use the *New Oxford Dictionary* and the *Century Dictionary* in the college library as books of reference; and own, if possible, *Webster's New International* — probably the most trustworthy single-volume dictionary — for your own use. A smaller volume, such as the *Webster's Secondary School Dictionary*, or the *Standard Desk Dictionary*, will be convenient for desk use.

Having a dictionary, know how to use it. Learn once for all the meaning of symbols and abbreviations, the order in which meanings are given, the references for variations in spelling and pronunciation. Know how to find the lists of synonyms, which are provided in good dictionaries, and make full use of illustrative quotations.

The Functions of Words

Once acquired a word is a tool, ready for use whenever needed. To use it effectively a writer should know something of the purposes which it is fitted to serve. Some words have the single function of standing as a symbol for a definite idea or relation, as exactly as the signs of a telegraph code designate letters of the alphabet; others are so rich in meaning that they can express several different ideas and can perform a variety of functions.

51. The Expression of Literal Meanings. A good dictionary gives first that meaning of a word which is fundamental in English. A technical term is likely to have no other meaning. Thus *hamamelis virginiana* means a particular shrub and that only. The popular term *witch hazel* may mean either the same shrub or a medicinal extract made from it. A word may have one or more literal meanings secondary to its primary meaning. The primary meaning of *fast* is firm, immovable; of *beat* is to strike. Yet fast has developed a secondary meaning, equally literal, namely, rapid or speedy. One may speak of fast colors and a fast life. Beat also means to conquer in wholly peaceful ways. The literal meaning, whether primary or derived, is what is technically known as the denotation of the word.

52. The Expression of Associated Meanings. Besides its denotation, a word may convey a cluster of associations, known as its connotation. The terms denotation and connotation have been borrowed from the terminology of logic, in which a term is said to denote its accepted meaning, the thing known (Latin *nota*) or named by it, and to connote the attributes of the same thing. The term lion denotes the wild animal sometimes called the king of beasts, and connotes, consequently, kingliness, courage, power — qualities which lions are popularly supposed to possess. In the study of style the term connotation is commonly used to include all the associations which a word may be able to call up — pictures of the mind, as Stevenson calls them in the paragraph cited among the specimens of style (see page 151) — and the feelings which they may evoke.

The literal meanings of a word are fixed by usage; its associations are necessarily individual and may differ widely with different persons, as in the case of Stevenson and his Chinese fellow-passengers. Yet much-used words tend to develop connotations which are felt by everybody. These connotations often determine the plane upon which a word shall be used, deciding, for example, whether a particular beast shall be called a *nag*, a *horse*, or a *steed*, and whether one shall write *cup* or *chalice*, *house* or *residence*, *lazy* or *indolent*. To illustrate further, the term *goose* means literally the domestic fowl *branta canadensis* and in a secondary sense, doubtless due to the shape of the handle, a tailor's smoothing iron. These are its denotations. By a familiar connotation it means a silly person, a well-meaning blunderer. To be called a goose is disparaging enough, but it implies no moral delinquency. The epithet *dog,* however, suggests the worst qualities that a cur can possess — cowardice, sneakiness, baseness. His good qualities are only partly implied in the adjective *dogged.* Obviously, to avoid pitfalls in diction and to write with vigor and freedom one must not merely know the dictionary meaning of a word but must also share with others a feeling for its associations.

53. General or Specific Meanings. A word may be relatively general or specific. A general term names a class or group, enabling us to speak of several things as united by a common identity and to generalize into a single concept a number of separate sense perceptions. A specific term names a member of a class or group. It tells about the thing itself rather than about its relation to other things. When an idea is to be expressed, we may want to make it highly specific or broadly general, according to the effect which we wish to produce. The same object or action may thus be designated by one of a number of terms.

General	Less General	Specific	More Specific
flowers	wild flowers	early wild flowers	blood root and violets
shrubbery	hedge row	privet hedge	neatly clipped privet hedge
dwelling	mansion	executive mansion	the White House
went	walked	strode	strode wrathfully

Observe that the general term has the greater denotation — *flower* names thousands of varieties of blooms; whereas the specific term is richer in connotation — *blood root and violets* can hardly fail to suggest associations with the

woods and the spring days. Each is effective in its own
way. When a poet likens life to " the frail duration of a
flower," nothing is to be gained by a more specific word
for flower. Since, however, the general term is usually
short, simple, and readily grasped, there is a temptation
for lazy thinkers to choose it when a more specific word
is really needed. If your purpose is to convey an exact
idea, particularly an idea of the look of an object, you
may safely make your diction specific.

	More General	*More Specific*
	(with difficulty)	toddle, totter, shuffle
		hobble, limp, grope
Go	(with vigor)	stride, stalk, march, walk
	(with carelessness)	saunter, stroll, ramble
	(with lightness)	dance, trip, skip.

54. Concrete or Abstract Meanings. An abstract term,
in the narrow sense of the word abstract, names a quality
or attribute apart from the thing to which the quality
belongs. Thus royalty sums up the qualities of a king.
A concrete term names the thing with its attributes.
(Compare Latin *abstraho* and *concresco*.) The terms
concrete and abstract are used in a more general sense,
however, to indicate the distinction between the tangible
and material, which can be imaged by the mind, and the
intangible, incapable of sense perception. In this sense,
words can be relatively concrete or abstract, the difference
going hand in hand with that between general and specific. *Boy* is the concrete term of which *boyhood* is the
corresponding abstract. But boyhood may be used in two
senses: as a general term summing up the years, say, from

five to fifteen; and as a pure idea meaning the qualities of that period of adolescence. Effectiveness in diction may depend upon the selection of a more or a less concrete word.

More Abstract	*More Concrete*
abstinence	self-denial
acceptation	acceptance
antiquity	old age
decadence	decay
decease	death
gravity	weight
mishap	accident
necessity	need
negligence	neglect
temerity	rashness

More specific without becoming more concrete
Nice day; nice day for a walk; too fine a day to stay indoors; finest March day I ever saw.
Strong man; physically powerful; strongest man in his class; man whose tests total 1250.

More concrete without becoming more specific
Evil; infamous; unspeakable.
Rendezvous; meeting-place; tryst.

More specific and more concrete
Pleasant days; clear days; "blue days and fair."
Strong man; brawny man; muscled like a blacksmith.

TYPES OF DICTION

55. The Literal Use of Words. Diction may be literal or imaginative. Literal diction is the result of the choice of words for their denotation, so that the language means what it says. Such choice of words gives (1) exactness and (2) simplicity.

1. Exactness is the precise adaptation of words to the thought. In technical writing it is gained by the use of terms that have a fixed denotation and little connotation.

The symbols that abound in mathematics and chemistry give exactness as well as brevity. The Latin and Greek names used in zoölogy and pharmacy, though often longer than common terms, are free from the connotations that cling to household words. The mastery of terminology is a first step in science, and the problem of finding exact technical terms and keeping them definite in meaning is an important element in research.

Literal accuracy in non-technical diction is attained only by insistence upon the exact, the specific, the unequivocal word. Such a command of words presupposes a wide vocabulary. The popularizing of special knowledge brings constantly into current use words which yesterday were the exclusive possession of a few. One should so far as possible know what such words mean — in order to read intelligently and, as occasion may demand, to write exactly. Strive to call things by their precise names — to say " the controller," not " the thing they use to stop and start the trolley car "; the " semaphor," not " the thing beside the track that signals trains " — and to avoid the necessity of alluding to something as a " what-you-call-it." The more words you know accurately the broader your education.

2. Simplicity is the result of using short, familiar words in their literal sense. Such words are instantly understood and draw no attention to themselves, conveying the thought through a transparent medium. Simple diction befits commonplace ideas; it is not unworthy of lofty thought or deep feeling. For an example of it, read aloud Ruth's avowal, " Intreat me not to leave thee," cited elsewhere (page 117), as an example of symmetry. It is not easy to write simply. When the matter is complex or technical, it is scarcely possible; but it is well to recognize the worth of the homely, everyday words and to prefer them whenever they express the idea.

56. The Imaginative Use of Words. Certain limitations

of literal speech are obvious. It is restricted to a known vocabulary, it lacks variety, and it cannot easily arouse interest or emotion. Imaginative diction is a natural recourse of those who lack words or who feel keenly and wish to stir the feelings of others. " The imagination," says Stedman, " begets original diction, suggestive epithets, verbs implying extended scenes and events, phrases which are a delight, and which as we say speak volumes, single notes which establish the dominant tone." Such diction is achieved by the choice of words for their connotation rather than for what they literally mean. It is pictorial rather than analytic, preferring a sense of fact to the fact itself and sacrificing literal accuracy for artistic truth. When Macaulay says of Goldsmith " He spent twice as much as he had," he is using a more forcible expression than the literally true, He spent more than he had. Stevenson says, " We live the time a match flickers; we pop the cork of a ginger-beer bottle, and the earthquake swallows us on the instant." This, though literally absurd, is in effect better than, " We live a brief time, we indulge in a few transitory pleasures and death takes us away suddenly." When the poet says of the skylark's song that it is " like a glow-worm golden," the deviation from literal truth is still greater. Diction which thus uses the connotation of the familiar, the specific, the concrete instead of literal statement is loosely known as figurative language, and specific departures from denotations are called figures of speech.

57. The Forms of Figurative Speech. Figures appear in a variety of forms and in speech of every type from the slang of the moment to the noblest verse. They may be classified, according to their divergence from the literal, as follows:

1. Figures of Immediate Association.

(*a*) Imitative words, which name a sound by echoing it,

technically called onomatopoetic words. The choice or coinage of such a word is one of the simplest appeals to imagination, for the association is inevitable. The *chug-chug* of a motor-boat is more suggestive of that obtrusive sound than the denotative expression *noisy exhaust,* the *crack* of a rifle than its *report*. The great majority of our sound words are obviously of imitative origin.

(*b*) Synecdoche. When a part of a thing or a member of a class is named for the whole, the deviation from the literal is slight. A few synecdoches are in common use; *e.g., tea* for a light supper, *wheel* for bicycle, *rum* for liquors of all kinds.

(*c*) Metonymy, a similar figure, in which the association is slightly more remote, as of material and the thing made of it, a cause and its effect, a place and its products. Examples are abundant: *glasses* for spectacles or tumblers, *steel* for sword, *bronzes* for bronze statues, *coppers* and *nickels* for one-cent and five-cent coins, *rubbers* for overshoes, *flannels* for woolen underwear; to read *Thackeray,* a genuine *Corot;* address the *chair*.

2. Figures of Imagined Resemblance.

(*a*) Simile (Latin *similis*). This figure is the assertion of connotative likeness. The two things compared are literally unlike — else we should have no figure at all — yet there is a resemblance which the imagination can seize upon. The simile abounds in the Bible and in classical literature, whence it came into use in English. A simile may be (1) explicit; *e.g.,* " Like a tree planted by the waters "; " He chased them as a sheep-dog chases sheep"; (2) condensed; *e.g., fan-like* jets of water; his *lion-like* courage; or (3) extended into the form called analogy, a likeness of relations.

(*b*) Metaphor differs from simile in asserting identity instead of likeness. It is, as the etymology hints, an exchange of terms. To thus give an unfamiliar or abstract thing the name of something more familiar which it faintly resembles is a primitive instinct in language, the natural resort of those who are at loss for a word. The metaphor may be (1) explicit, naming both the literal and the figured, *e.g.,* " Our *birth* is but a *sleep* and a forgetting." " Thy *word* is a *lamp* to my feet "; (2) implied, naming only one; *e.g.,* Come blessed *barrier* between day and day; (3) incidental; *e.g.,* " It is only from *its roots* in the living generations of men that a language can be reinforced with fresh vigor for its needs "; (4) an epithet, *e.g.,* " Or like stout Cortez when with *eagle* eyes. . . . "

(*c*) Personification attributes life where none exists or life of a totally different kind. It is an extremely common and useful figure, appearing readily in everyday speech. The personality may be (1) merely implied, as in, A sudden fear smote me; or (2) explicit; *e.g.,* " When that churl Death my bones with dust shall cover."

(*d*) Allegory extends the resemblance into a parallelism. This may be brief, as in the proverb, " The rolling stone gathers no moss," or long and elaborate, as in such works as *The Faerie Queene* and *Pilgrim's Progress*.

58. Fossil Figures. A figure of speech is an effective spur to the imagination only while it is fresh. The association that underlies it will seem to the reader so apt and striking that he may wonder why he did not think of it himself; yet he did not think of it himself. A figure which, because of its convenience or expressiveness is used repeatedly, soon becomes a literal designation. It is a dead figure. If its connotative origin is obscured by linguistic change so as to be recognized only by scholars, the word becomes what has been aptly termed a fossil figure. It is of such fossils that language consists. In a few very old words the origin is lost beyond the conjecture of philologists; in most words there remains the distinct image of what was once a bold and luminous figure. If a poet writes of " a vaulting ambition that o'erleaps the moon," he uses a vivid figure. When we speak of *high hopes and expectations,* the figure, though easily recognizable, is dead. It is scarcely more imaginative than earnest hopes. To describe somebody's aims as *extravagant* is to use a fossil figure. Only one who remembers something of his Latin will observe that the ambitions are really spoken of as wandering beyond bounds, and will think of a kinship with *vagary.* The reputable word *attention* and the slangy *rubber-neck* come from the same image of one stretching toward what interests him.

59. Figures of Heightened Feeling. Akin to the figures based upon associations are those which suggest a stronger emotion or greater sincerity by a deviation from the ordinary, literal form.

1. Exclamation. The force of an impression has been great enough to cause the abrupt expression of it. " How infinite in faculty! "

2. Rhetorical Question. " Could anything be more miraculous than an actual, authentic ghost? "

3. Overstatement, technically known as hyperbole. " I beg a thousand pardons."

4. Understatement, technically litotes. " Is it cold? " " Well, slightly."

5. Apostrophe, the imaginative address to a person or thing as if present or capable of hearing.

6. Vision, the imaginative seeing of what it is impossible to see.

7. The Historical Present, a sudden turning to the present tense in narration to give vividness.

60. The Use and Misuse of Figures. A good figure of speech is not merely decorative; it springs from a sense of the inadequacy of literal diction. The little girl who said that soda-water tastes " as if your foot's asleep," had no words in her vocabulary to express the idea literally.

In a particularly moving sermon Jonathan Edwards likened a sinner in God's hands to a spider held between the fingers. He felt the need of a concrete image of the loathsomeness of sin. Professor Royce, endeavoring to convey an idea of infinity, pictures a spider patiently spinning with her web radius after radius of a circle. He used the same insect to make clearer an unusually difficult abstract notion. Poets use imaginative diction because it is only so that they can express the meaning of life.

To be effective a figure must be clear. When an old lady enveloped in a shawl is likened to a caddis worm, most readers are not enlightened. The angry partisan who wrote, "What observant men perceive in this dangerous situation is a cataclysm trained and bridled for Theodore Roosevelt to bestride and run amuck," may have had a mental picture of a docile cataclysm, but his readers found the image vague.

The misuse of figures springs in general from a dull sense of reality, a disposition to think in symbols rather than in images. It takes various forms.

1. Frigid figures are the product of obvious artifice, the unreal imitation of genuine imaginative phrasing. "The ambition to get an A became my guiding star and beacon." "Divine Philology became his goddess and he worshipped her ten hours daily."

2. Inapt or inappropriate figures are incongruous with the context. A student described the driver of a fire-engine as leaning eagerly forward over his horses, "spurring them on." The figure was too close to the literal to succeed as a metaphor. "China has awakened from her sleep of decadence to a dream of revolution and a republic," wrote another.

3. Mixed figures are commonly spoken of as mixed metaphors; but of course similes and personifications may be mixed also. Such figures blend two incongruous resem-

blances. They may result from a very active imagination which crowds images too closely, as well as from a dull one which fails to conceive them clearly. The student who spoke of his decision to go to college, "And so I embarked upon the road of learning," and the other who wrote confidently, "I could cite instances without number where men with a good college education have left the lower rounds of the ladder of fame and are now soaring at the top," failed to realize their figures. An unusual affluence of image seems to have inspired one of their classmates who wrote of his native town: "Seated in the valley of contentment, where joy and sunshine reign, stands the city of Cumberland clothed with beautiful buildings and cottages."

4. Trite figures are obvious resemblances which have been used so often that they are worn out. Mark Twain, in a figure that is not trite, described such overworked expressions as "burnt out carbon filaments which do not give a ray of light." However fitting it may once have been to speak of flames as the devouring element, a green lawn as velvet, or a distant stream as a ribbon of silver, it is now worse than useless. If the analogy is so apt that you are unwilling to give it up, it may possibly be made fresh and connotative by a revivifying touch. So Henry James, telling of the various kindly offices rendered by the guards at a French bathing beach, describes them as "like ministering and *trickling* angels."

The Qualities of Diction

The reader, whose point of view we must now endeavor to take, judges a piece of writing by the impression which it makes upon him. His approval will depend on one or more of three important considerations; namely, whether he understands it readily, whether he is interested in it, and whether he is pleased by it. Hence the three fundamental qualities of style; clearness, the intellectual quality, force or interest, the emotional quality; ease or elegance, the esthetic quality. All of these qualities are relative, and are to be achieved, not merely by overcoming the inherent difficulties of the art of writing, but also by carefully adapting the choice of words to the needs and tastes of the readers for whom it is designed.

61. Clearness. Lucidity whether of arrangement or diction is the fundamental quality of style. As influenced by the choice of words, clearness is an exacting requirement. To use words that can mean what you intend to say is not enough; they must mean that only, and any but a wilfully stupid reader should be unable to misunderstand them. Clearness is promoted by:

1. Precision. When the idea is sharply defined in the writer's thought, it will always be possible to give it exact expression. Vagueness is usually the result of lazy thinking. Lazy thought is content with a worn and overworked vocabulary. It calls everything a *feature* or a *factor,* loves vague abstracts like *condition* or *proposition,* and escapes the necessity of searching for the exact word by having no exact idea.

2. Repetition. No word is superfluous if it is necessary to make the meaning clear. A difficult notion is often better expressed by the use of synonyms, which though they differ in effect and overlap in denotation, may combine to express the idea that is intended. So a technical term and the popular name may go hand in hand, the one limiting and the other explaining and making concrete. A scientist, speaking of the feathers in a bird's wing says, " The tubular form of the barrel (toothpick part) and the pithy nature of the shaft are brought about by these demands." A lawyer in a popular article writes, " Torts **or** private wrongs, the criminal law or the law of public wrongs."

3. Figures of Speech. An illuminating figure often makes a difficult matter clear. Addison (see page 147) writes, " The fancy must be warm to retain the print of those images it hath received," and likens a dull imagination to weak sight. A good figure gives both light and heat. It is resorted to as often by a writer who is struggling to be understood as by one whose feelings overleap the limits of literal speech.

62. Interest. A piece of writing may have interest — the quality that wins and holds attention — quite independent of its style. The guide book when you have lost your way or a pamphlet on first aid when your companion has been injured will be absorbing enough, however crudely written. But most writing must have intrinsic interest if it is to have readers.

63. Interest and Force. The sources of interest are not easy to define. The secret of force, according to Professor Wendell, is connotation; but literal speech as well as imaginative may possess it. Novelty of subject-matter naturally creates interest; yet the magic of style can make the most unpromising material readable. In general, it may be said that style is interesting if it gives a sense of reality. Parkman's explanation of the method of shooting a buffalo has such interest. So has Mr. Howells's account of a very commonplace experience, waiting for a steamboat. Both of these excerpts, it will be noticed, are literal and specific. Style will be interesting, also, if it can stir the feelings. Ruth's " Intreat me not to leave thee " and Bunyan's account of the man who cried " What shall I do? " are forcible for this reason, yet both are utterly simple. On the other hand, the selections from Hawthorne, Newman, and Stevenson illustrate the force of imaginative diction.

64. Hindrances to Force. Interest is lessened by any-

thing that needlessly intervenes between the reader and
the effect desired, that prevents the thought from taking
shape in what Mr. Benson calls " a perfectly pure medium
of language." Three such hindrances may be noticed.

1. Redundancy, the use through carelessness and un-
guided fluency of too many words.

(*a*) Tautology; *i.e.,* sameness, the fruitless repetition of
the same idea in other words.

1. Polyglot tautology — the use of words whose sameness in meaning is obscured by their different linguistic
origin; *e.g.,* He *first initiated* the movement. They vol-
unteered of their own *free will.* The *umbrageous shade.*

2. Approximate tautology — the use of words which
mean so nearly the same thing as to make one of them
unnecessary; *e.g.,* Our work in rhetoric surpassed that of
previous years both in *scope* and in *comprehensiveness.*

3. Idiomatic tautology — the use of doublets that have
come to have a single denotation. One member may be
archaic when used alone, as *kith* and *let.* These expressions
are not always really redundant; they are used freely in
oral English, and sometimes agreeably fill out a phrase in
writing. They are always, however, under suspicion.

Bag and baggage	part and parcel
end and aim	pains and penalties
intents and purposes	rules and regulations
kith and kin	safe and sound
let or hindrance	sum and substance
metes and bounds	to have and to hold
null and void	try an experiment

(*b*) Pleonasm — the use of more words than are needed
to express a thought.

1. Extra-structural words. Avoid useless initial *there*
and final *one; e.g., There* are two kinds of drawings which
have to be made. His characters are all excellent *ones.*

Omit other words not needed by the construction: It was thirty years *later* before the truth became known. This trick is harder than you think *for*. There can be no doubt *but* that newspapers *at present* are read too much.

2. Improper comparisons. Words that express an absolute or a superlative sense should not be compared. *Somewhat unique.* The *larger half. Rather complete.* Some such comparisons are idiomatic as in " I show you a more perfect way." Superlatives tend to weaken and to need props. So, colloquially, complete means nearly complete.

3. Pleonastic adjectives are already included in the meaning of the word which they modify; *e.g.,* There is an *esthetic beauty* about the new district. *Potent powers.*

4. Expletives — words used merely to fill out a phrase for emphasis. These are natural colloquialisms and are employed for force. They are usually redundant in written style and are often undesirable in speech. Hurry *up*. Finish *off*. Fill *out*.

(*c*) Verbosity, general wordiness, is not so much a fault in specific sentences as a habit of diction. It is most common in a preference for circumlocution.

1. The pronoun I. Roundabout expressions to avoid using *I*, such as *the writer, the author, the present writer*, are undesirable. Either frankly say *I* or avoid all personal reference.

2. General words. In the sporting news it is apparently improper to call the team a team or the ball a ball. Yet the repetition of a really needed word is not undesirable. Avoid the feeble circumlocutions, *better half, life partner, fair sex, tiller of the soil.*

3. Euphemisms, expressions that soften the effect of unpleasant or indelicate terms. Some use of such words is desirable. There are times when *intoxicated* is better than drunk, *passed away* than died, *irregularity* than

theft; but constant preference for euphemisms is a ridiculous habit.

2. *Over-Abstractness.* Abstract nouns are usually easier to think of than the corresponding concrete expressions. They necessarily lack reality and sense-appeal. Prefer the concrete when it is available.

Over-Abstract	*Better*
A presidential possibility	a possible candidate for president
His rendition of Old Black Joe	his singing of or he sang
Inclement weather conditions	bad weather or rain
No matter what the condition of his health	whether sick or well

3. *Triteness.* Overworked phrases, faded figures, and stale quotations or allusions are hindrances to force. They are expressions which seemed neat or striking when first used and which have consequently been overworked until they are conventional, the refuge of the indolent and a weariness to discriminating readers. The use of trite ornament and exaggerated description is called fine writing. It is doubly objectionable, being both insincere and over familiar.

Trite Phrases	*Trite Quotations*
Acid test	Cup that cheers
Along this line	Far from the madding crowd
Bathed in tears	In maiden meditation
Checkered career	Last rose of summer
Dastardly deed	Method in his madness
Filthy lucre	Monarch of all I survey
Long-felt want	Not wisely but too well
One fell swoop	Poor thing but mine own
Psychological moment	Proverbial needle in a haystack
Replete with interest	Sadder and a wiser man
Student-body	Sound mind in sound body
Words fail me	Trip the light fantastic

65. Resources of Force. The effectiveness of diction is increased by:

1. Conciseness. The fewer the words with which an image can be presented or a thought made clear the better the effect. Like clearness, however, conciseness is relative. In certain kinds of subject-matter words can be more easily spared; namely:

(*a*) Description. Few details are better than many, and the omission of relation words will increase the value of the pictorial words.

(*b*) Routine exposition. Reference books and reports condense material given according to a repeated pattern.

(*c*) Poetry may be more concise than prose. Compare Shakespeare's "Winter" (*Golden Treasury,* Book I) with Leigh Hunt's "Now" on a Cold Day. Conciseness is furthered by the omission of unnecessary predicates; *e.g.:*

(When you are) In Rome, do as the Romans do.
When (you are) in doubt, call a physician.
Having no other course, I did as I was told.
He is going to build a house and the plans call for a slate roof.
Better: He is going to build a slate-roofed house.

2. Concreteness. The use of the concrete to stir the imagination has already been discussed. It is, of course, one of the most effective means of creating a sense of reality, particularly when combined with abstracts:

"The Puritan was made up of two different men, the one all self-abasement, penitence, gratitude, passion; the other proud, calm, inflexible, sagacious. He prostrated himself in the dust before his Maker; but he set his foot on the neck of his king."

3. Freshness and variety make style readable. They are a kind of minor originality not restricted to genius. Phrases to describe the exhilaration of alcoholic drinks are abundant, yet Stevenson when he spoke of a passing singer in the night as " internally lit with wine " contrived to find an unhackneyed expression for it.

4. Connotative Words. Force is heightened sometimes at the expense of ease or exactness by the use of words which for any reason are vigorous in connotation. An old gentleman is easily aroused to anger. Shall we call him *testy* or *hot-tempered?* Clearly the second is more forcible. But suppose I say he is *peppery?* The description is still more connotative. *Gaunt* is a stronger word than *emaciated.* *Skinny* is more forcible than either, though less dignified. It is usually safer to say that a man prevaricates or falsifies than that he lies.

66. Ease. For the esthetic quality of style, that which makes writing agreeable to read, no entirely satisfactory name is available. It is a matter partly of good taste and proportion. The deliberate pursuit of charm of style is for most of us undesirable if not futile. It is best regarded as a negative quality, and no name is more appropriate than ease, the lack of that which disturbs or offends.

67. Violations of Ease. Certain faults should be avoided by the writer who desires an easy, agreeable style:

1. Over-conciseness. The omission of words may heighten force at the expense of ease. A compact construction is sometimes awkward though entirely clear. Avoid the omission of

(*a*) Words essential to grammar or logic.

1. This is one of if not her best song. (Say, this, if not her best song, is one of the best.)
2. I am as tall, if not taller than James.
3. He said he would come. I know he won't disappoint me. (Colloquial. In written style the mark of the lighter tone.)
4. I saw at once something was wrong with him.
5. That is the man told me the way.
6. The good which men have always sought and always will.
7. I never said it and what's more, I never could.

(*b*) Words essential to a series.

1. He started down town with me, walked as far as the *Sun* Office, when he suddenly turned back.

2. I took it with me on journeys, on my walks, and visits to my friends.

3. Yet the regular physicians decline to recognize the osteopaths, refuse to consult with them, or call in any trained nurse who attends osteopathic patients.

2. *Faulty Euphony.*

(*a*) Harshness in words or in combinations of words. Certain words are harsh in themselves: *statistics, piousest, difficultly, doubtlessly.* Others are disagreeable when combined: the *richly arched church;* traveled *comparatively inexpensively.*

(*b*) Flat repetition or inadvertent rime. Skilful repetition is useful for clearness or force. Rime is serviceable in poetry to bring out the symmetry of the verse. When these devices are used undesignedly, they are objectionable.

1. All the children were *excited* and *delighted.*

2. You should avoid the *appearance* of *incoherence.*

3. We *accord* him a *cordial* welcome.

4. When I look out of my window and see the moonlight shining through the *trees,* the stars on their beautiful blue background seem to dance among the *trees* which sway in the newly arisen *breeze.*

3. *Faulty Fluency.*

(*a*) Awkward suspense.

1. In view of his thus for the first time disclosed animosity, I must decline.

2. The long journey to and the tiresome stay at his aunt's home were an unpleasant prospect.

(*b*) Heavy parenthesis.

4. *Violations of Idiom.* An idiom depends upon usage and is explainable only by usage. Unidiomatic expressions

attract attention to themselves and thus violate both force and ease.

1. I wish to speak a few remarks on this subject.

2. The refugees were insufficiently clad and with a scanty or no supply of food.

3. When a poor man gets out of labor, he is helpless.

5. *Violations of Simplicity and Good Taste.*

1. The politicians strive to bring about the demise of conditions approaching equality at the polls.

2. The ambitious literary activities of the Hub evidently ruffled a little at that time the literary aspirations of the neighboring spokes of the wheel, as a red rag is said to disturb the equanimity of a male bovine.

3. After their match win of yesterday Waid and Wright are naturally stronger than ever favorites for to-day's event, the win of which will go far to strengthen the impression that they are America's premier pair at the doubles game.

SPECIMENS OF STYLE

I

THE MAN CLOTHED WITH RAGS

As I walked through the wilderness of this world, I lighted on a certain place where was a Den: and I laid me down in that place to sleep: and as I slept, I dreamed a dream. I dreamed, and behold, I saw a man clothed with rags, standing in a certain place, with his face from his own house, a book in his hand, and a great burden on his back. I looked, and saw him open the book, and read therein; and as he read he wept and trembled; and, not being able longer to contain, he brake out with a lamentable cry, saying, "What shall I do?" — BUNYAN in *Pilgrim's Progress.*

II

THE FORCE OF WORDS

It may be here worth our while to examine how it comes to pass that several readers, who are all acquainted with the same language and know the meaning of the words they read, should nevertheless have a different relish of the same descriptions. We find one transported with a passage, which another runs over with coldness and indifference; or finding the representation extremely natural, where another can perceive nothing of likeness and conformity. This different taste must proceed, either from the *perfection of the imagination* in one more than in another, or from the different ideas that several readers affix to the same words. For, to have a true relish, and form the right judgment of a description, a man must have well weighed the force and energy that lie in the several words of a language, so as to be able to distinguish which are the most significant and expressive of their proper ideas, and what additional strength and beauty they are capable of receiving from conjunction with others. The fancy must be warm to retain the print of those images it hath received from outward objects; and the judgment discerning, to know what expressions are most proper to clothe and adorn them to the best advantage. A man who is deficient in either of these respects, though he may receive the general notion of a description can never see distinctly all its particular beauties; as a person with weak sight may have the confused prospect of a place that lies before him, without entering into its several parts or discerning the varieties of its colors in their full glory and perfection. — ADDISON in *The Spectator,* No. 416.

III

SHOOTING A BUFFALO

The buffalo have regular paths by which they come down to drink. Seeing at a glance along which of these his intended victim is moving, the hunter crouches under the bank within fifteen or twenty yards, it may be, of the point where the path enters the river. Here he sits down quietly on the sand. Listening intently, he hears the heavy monotonous tread of the approaching bull. The moment after, he sees a motion among the long weeds and grass just at the spot where the path is channeled through the bank. An enormous black head is thrust out, the horns just visible amid the mass of tangled mane. Half sliding, half plunging, down comes the buffalo upon the river bed below. He steps out in full sight upon the sands. Just before him a runnel of water is gliding, and he bends his head to drink. You may hear the water as it gurgles down his capacious throat. He raises his head and the drops trickle from his wet beard. He stands with air of stupid abstraction, unconscious of the lurking danger. Noiselessly the hunter cocks his rifle. As he sits upon the sand his knee is raised, and his elbow rests upon it, that he may level his heavy weapon with a steadier aim. The stock is at his shoulder; his eye ranges along the barrel. Still he is in no haste to fire. The bull, with slow deliberation, begins his march over the sands to the other side. He advances his foreleg, and exposes to view a small spot, denuded of hair, just behind the point of his shoulder; upon this the hunter brings the point of his rifle to bear; lightly and delicately his finger presses the hair trigger. The spiteful crack of the rifle responds to his touch, and instantly in the middle of the bare spot appears a small red dot. The buffalo shivers; death has overtaken him he cannot tell from whence; still he does not fall, but walks heavily forward, as if nothing had happened. Yet before he has gone far out upon the sands, you see him stop; he totters; his knees bend under him, and his head sinks forward to the ground. Then his whole vast bulk sways to one side; he rolls over on the sand, and dies with a scarcely perceptible struggle. — FRANCIS PARKMAN in *The Oregon Trail*.

IV

IN A BOAT WOMAN'S KITCHEN

We despatched our visit so promptly that we got back to our boat-woman's cottage a full hour before our steamer was to call for us. She had an afternoon fire kindled in her bright range, from the oven of which came already the odor of agreeable baking. Upon this hint we acted, and asked if tea were possible. It was, and jam sandwiches as well, or if we preferred buttered tea-cake, with or without currants, to jam sandwiches, there would be that presently. We preferred both, and we sat down in that pleasant parlor-kitchen, and listened, till the tea-cake came out of the oven, and was split open and buttered smoking hot, to a flow of delightful and instructive talk. For our refection we paid sixpence each, but for our edification we are still, and hope ever to be, in debt. Our hostess was of a most cheerful philosophy, such as could not be bought of most modern philosophers for money. The flour for our tea-cakes, she said was a shilling and fivepence a stone, "And not too much for growing and grinding it, and all." Every week-day morning she rose at half past four, and got breakfast for her boys, who then rode their bicycles, or, in the snow, walked, all the miles of our voyage into York, where they worked in the railway shops. No, they did not belong to any union; the railway men did not seem to care for it; only a "benefit union." She kept the house for her family, and herself ready to answer every hail from the steamer, but in her mellow English content, which was not stupid or sodden, but clever and wise, it was as if it were she, rather than the archbishop, whose nature expressed itself in a motto on one of the palace walls, "Blessed be the Lord who loadeth us with blessings every day." — W. D. Howells in *Harper's Magazine,* July, 1909. Used by permission.

V

Shooting an Oil-Well

In the afternoon of a dull February day I stood with a companion in the center of a level space of farm land in southeastern Illinois. A heavy mist, hesitating on the border line between fog and rain, subdued the landscape to a gray monotone, its only bright spot the ruddy flare of a natural-gas flame in a distant farm-yard. From a shadowy group of low buildings across a field the measured beat of a giant heart punctuated the stillness, its sound reproduced in diminishing emphasis from points farther and farther away through the dusk. Here and there in the fields about this common center, some near, some distant half a mile or more, stood a company of strange beings, their curious outlines magnified into threatening mysteries by the fog. In syncopated rhythm with the great heart-beat, they executed slow movements like giant sawhorses gravely rising on their hind legs to solemn music. The Knight of La Mancha would have found as stirring provocation to righteous wrath in this band of balancing wooden-headed Centaurs as ever in his windmill giants. A hundred yards before us rose a tall mast, flanked by a small shanty, a wheeled boiler, and an engine with a simplified steamboat walking beam. At the foot of the mast four men stood idly about watching another who seemed engaged in mysterious rites. The center of their interest and ours was a new oil well. The well had been sunk until the "pay sand"

was reached, and the busy little man was completing his preparations to " shoot " it.

Oil occurs in the crevices of certain kinds of porous rock from
three hundred to two thousand feet below the surface. An oil
well is a hole in the ground, a foot in diameter at the top, six
inches at the bottom, tapping the rock containing the oil and
affording an outlet through which the oil may flow, or, more
usually, be pumped to the surface. The boring of the well is
done by a steel drill, measuring with its fittings thirty feet in
length, and weighing from half a ton to a ton and a half. This
drill is continually lifted and dropped in the hole, the force of
its impact pulverizing the rock into sand. At intervals the debris
is removed by a sand pump, which is not a pump at all, but a
tube with a valve at the bottom, which is lowered into the hole
and drawn out, bringing the sand with it. When the oil rock is
reached, sometimes, the pressure is sufficient to bring the oil to
the surface with a rush, and to keep it flowing indefinitely.
Generally, however, the oil either does not flow at all or flows
only in small quantity. In either case the well is " shot." By
exploding a charge of nitroglycerine at the bottom of the hole
the surrounding rock is broken up and the flow of the oil
stimulated.

The busy little man was the " shooter " engaged in lowering
into the well two hundred quarts of " glycerine " contained in
ten cylindrical shells. The premature explosion of only a small
fraction of the thick yellow fluid which he was pouring so calmly
into the shells would have sufficed to eliminate not only him but
most of the surrounding apparatus. By mutual consent, then, my
companion and I viewed proceedings from our remote point of
vantage. His experience of twenty years in the oil fields led me
to accept without question his estimate of a satisfactory distance
for observation.

After a couple of hours of steady work the ten shells were
safely in position, and the well filled for a couple of hundred feet
above them with water to " tamp " the charge. The shooter,
ready with his " jack squib," a long slender shell filled with a
small charge of glycerine, a fulminating cap, and a slow-burning
fuse, lighted the fuse and started the squib on its downward
course to arouse the sleeping energies of those two hundred
quarts of yellow earthquake essence. Then even the shooter
forsook his nonchalant calm and joined us without delay in our
retirement. In a moment a heavy shock stirred the earth be-

neath us, accompanied by a dull, muffled report. From the well a jet of muddy fluid leaped a hundred feet in the air, was swept away by the wind, and fell in a scattered shower, the sound of its fall accented by the thud of chunks of rock hurled out with a force that plunged them bodily into the earth.

Rapidly the jet died down; and the drillers went briskly to work to finish lining the well with iron piping, and to connect it up to a receiving tank. In a few hours, if it proved in any degree a flowing well, oil from it would be accumulating and the well would have begun to pay for its drilling. In another day its pump would be installed, adding another to that scattered group of solemn Centaurs; an iron rod would lead three or four hundred yards to the low building across the field, connecting the " jack " of the pump with the gas engine there, the beat of whose strokes revealed the heart of the system of wells of which this was numbered twenty-one; if the well produced gas in addition to oil, it would be piped to the engine, and the well would do its own pumping. — HAROLD J. HOWLAND. From "Standard Oil" in *The Outlook*, September 28, 1907. Used by permission.

VI

CHINESE FELLOW-PASSENGERS

For my own part, I could not look but with wonder and respect on the Chinese. Their forefathers watched the stars before mine had begun to keep pigs. Gunpowder and printing, which the other day we imitated, and a school of manners which we never had the delicacy so much as to desire to imitate, were theirs in a long-past antiquity. They walk the earth with us, but it seems they must be of different clay. They hear the clock strike the same hour, yet surely of a different epoch. They travel by steam conveyance, yet with such a baggage of old Asiatic thoughts and superstitions as might check the locomotive in its course. Whatever is thought within the circuit of the Great Wall; what the wry-eyed, spectacled schoolmaster teaches in the hamlets round Pekin; religions so old that our language looks a halfling boy alongside; philosophy so wise that our best philosophers find things therein to wonder at; all this travelled alongside of me for thousands of miles over plain and mountain. Heaven knows if we had one common thought or fancy all that way, or whether our eyes, which yet were formed upon the same design, beheld the same world out of the railway windows. And when either of us turned his thoughts to home and childhood, what a strange dissimilarity must there not have been in these pictures of the mind — when I beheld that old, gray, castled city, high throned above the firth, with the flag of Britain flying, and the red-coat sentry pacing over all; and the man in the next car to me would conjure up some junks and a pagoda and a fort of porcelain, and call it, with the same affection, home. — STEVENSON in *Across the Plains*. Used by permission of Charles Scribner's Sons.

VII

EMERSON LECTURING

Many years ago the Easy Chair used to hear Ralph Waldo Emerson lecture. Perhaps it was in the small Sunday-school room under a country meeting house, on sparkling winter nights, when all the neighborhood came stamping and chattering to the door in hood and muffler, or ringing in from a few miles away buried under buffalo skins. The little low room was dimly lighted with oil lamps, and the boys clumped about the stoves in their cow-hide boots and laughed and buzzed and ate apples and peanuts and giggled, and grew suddenly solemn when the grave men and women looked at them. At the desk stood the lecturer and read his manuscript, and all but the boys sat silent and en-thralled by the musical spell.

Some of the hearers remembered the speaker as a boy, as a young man. Some wondered what he was talking about. Some thought him very queer. All laughed at the delightful humor of the illustrative anecdote that sparkled for a moment on the surface of his talk; and some sat inspired with unknown resolves, soaring upon lofty hopes as they heard. A noble life, a better manhood, a purer purpose wooed every listening soul. It was not argument, nor description, nor appeal. It was wit and wisdom, and hard sense and poetry, and scholarship and music. And when the words were spoken and the lecturer sat down, the Easy Chair sat still and heard the rich cadences lingering in the air, as the young priest's heart throbs with the long vibrations when the organist is gone. — G. W. CURTIS in *From the Easy Chair*. Used by permission of Harper and Brothers.

VIII

THE CONCORD RIVER

Perhaps the reader — whom I cannot help considering as my guest in the Old Manse, and entitled to all courtesy in the way of sight-showing — perhaps he will choose to take a nearer view of the memorable spot. We stand now on the river's brink. It may well be called the Concord — the river of peace and quietness — for it is certainly the most unexcitable and sluggish stream that ever loitered imperceptibly toward its eternity the sea. Positively, I had lived three weeks beside it before it grew quite clear to my perception which way the current flowed. It never has a vivacious aspect except when a north-western breeze is vexing its surface on a sunshiny day. From the incurable indolence of its nature the stream is, happily, incapable of becoming the slave of human ingenuity, as is the fate of so many a wild, free mountain-torrent. While all things else are compelled to serve some useful purpose, it idles its sluggish life away in lazy liberty without turning a solitary spindle or affording even water power enough to grind the corn that grows upon its banks. The torpor of its movements allows it nowhere a bright pebbly shore, nor so much as a narrow strip of glistening sand in any part of its course. It slumbers between broad prairies, kissing the long meadowgrass, and bathes the overhanging boughs of elder bushes and willows or the roots of elms and ash trees and clumps of maples. Flags and rushes grow along its plashy shore; the yellow water-lily spreads its broad flat leaves on the margin, and the fragrant white pond-lily abounds, generally selecting a position just so far from the river's brink that it cannot be grasped save at the hazard of plunging in.

It is a marvel whence this perfect flower derives its loveliness and perfume, springing as it does, from the black mud over which the river sleeps, and where lurk the slimy eel and the speckled frog and the mud-turtle whom continued washing cannot cleanse. It is the very same black mud out of which the yellow lily sucks its obscene life and noisome odor. Thus we see, too, in the world that some persons assimilate only what is ugly and evil from the same moral circumstances which supply good and beautiful results — the fragrance of celestial flowers — to the daily life of others.

The reader must not from any testimony of mine contract a

dislike toward our slumbersome stream. In the light of a calm and golden sunset it becomes lovely beyond expression — the more lovely for the quietude that so well accords with the hour, when even the wind after blustering all day long, usually hushes itself to rest. Each tree and rock and every blade of grass is distinctly imaged, and, however unsightly in reality, assumes ideal beauty in the reflection. The minutest things of earth and the broad aspect of the firmament are pictured equally without effort and with the same felicity of success. All the sky glows downward at our feet; the rich clouds float like heavenly thoughts through a peaceful heart. We will not, then, malign our river as gross and impure, while it can glorify itself with so adequate a picture of the heaven that broods above it; or if we remember its tawny hue and the muddiness of its bed, let it be a symbol that the earthiest human mould has an infinite spiritual capacity and may contain the better world within its depths. But, indeed, the same lesson might be drawn out of any mud-puddle in the streets of a city; and being taught us everywhere, it must be true. — HAWTHORNE in *The Old Manse*.

IX

A VIEW OF ATTICA

A confined triangle; perhaps fifty miles its greatest length and thirty its greatest breadth; two elevated rocky barriers, meeting at an angle; three prominent mountains commanding the plain, — Parmes, Pentelicus, and Hymettus; an unsatisfactory soil; some streams, not always full; such is about the report which the agent of a London company would have made of Attica. He would report that the climate was mild; the hills were limestone; there was plenty of good marble; more pasture land than at first survey might have been expected, sufficient certainly for sheep and goats; fisheries productive; silver mines once, but long since worked out; figs fair; olive oil first-rate; olives in profusion. But what he would not think of noting down was, that the olive tree was so choice in nature and so noble in shape that it excited a religious veneration; and that it took so kindly to the light soil, as to expand into woods upon the open plain and to climb up and fringe the hills. He would not think of writing word to his employers how that clear air, of which I have spoken, brought out, yet blended and subdued, the colors on the marble, till they had a softness and harmony, for all their richness, which in a picture looks exaggerated, yet is after all within the truth. He would not tell how that same delicate and brilliant atmosphere freshened up the pale olive, till the olive forgot its monotony, and its cheek glowed like the arbutus or beech of the Umbrian hills. He would say nothing of the thyme and thousand fragrant herbs which carpeted Hymettus; he would hear nothing of the hum of its bees; nor take much account of the rare flavor of its honey, since Gozo and Minorca were sufficient for the English demand. He would look over the Aegean from the height he had ascended; he would follow with his eye the chain of islands, which starting from the Sumian headland seemed to offer the fabled divinities of Attica, when they would visit their Ionian cousins, a sort of viaduct thereto across the sea; but that fancy would not occur to him, nor any admiration of the dark violet billows with their white edges down below; nor of those graceful fan-like jets of silver upon the rocks, which slowly rise aloft like water spirits from the deep, then shiver, and break and spread, and shroud themselves, and disappear, in a soft mist of foam; nor of the gentle incessant heaving and panting of the whole liquid plain; nor of the long waves keeping steady time, like a line of soldiery, as they resound upon the hollow shore, — he would not deign to notice that restless living element at all, except to bless his stars that he was not upon it. Nor the distinct detail, nor the refined coloring, nor the graceful outline and roseate golden hue of the jutting crags, nor the bold shadows cast from Otus and Laurium by the declining sun; our agent of a mercantile firm would not value these matters even at a low figure. Rather must we turn for the sympathy we seek to yon pilgrim student come from a semi-barbarous land to that small corner of the earth, as to a shrine, where he might take his fill of gazing on those emblems and coruscations of invisible, unoriginate perfection. It was the stranger from a remote province, from Britain or from Mauritania, who in a scene so different from that of his chilly swamps, or of his fiery choking sands, learned at once what a real University must be, by coming to understand the sort of country which was its suitable home. — NEWMAN in *The Idea of a University.*

X

THE ENGAGING SCARAB

This strange predilection for beetles has been lasting. Even yet a June-bug gives me a thrill, and the grip of his horny legs on my finger will set my associative memory working as will few things else. For me he is a living question, a puzzle, a hard little lump of primeval nature, that stands for the flower in the crannied wall. Above all, he is a scarab. Around his foolish head lingers a glory visible only to the mind's eye, but made up of vestiges of Karnak and Thebes, or Isis and Orus and the dog Anubis, of the old moon-mountains African. Just as now this evening he booms athwart the thicket lone, and bumps his dunderhead against mine, so his cousin *scarabæus sacer*, wheeling his droning flight some millenniums ago over papyrus and lotus and sand, collided as impolitely with the cranium of a Shepherd King, or a Ptolemæus Soter, or a Hermes Trismegistus. The Egyptians embalmed *sacer* and cut effigies of him in costly stone, fabling him to be an emblem of fertility and eternity; and all because he was a tumble-bug, depositing his eggs in dung, and burying them in the ground for warmth and safekeeping. I cannot follow all the ramifications of their symbolism: I only wonder whether at the age of three I already felt in the presence of a scarab some vague fore-feeling of that love for the old and the strange that later I experienced so keenly in the presence of the relics of the Egyptians themselves.

There is, however, quite enough of engaging simplicity and pertinacity about the scarab family to make them attractive. Their peculiarities are more ancient and more permanent than pyramid or sphinx. The experience of millenniums has not taught them to "stryve noght, as doth the crokke with the wal." They continue to strive, but, unlike "the crokke," seem never to get hurt. Too insignificant even to fear extermination, while the mountains wear away and the forests are cleared, and the river is dammed and diked, and the lion and the bison go the way of the dodo, the little scarabee has crawled yearly out of the sod, tried his wings, and soared away in a bee-line for the nearest or brightest light, be it Pharos or Eddystone or only the modest beam of my desk-lamp. Year in, year out, while all else goes merrily sliding down the ringing grooves of change, he continues to bump his dusky carapace against window and wall, falling on his back, wildly waving his crooked legs, blundering into corners, under tables, down people's necks, up their sleeves, into their ink, their waste-baskets, their soup. Eternally ridiculous, he has in him, nevertheless, a spark of divine aspiration, sharing the desire of the moth for the star or the flame. In my symbolism, he stands for a class of people, familiar though not numerous, stupid but lovable, who blunder their way through life, seeking the light with utmost seriousness, but leaving a wake of laughter behind them. — ROBERT M. GAY, in *Entomological, The Atlantic Monthly*, August, 1912. Used by permission.

EXERCISES IN DICTION

I

Test the range of your vocabulary of learned words by means of this exercise. Write, without previous study of the words, a clue to the meaning of each and then verify your answers by consulting a dictionary. A college freshman should know, in a general way, the correct meaning of more than half of the list.

1. antipathy	14. acumen
2. shoddy	15. indigenous
3. tenuous	16. plethora
4. aphasia	17. repatriation
5. agrarian	18. histrionic
6. venison	19. lenity
7. cataclysm	20. parvenu
8. quinquennial	21. limn
9. diurnal	22. imprimatur
10. bursar	23. refectory
11. extrinsic	24. scarify
12. factotum	25. rubric
13. gerrymander	

Test your acquaintance with technical vocabularies by means of the following words. You should know not less than half the words in each of these special lists.

Housewife's	Physician's	Clergyman's
meringue	fracture	heresy
sateen	asepsis	predestination
smock	bacillus	Pentateuch
taffeta	anesthesia	homiletics
carafe	neurasthenia	vicarious
gusset	anemia	Septuagint
shirr	prophylaxis	Exegesis
dimity	amnesia	latitudinarian
casserole	prognosis	eschatology
ramekin	endemic	teleology

Lawyer's	Automobilist's	Druggist's
affidavit	blow-out	decolor
indictment	spark-plug	decoction
codicil	clutch	dehydrate
demurrer	generator	febrifuge
chattel	carburetor	antipyretic
habeas corpus	accelerator	triturate
subpoena	commutator	rubifacient
talesman	gasket	deliquescent
tort	differential	desiccative
escrow	ammeter	emollient

Test your familiarity with foreign words in English speech by this list. You should know at sight the meaning and pronunciation of not less than half of them.

1. exit	14. confrere
2. finis	15. nuance
3. alibi	16. dilletante
4. chef	17. distrait
5. fiancé	18. entrepreneur
6. alias	19. soi-disant
7. ennui	20. argumentum ad hominem
8. bizarre	21. pari passu
9. fiasco	22. gaucherie
10. éclat	23. noblesse oblige
11. quasi	24. recherché
12. blasé	25. rechauffé
13. bourgeois	26. bête noir

These words are so much used as to be colorless in the speech of many persons. Can you tell at sight the precise meaning of each?

1. fine
2. nice
3. grand
4. splendid
5. elegant

6. factor
7. feature
8. element
9. condition
10. proposition

II

Rewrite the following sentences, making such changes as seem desirable. In case of ambiguity, give two improved versions.

1. He is interested in the willing unemployed.
2. Such ideas as he expresses are wrong.
3. Outside of you and me there isn't anybody he can apply to.
4. The appointments committee finds opportunities for securing positions that will help to finance an education.
5. By exercise a man's muscles and whole physic is developed so that in later life he will be able to resist decease.
6. Again, the effect of a Pan-Hellenic council on the whole student-body will be very beneficial also.
7. The children about to be punished wore a look of painful anguish.
8. Now and then one could see the snow-plows busy cleaning the tracks for the cars and at the same time sending a shower of dirty snow to each side.
9. It costs a large sum of money to pump a large quantity of water a long distance.
10. The chairman was a man of strong social qualifications and was a great factor in Bosworth.
11. Clarke, has worked out a plan by which he will be able to keep Wagner in the lime-light for many years more which consists of nothing less than transferring the premier shortstop to the initial bag.
12. The constitutional convention is a Democratic organization proposition.

13. I ask you to consider whether or not the country shall go wet or dry.

14. Both Rosalind and Orlando fell in love with each other at first sight.

15. This will gain him a position of influence among all of his fellow-associates.

16. We do not know much about his interview except it was long and protracted and did not end till the break of day.

17. A man's habits, tastes, and ideals are shown by the condition, pictures, and decorations of his room.

18. A serious collision was possible, for both vehicles were approaching each other too swiftly to be suddenly stopped.

19. On June 17 of this year, he, without warning and with no cause left his home and young wife.

20. As Smith embarked upon the road of learning he found his duties elbowing his pleasures out of his path.

21. It seems a lack of reverence for Hawthorne's rich style to break his thoughts into fragments and then dig up the roots of these fragments.

22. Although some were not very interesting the majority were very interesting.

23. Longfellow's *Evangeline* was more appreciated by me than any other character described by him.

24. All this flashed into my mind as the truth of the message flashed upon the telegraphic instrument came to me.

25. In choosing a subject for debate you should be very careful that it contains only one subject and that that one is a debatable one.

26. Upon this grave stood a battered iron cross badly rusted by the tooth of time.

27. At the witching hour of midnight, the assembled multitude who had been tripping the light fantastic toe and gliding through the dizzy mazes of the waltz, wended their way homeward.

28. Three respected and influential residents of Anderson have succumbed to the grim reaper during the week. Colonel Browse passed to the great beyond on Tuesday; Mr. W. G. Browne was called to his eternal rest on Wednesday as a result of being overheated; and the spirit of the widow Jones was wafted to her Maker yesterday morning.

29. If he had been only a stock broker, his earthly renown would not have long survived his earthly existence. His work is scholarly, whether it be written to meter or without any attempt at measured cadences.

30. The defendant's old mother, who had passed eighty milestones along life's weary path, gave her testimony in her boy's behalf.

III

1. Arrange in a table synonyms for each of the following ideas, showing terms that will make the meaning (a) stronger, (b) weaker, (c) more abstract, (d) more concrete: strong, pure, interesting, glad, loyal, courage, fidelity, durability, beauty. For example, using the word *strong*:

Stronger: powerful, irresistible, invincible.
Weaker: helpless, feeble, weak, weakened.
More abstract: able, virile, mighty, potential.
More concrete: muscular, brawny, iron-thewed.

2. List and discuss synonyms for the following general terms: good to eat; agreeable to hear; an unfortunate happening; cold weather; a good friend; a good soprano voice; perseverance; decorated; talkative; not true; not active; an unwise policy; uncompanionable; eccentric; precious; of little importance; humble; competent; difficult to learn; not to be avoided.

3. Discuss the shades of meaning by which these synonyms differ, and use them in sentences which will make the distinctions clear.

(a) Frank, artless, candid, sincere, ingenuous.
(b) Wise, discreet, learned, discerning, shrewd, acute.
(c) Good, virtuous, pious, upright, just, righteous.
(d) Fast, rapid, quick, fleet, expeditious, swift.
(e) Save, ransom, rescue, recover, free, redeem.
(f) Abate, lessen, decrease, lower, reduce, lighten.
(g) Angry, wrathful, furious, resentful, fierce, bitter.
(h) Enough, sufficient, plenty, abundance, surfeit.
(i) Dark, dim, dismal, opaque, obscure, gloomy.
(j) Annul, cancel, repeal, nullify, quash, kill.

4. The English prefix a- may come from old English, from Latin, or from Greek, with a different meaning in each case. Learn from the dictionary what these meanings are, and list and discuss several words that will illustrate them.

5. Find, discuss, and illustrate five other prefixes from the Greek.

6. Distinguish in meaning the following doublets: Prudent, provident; pursue, prosecute; gentle, genteel; human, humane; penalty, punishment; corporation, body; limitation, limit.

7. Learn what you can of the origin and meaning of these phrases: " sweetness and light," the square deal, America first, " a scrap of paper," Machiavellian policies.

8. Examine as to etymology the terms riddle, rebus, enigma, charade, puzzle, rune.

9. List and discuss as to origin and use several words of each of the following classes: (1) group words: swarm, herd, flock, and the like; (2) family names indicating occupations: Webster, Fletcher, and the like; (3) names of writing materials; *e.g.*, paper, vellum, book; (4) names of fabrics; (5) military terms for bodies of soldiers; (6) names of common birds.

10. Find out the fossil metaphors in the following words: *assassin, chum, companion, dandelion, daisy, geranium, vipers bugloss, ammonia, vinegar, whiskey, ostracize.*

IV

Find in your dictionary:

1. Whether *beak* (bill of a bird) and *beaker* (glass vessel) are related words.

2. How these articles came to be so named: *boycott, derrick, fuchsia, guillotine, macadam, silhouette, watt.*

3. Why these fabrics are so called: *calico, cambric, cheviot, damask, muslin, poplin, worsted.*

4. The origin of the slang terms: *buncombe, chump, cinch.*

5. The meaning of allusions to *Allan-a-Dale, Bellerophon, Cerberus, Croesus, Huns, Hydra, Tory, Whig.*

REFERENCES

Words and their Ways in English Speech by Greenough and Kittredge (Macmillan); *The Making of Speech* by Henry Bradley (Macmillan); *The Romance of Words* by Ernest Weekley (John Murray); *The Century Vocabulary Builder* by Greever and Bachelor (Century); *Modern English* by G. P. Krapp (Scribners).

CHAPTER VI

STRUCTURE AND STYLE IN EXPOSITION

THE NATURE OF EXPOSITION

68. Exposition as a Form of Discourse. Since words, phrases, and sentences are the elements of which every piece of writing is built up, the general study of style is merely the mastery of necessary tools. Whatever your purpose in writing, whatever your material, some such mastery must be acquired, by one means or another, before you can succeed. The principles of style which we have thus far considered are common to all forms of writing and are employed consciously or unconsciously by all who write effectively. There are, however, certain well-recognized types of writing so different from each other that in the further study of style they must be considered separately. Each of such forms serves its own purpose and has its own methods and technic. As commonly named and distinguished they are exposition, description, narration, argument, and persuasion.

The purpose of exposition is to explain, to lay out before the mind as one unrolls a chart or sets forth merchandise. In that its appeal is to the understanding it is akin to argument. The aim of both is the truth. Exposition seeks to make the truth known; argument to get it believed and accepted. Although, like description, exposition may deal with concrete things, its concern is not with their impression upon the senses but with their meaning and their relation to other things. An airplane whirring in the blue may in the same paragraph be both described and explained. Description deals with it as an object of sense, to be portrayed for the imagination of the reader. Exposition deals with it as an idea to be analyzed or defined.

Being more purely intellectual than any other form, exposition is in a sense the typical form of discourse, for language is an intellectual medium. Very little writing of any kind is wholly unmixed with exposition. The setting and the characters of narrative often have to be explained. Description, when not merely incidental to other writing, frequently depends for coherence upon an expository frame. Argument and exposition are sometimes to be distinguished only with reference to the attitude of the reader, and are in practice commonly intermingled. It is not accidental that selections used to illustrate structure are chiefly exposition; the deliberate ordering of parts is an expository process, and all carefully planned structure makes use of the methods of exposition.

69. Exposition as a Practical Art. Skill in explanation is a useful everyday art of the utmost importance and value. By means of it organized society is made possible and the accumulated knowledge of one generation is preserved for the next. Science cannot push forward the boundaries of knowledge without an adequate vocabulary and a serviceable style. The commerce of the world depends upon organization, which is the product of clear thinking and lucid explanation. Indeed, our power to think clearly is apparently conditional to a great degree on the corresponding power of clear expression.

This power to write clearly is consequently required of every educated man. The practice of literature as a fine art is reserved — like the other fine arts — for those persons who possess the necessary taste and skill. A man may never in all his life feel called upon to attempt a story, a poem, or a literary essay. He may not often have occasion to write an argument. But he must play a small part in the world if he does not frequently find it necessary in letters, reports, speeches, or advertisements to make clear to others his own understanding of some part of his experience. It follows that a reasonable mastery of the art of exposition can be achieved by anybody. It is not easy to be clear, but clearness does not depend upon any special aptitude. A student who can master facts enough to pass an examination can also master the form in which the facts should be presented. Neither he nor his instructor should be satisfied with anything less than excellence in this regard, for the world has a right to expect that an intellectual worker shall know how to use his tools.

THE MATERIAL OF EXPOSITION

70. Gaining the Facts. Knowledge about a particular subject we may get in two ways: at first hand, by seeing and hearing for ourselves, by asking questions, and by collecting original sources of information; or at second hand, by adapting to our particular purpose facts already collected and ordered by others. Knowledge got at first hand may have already come to us incidentally, so that our task is to recall and arrange the facts, or it may have to be sought for specifically for use in a projected piece of writing. In either case what has already been said about structure is of importance. Determine as promptly as possible what your fundamental idea really is. It will lead you to such facts as you can use and will exclude those that are useless. A student who has decided to tell how to install an electric door-bell will not waste time reflecting about the usefulness of electric bells or the great variety of purposes that they serve. He will jot down on paper a list of the parts of such a bell and of the steps in the process of setting them up. If he is to write about the high school that he attended last year, the limitation of his subject to the school as an organization or as a public institution will make it easier rather than harder for him to find the facts.

An assignment to get the facts and write them up is a somewhat different problem. The fundamental idea may not be easily determined until some of the facts are known, but it should be constantly sought for. When Mr. Howland was sent by a periodical to write an article on the Standard Oil Company (see page 149), he may conceivably not have decided in advance upon his point of view. He can hardly have inspected oil-fields long, however, before he decided to write about the company as a middleman between the producer and the consumer. The decision at once excluded from his article many of the interesting things that he saw. A student sent to learn about the organized charities of a city felt at a loss as various agencies were explained to him and reports and circulars were thrust into his hands, until he hit upon the fact that the central idea of modern charity is to find and remove the cause of poverty rather than merely to alleviate it.

Material derived from printed sources differs from that obtained by our own observation and inquiry chiefly in that it has already been collected and arranged by somebody else. Our only excuse for rehandling it is our ability to use it in new combinations and for new purposes. Such material, stored up in libraries and constantly augmented in new books and periodicals, is so overwhelmingly abundant that our greatest problem is how to find the facts that we want.

1. Books. In a good library, go first to the card catalog. If, as is usually the case, it is what is known as a dictionary catalog, you will find that each book is represented by at least three cards, which list it by the name of the author, the title and the subject. Under the subject heading you will find cards for all the books in the library on your general subject. Special bibliographies are compiled by the Government and by other agencies. Look for references to these in the American Library Association Annual.

2. Periodicals. In a good library bound volumes of the more important periodicals will be available. For references to articles in them use,

The Reader's Guide to Periodical Literature. (From 1900 in five-year and annual cumulations.)
Poole's Index to Periodical Literature. 1882–1906.
The Annual Magazine Subject Index. (Supplementary to the Reader's Guide, listing special topics and less general periodicals.)

3. Reference Books.

Murray's New English Dictionary (Oxford).
The Century Dictionary and Cyclopedia.
Webster's New International Dictionary.
The Standard Dictionary.
The Encyclopedia Britannica.
The New International Encyclopedia.
Lippincott's Pronouncing Biographical Dictionary.
Hastings' Dictionary of the Bible.
Hastings' Encyclopedia of Religion and Ethics.
Harper's Dictionary of Classical Antiquities.
Who's Who (British. Living persons only).
Who's Who in America.
The World Almanac.

Besides these works a large library will contain a great variety of special dictionaries, handbooks, and almanacs, which a student should learn to know by browsing among them. Do not hesitate to appeal to the library attendant for help when you fail to find what you want.

Information found in books and periodicals should be tested in two ways — as to its trustworthiness and as to its relevancy. A college education should teach you not only to know and to love books but also to distrust them. Overcome the juvenile feeling that whatever is said in print must on that account be true. Form the habit of noting carefully the names of the authors and the publishers of what you are reading. As to the author, ask whether he is a recognized authority, whether he is reporting fact or expressing opinion, whether he writes from personal knowledge or from hearsay, and whether he is judicial or partisan. A work that bears the imprint of a reputable publisher is likely to have been scrutinized carefully before publication. In the case of current events put more confidence in later reports and summaries than in the first dispatches, and make allowance for sensationalism and partisan bias as well as for the haste of news-writing. Do not depend, in a question of fact, upon a single source. Test the opinion of one authority by another. Finally, do not include in your material any fact, however true or interesting, that does not bear upon your fundamental idea and have a logical place in the plan of your work.

As facts accumulate they must be arranged and preserved according to some system. If more than half a dozen separate items are to be recorded, cards or the pages of a small loose-leaf notebook will be found convenient. Devise a method suited to yourself and follow it faithfully. Do not, on the one hand, burden yourself with some needlessly elaborate system because it is recommended, or, on the other hand, waste your energy trying to do good work with memoranda made on scraps of paper and the fly-leaves of books. Note down carefully every reference while the exact pages and dates are before your eyes, and keep your facts in such a form that they can be readily arranged in the finished work according to the structure which your analysis of the subject discloses.

The Methods of Exposition

71. The Direct Methods. A matter that needs explanation may be made clear directly or indirectly. The direct method proceeds by analyzing the ideas and relations involved in it; the indirect method by representing or suggesting it. The first is abstract, the second concrete. Each supplements the other. Thus a spark plug is explained directly by an enumeration of its parts and a setting forth of their functions and the principles on which they operate; it is explained indirectly by a simile, a mechanical drawing, a picture, or by the exhibition of an actual plug. The direct methods include:

1. *Classification.* A first step in the mastery of miscellaneous facts is the making of serviceable classifications. The incoming letters in a post-office would accumulate in a confused and futile heap if they were not constantly grouped and regrouped into convenient classes. The principle of this grouping is in every case some significant similarity. The letters of one large group are alike in being designed for general delivery; of another in being intended for distribution in private boxes. The same set of facts is capable of classification by means of several different kinds of similarity, as playing cards can be grouped according to suit, color, or degree and the subscribers for a periodical according to state, length of subscription, or date of expiration.

Classification for practical purposes uses any principle that proves convenient. It does not hesitate to ignore unimportant groups. Scientific classification is exact, insisting upon similarities that can be recognized with unfailing accuracy and seeking constantly for systems that will have a place for every individual that can be discovered. A popular manual successfully classifies wildflowers according to color. A botanist requires more

precise distinctions and such a multiplication of groups as
enables him to identify any blossom that he finds.

2. *Division.* An already recognized class or a unit
capable of separation into parts is made clear by division,
a process complementary to classification, from which it
differs in point of view.   Most general terms may be
divided into other less general terms, and all are divisible
into the units which compose them.   The term *States of
the American Union* admits of division into geographical
sections, such as New England States, Middle Atlantic
States, Southern States, Central States, Northwestern
States, and Southwestern States, as well as into the forty-
eight individual states which comprise the Union.   The
division of a subject so that it may be discussed part by
part has already been dealt with in the chapters on structure and has been adequately illustrated in various outlines
of articles.

3. *Definition.*   Classification might have been defined as
the creation of classes.   It looks at the groupings of facts
from below and relates them on the basis of similarity.
It is the means by which ordered knowledge comes into
existence.   Division might have been called the recognition
of classes.   It approaches the same groupings from above,
distinguishing them by means of dissimilarity.   When these
two principles are applied to the same term it is possible
to fix its relation to other terms with such exactness that
the process is called definition, literally, the setting of
limits.   A term is defined by (*a*) being classified, that
is, put into the group to which it belongs by reason of
its similarity to the other members of that group, and (*b*)
being identified, that is, separated from the other members
of its class by some dissimilarity that distinguishes it.   The
class to which a term is assigned is called by logicians the
genus — usually the proximate (nearest) genus — and the
characteristic dissimilarity that sets it off is termed the

differentia. A definition consisting of a term, its genus, and an adequate differentia is known as a logical definition. For example:

Term	Genus	Differentia
Play is	exercise, mental or physical	undertaken for amusement
Chemistry is	the science	of the composition and changes of substances
A ballad is	a story	told in song

The requirements of a logical definition are exacting. It must (*a*) include everything that belongs to the idea defined, (*b*) exclude everything else, and (*c*) use words that are simple and clear. The definition, " Taxes are charges levied by a government on the owners of real estate," violates (*a*), for it does not include personal property taxes, income taxes, and various others. " Taxes are portions of private property taken by a government for public purposes " violates (*b*), since it includes fines and condemnations. " Life is the summation and aggregate result of all the properties of living matter " is neither clear nor simple. In order to fulfil these requirements, the definition must be correct in form. " Man is a rational human being " is not successful, because the genus is not large enough. " Man is a rational being " is open to criticism because the genus is too large. It does not exclude deity. " Man is a rational animal " is more satisfactory, because animal is the proximate genus. The differentia must really discriminate. In " Man is a featherless biped " we have a whimsical distinction rather than an essential difference between man and all other animals.

From all this it is obvious that a wholly satisfactory logical definition is sometimes difficult to frame. Most dictionary definitions are mere approximations, like that which defines man as " a human being; a member of the human race "; for it is the office of the dictionary to tell us the meanings of words rather than the precise limits of the ideas for which words stand.   The difficulty in phrasing a precise definition most often occurs in the differentia.   " A gentleman is a man who . . ." is all very simple.   When one attempts to complete the sentence, he discovers that the term *gentleman* means several different things, and after he has decided just what it means for him, he may, like Newman, find it necessary to use several pages to make his differentia exact.   Except in the terminology of the sciences, in which accurate classification is a matter of course, we must often be content with less than a logical definition and sometimes even with a substitute for a definition.

72. The Indirect Methods.   The direct methods of exposition, though essential to precise thinking, are subject to all the disadvantages of abstract language.   For practical purposes they ordinarily need to be supplemented by some use of concrete explanation, which is more easily grasped. For this reason popular exposition often relies wholly upon the indirect methods.   The most used of these methods are:

1. Example.   There is no readier means of making explanation concrete than by citing typical examples and instances.   When all the members of a class are alike, as in the case of machine-made articles, the example is as exact as a detailed specification.   In a less homogeneous class, the example, though not so precise, has still the immense advantage of being easily understood.   This advantage is qualified by two defects.   One is the danger that an example may be thought more typical than it really is.   One who has never seen a rose might assume from a single example that all roses are alike in color, size, and fragrance. Professor Royce (in *The Philosophy of Loyalty*), striving to illustrate by example his definition of loyalty, was dissatisfied with the case of the captain who is the last to leave his sinking ship, because such fidelity is a part of the captain's duty. The other defect lies in the careless observation which may overlook typical characteristics. Many persons read and enjoy sonnets without noting that they have exactly fourteen lines and certain definite arrangements of rimes, and not infrequently a writer who essays to write a sonnet betrays the fact that he has failed to observe his models closely.

Examples are most useful as a means of amplifying and reinforcing a logical definition. A botanist writes, "A cluster in which the flower stalks all spring from apparently the same spot, *as in the milkweeds,* is called an umbel." Examples may also serve in the place of a formal definition. The writer of an article on Mark Twain, wishing to make use of the term *famous man of letters,* cited Kipling, Bernard Shaw, and Tolstoi as living members of the class and compared each in turn with Mark Twain. A logical definition of the term was thus made unnecessary.

2. Comparison and Contrast. To measure what is unfamiliar by something better known that is strikingly like or unlike it is often the simplest means of making it clear. The comparison may be of interest in itself, for it constitutes a kind of classification; but it is of value also as a means of making the exposition concrete. When a writer on Japan, wishing to make us understand the remarkable uniformity of the Japanese population, remarks that with the exception of certain aborigines one can hardly find among the Japanese " any difference more pronounced than those which might distinguish New Hampshire from Connecticut " he gives his thought a reality which it could not otherwise possess.

3. Illustration. Resemblances more remote than those upon which example and comparison are based are freely used in a variety of forms to throw light on what is obscure or abstract. Perhaps the most exact is analogy, a similarity, not of things themselves but of the relations between them. The human body and a steam engine are distinctly unlike, but the relation of the body to food is in certain respects so strikingly like the relation of the engine to fuel that a physiologist may find the analogy helpful in explaining nutrition. All good illustration exhibits in simpler or more familiar circumstances the principle that needs to be made clear. It is exemplified in the parables of the sower and of the prodigal son, in the fable of the frogs and their kings, in the allegories which represent life as a pilgrimage or a battle, in the proverbs of the pitcher that goes often to the well and the early bird that gets the worm, and even in the symbol that embodies a vague reality, like the circle to suggest infinity, or the triangle, completeness.

4. Pictures and Drawings. A picture, since its usual office is to represent the appearance of something, ordinarily supplements or takes the place of description in words. But pictures may also supplement exposition, serving to present examples or illustrations more correctly than words alone could do; and in certain forms pictures become pure exposition. This is the case when statistics are expressed pictorially, as the relative sizes of armies by the figures of soldiers drawn in proportion or the output of a factory by a pile of boxes dwarfing the Woolworth Building. Such pictures are merely symbols. Most cartoons use a similar symbolism — a candidate for nomination to Congress defeated because of his pro-German leanings is represented as kicked off the Congressional limited with his pet dachshund — and may be regarded as expository pictures. Outline drawings, ground plans, and maps are forms of pictorial analysis which go hand in hand with explanation in words and are often essential to it. Some writing illustrated in this manner should be undertaken by every student, no matter what his prospective calling.

73. Expository Description. Practical description, designed to identify and explain the object described, is so different in its purpose and method from artistic description that it is best studied as a form of exposition. Such description is exact and objective, uninfluenced by the writer's feelings and not addressed to the emotions of the reader. In method it is usually analytic, cataloging the details of an object after the manner of exposition. Its unity is the unity of idea rather than of impression, and complexity does not necessarily defeat its success.

The description of a type enumerates characteristics observable in all members of the class. This enumeration approaches, and sometimes attains, the exactness of logical definition. To say that a robin is a familiar bird with a red breast is to fall short of a definition; but when a popular work on birds describes the humming bird family as " very small birds with green plumage (iridescent red or orange breast in males), long needle-shaped bill for extracting insects and nectar from deep-cupped flowers, and exceedingly rapid, darting flight," the details constitute an adequate differentia. A similar work on trees says of the flowering dogwood, " The leaves are from three to five inches long and have indented whitish ribs nearly following the general curve of the edges; they turn a rich red in autumn." The test of such a description is the certainty with which it identifies members of the class described.

Expository description of an individual object lists essential details, with exact dimensions and, so far as possible, in technical language. It does not ordinarily attempt to give a general impression. This can be done so much better by a picture that an expository description often accompanies and supplements a photograph or a drawing. A description designed to enable the reader to identify the object emphasizes details that are characteristic and suppresses those that belong to all objects of the same class. A description of an object to be offered for sale or to be used as a pattern, on the other hand, will be systematic and complete. The following are typical:

LOST: a launch named Brentwood, 18 ft. long, 5 ft. wide, painted lead color, equipped with 3 H.P. Mianur gas engine.

The entrance to the house is merely an angular pediment supported by plain pilasters over a semi-colored door. It is of wood, painted deep cream. A semi-circular brick step before it adds a touch of color.

FOR SALE: two auto folding chairs, steel frame, seat and back padded with felt and upholstered in black art leather. Size of seat, 11 x 12 inches; back, $12\frac{1}{2}$ x $3\frac{1}{2}$ inches; height of seat, 16 inches; folds to $12\frac{1}{2}$ x 20 x 2 inches.

EXERCISES IN EXPOSITION

1. Examine the card catalog of the library and write a brief explanation of the system of numbering and indexing books.

2. Report in writing the result of an examination of the catalog for information on one of the following topics: George Washington; The French Revolution; Romanticism; Steel; The League of Nations.

3. Spend ten or fifteen minutes among the reference books looking for information about one of these topics and noting down all references. Write a brief account of your search, giving the more important sources: Rheims in the War; The Single Tax; The Monroe Doctrine; The French Academy; The Daylight-Saving Plan; Zeppelins.

4. Define as precisely as you can one of these terms: a first mortgage; insurance; income tax; incorporation; the consent of the governed; matriculation in college; the college of arts and sciences; a profession; autocracy.

5. Fix the meaning of one of the following expressions:

" making " a team; a yellow streak; to get by with it; a square deal; a raw deal; pep; to have the punch.

6. Identify one of these quotations and tell, as precisely as you can, what you think it means: (*a*) " What's in a name? "; (*b*) " Full many a flower is born to blush unseen "; (*c*) " As good almost kill a man as kill a good book "; (*d*) " They also serve who only stand and wait "; (*e*) " . . . hear old Triton blow his wreathed horn."

7. Give explicit directions for the carrying through of some simple process. If the subject is too large for treatment in a short theme, limit it. Above all, be clear. Use sketches or diagrams whenever they will help. Tell how to:

1. Build a campfire	11. Serve in tennis
2. Make coffee	12. Make caramels
3. Bake potatoes	13. Train for hare and hounds
4. Paddle a canoe	14. Solicit for advertisements
5. Cure a pelt	15. Crank an engine
6. Plug a punctured tire	16. Read a gas meter
7. Fly a kite	17. Renew worn-out batteries
8. Make a forward pass	18. Gig for eels
9. Make a flying tackle	19. Trap rabbits
10. Kick a goal	20. Develop photographs

8. Explain clearly the principle of some simple mechanical device. Do not try to explain a matter too complex for your space. Use a diagram or a slight sketch when it seems desirable. Write from personal knowledge and observation, so far as possible.

1. Electric door bell	10. Fireless cooker
2. Thermos bottle	11. Baking powder
3. Vacuum cleaner	12. Yeast
4. Ice cream freezer	13. Arc-light
5. Telephone receiver	14. Aneroid barometer
6. Block signals	15. Hot-water heating
7. Hydraulic ram	16. Coffee percolator
8. Syphon	17. Electric burglar alarm
9. Camera	18. Combination lock

19. Electric self-starter
20. Air-brake
21. Safety razor
22. Ice-boat
23. Automatic switch
24. Steam turbine
25. Compound steam engine
26. Hot-air engine
27. Coaster brake
28. Water filter
29. X-Rays
30. Hydroplane
31. Telautograph
32. Self-filling fountain pen
33. Heliograph
34. Spectroscope
35. Pedometer
36. Bunsen burner
37. Pocket flash-light
38. Turbine water-wheel
39. Wireless waves
40. Speedometer

9. Explain a simple business device or process. The theme may consist of a definition exemplified by some detail.

1. Taxes on real estate
2. Bank checks
3. The clearing house
4. Income tax
5. Bill of lading
6. Bank draft
7. Promissory note
8. Passport
9. Travelers' checks
10. Letter of credit
11. Ground rent
12. Royalty
13. Patent
14. Copyright
15. Loose-leaf ledger
16. Joint stock company
17. Fire insurance
18. Mortgage
19. Naturalization
20. Primary election

10. Write from your own observation an expository description of a pair of English sparrows; an easy chair; a beech tree; an athletic field suitable for a small country club; a proposed memorial to soldiers who fell in the War.

REFERENCES

1. To Text-books: *Expository Writing*, by M. G. Fulton (Macmillan); *A Handbook of Exposition*, by R. A. Jelliffe (Macmillan); *Exposition*, by F. M. Perry (American Book Co.); *The Theory and Practice of Technical Writing*, by S. C. Earle (Macmillan); *The Method and Practice of Exposition*, by T. E. Rankin (Macmillan).

2. To Specimens of Expository Writing: *Essays in Exposition*, by B. P. Kurtz and Others (Ginn); *A Book of Exposition*, by H. H. Nugent (Harcourt, Brace); *Modern Essays*, by J. M. Berdan and Others (Macmillan); *English, Science and Engineering*, by Eason and Weseen (Doubleday, Page).

CHAPTER VII

STRUCTURE AND STYLE IN DESCRIPTION

THE NATURE OF DESCRIPTION

74. Description as a Form of Discourse. Both description and narration endeavor to suggest by means of words impressions received by the senses. It is not their purpose to inform or persuade. Writing that portrays or recounts in order to give information is best regarded as exposition. When a war-correspondent enumerates the parts of a gun or records its performance in a battle in order to give us the facts about it, he is writing exposition. When he tells how he saw and heard the battery in action, and strives to reproduce for us some of the vivid interest of the actual experience, he is writing description and narration.

The two forms are interdependent. It is not easy for us to be interested in events unless we can form some mental image of the persons and things involved in them. Consequently narration is usually helped by description. We soon grow tired, also, of objects, however vividly described, that do not take part in some kind of action. Consequently extended descriptions unrelieved by a thread of story are not common. We have seen that the structure of description hinges upon changes in the point of view. To record and make clear these shifts in point of view, it is necessary to mingle with description some elements of both narration and exposition.

75. Description as an Art. The fine art of literature, since it must powerfully affect the feelings, makes more use of narration and description than of the other forms of writing. Words as a medium of art can directly represent only sounds; and description makes the most of our large vocabulary of imitative words. Other senses than hearing they must reach indirectly by suggestion. For the portrayal of still objects, literary art is in some respects less satisfactory than painting and sculpture, which can appeal immediately and vividly to the sense of vision. In the suggestion of motion and in appeals to the minor senses it is more successful than the other arts. As compared with actual experience, however, description in words is inherently weak in two respects: first, in that it must record impressions slowly and one at a time, thus losing the swift unity with which sensations crowd upon us; and, secondly, in that it uses an indirect and intellectual medium which necessarily robs perceptions of much of their vividness. The two great problems, therefore, which confront a writer of description are how, through a tardy and piecemeal report of sensations, to achieve singleness of impression; and how, at the same time, to charge words with such power of connotation as will win some degree of reality of impression.

THE QUALITIES OF DESCRIPTION

76. Singleness of Impression. Much descriptive writing is so incidental and so brief that the problem of unity seems unimportant. Often all the portrayal necessary to give reality to an action can be expressed in a single phrase. When, however, several details must be combined, it becomes apparent that the unity of description is a different thing from the unity of exposition and more difficult to attain. If I wish to make clear the nature of a class of five objects — five college buildings, let us say — I can secure unity by an orderly explanation of each member of the class in turn. Completeness is essential to this unity; if I omit one building altogether, I have really explained a different class, composed of four objects. Complexity, though it may make unity less easy, does not defeat it so long as the structure is kept clear. When I wish to describe the same objects, I find that a detailed description of each in turn fails to give an impression of the group as a whole. Completeness does not give unity and is not essential to it. Complexity in description so distracts a reader's attention that it usually makes any singleness of impression impossible. Those descriptions of persons, sometimes found in crude fiction, which consist of a detailed catalog of features fail utterly to portray a living face or to convey a sense of personal beauty. What is required in description is not, as in exposition, a unity of idea, but a unity of effect. Such unity, always increasingly difficult as the description is extended, is secured or furthered by the following devices.

1. A Consistent Point of View. One who writes description or narration is supposed to have been in a position to receive the impressions which he records. If we are to share those impressions with him, we must be able to imagine ourselves similarly situated, that is, to have the same point of view. Unless the point of view can be inferred, as in the case of an article small enough to be held in the hand, the reader must be plainly told what it is and must, of course, be informed whenever it is changed. If you wish, in a letter home, to describe your first view of the college buildings, you will perhaps tell how from the window of the motor-bus you saw a vista of colonial brick buildings, great masses of trees, and a noble white clock-tower, gleaming in the sunlight. These impressions belong together and make up one unit of your description. What you saw and heard as you walked toward the main building will make another, and the view that you had of the grounds from the steps at the entrance will be a third. In each of these units you will include only those impressions that you could receive from that point of view. In a description of the front of the library building you will not mention the sundial that stands in the garden behind it, even though the dial was erected by your Uncle Ned's class and seems suddenly to have a claim on your attention.

Changes of point of view may be required because the objects which you describe move while you remain stationary, as in the case of a vessel approaching a wharf or a parade passing your window. They may be made as you look from right to left or from foreground to background. They may even hinge upon a change of attention from one sense to another. Suppose you climb to the topmost floor of the tower on the main building. You will look down first upon roofs and tree tops and quadrangles, then to ranks of dwellings and apartment houses beyond, and finally to spires and buildings on a smoke-dimmed horizon. You hear a whirring of clock-mechanism, and bells over your head thump and clang the quarters and boom out the hour. The smell of burning leaves may hang in the autumn air, tinged perhaps with odors less agreeable drifting over from the city. These mingled sensations may come to you in some confusion. You will not find it easy to suggest them to your reader unless you unify them in groups by means of definite points of view.

2. *A General Impression.* Separate details of a portrayal may be gathered into a single impression much as the parts of an explanation are unified by a topic sentence. Froude, describing the sailing of the Spanish Armada, begins, "The scene as the fleet passed out of the harbor must have been singularly beautiful," and goes on to give specific details for which the phrase *singularly beautiful* has prepared us. The same method is often useful in the

description of persons. " There never was a man so unlike a professional writer," says Percy Fitzgerald at the beginning of a description of Charles Dickens. Thackeray's well-known picture of Beatrix Esmond begins with such a general impression: " Esmond had left a child and found a woman, grown beyond the common height; and arrived at such a dazzling completeness of beauty, that his eyes might well show surprise and delight at beholding her." Sometimes the general impression is reserved with good effect until the end, where it summarizes the details. An American journalist, describing his first journey in an English railway train sums up his impressions with a whimsical comparison: " I didn't feel that I was in a train half as much as I did that I was in a string of baby carriages."

3. *A Fundamental Image.* The use of an imagined outline to make clear the relative positions of objects or parts of objects goes back at least as far as the ancient astronomers who employed it in describing the constellations. It is frequently a convenient device for unifying separate details. The image may be a simple geometric figure. Gibbon saw Byzantium as a triangle. The streets of Washington have been described as the spokes of a wheel, radiating from the Capitol, superposed on a gridiron. A baseball field is familiarly spoken of as a diamond. Frank Hopkinson Smith represents a character in *Caleb West* (see page 192) as looking down upon Keyport village, " built about a rocky half-moon of a harbor." More often the fundamental image is some familiar object. Victor Hugo in a description of Paris seen from a lofty tower (in the Second Chapter of his *Notre Dame de Paris*) adopts the suggestion that the Island of the City is like a ship aground in the Seine. Henry James (in his *Portraits of Places*) finds it convenient to liken the race track at Epsom to the crater of an extinct volcano. The image

may be merely a fundamental figure of speech, underlying unifying various specific details. So Jeffrey Farnol, describing a storm (in the *Broad Highway*), maintains through three paragraphs the figure first introduced by the words, " Down in the woods was a faint rustling, as if *some giant* were stirring among the leaves."

4. Unity of Tone. Out of the multitude of details that an observer could see in an object, he will actually see only those that interest and impress him. And of those that he does see he must select for use in description a few of the more significant. If the selected details are so chosen as to emphasize a particular aspect or quality of the object described he may give his portrayal a tone that will pervade and unify it. In the following description of a plant for the manufacture of dynamite, details have been chosen so as to emphasize the silence and apparent solitude of the place.

Isolated and avoided, the high explosive plant lies half hidden in a waste of sloughs and sand dunes. Like the barren country that surrounds it, the plant itself seems a part of desolate nature, stunted and storm-beaten as the wind-swept hills. Against the straight line of the horizon rise no massive structures of steel or stone; no sound of man or machine breaks the soft stillness; no smoke clouds stain the blue of the autumn sky. Half buried in the rolling sand a hundred small green buildings scatter in wild disorder along winding paths among the scrub oaks. The voices of undisturbed wild fowl rise from the fens and marsh land. — JOSEPH HUSBAND in *America at Work*. By permission of Houghton Mifflin Company.

This description, though deliberately unified in tune, is objective and faithful. The writer does not permit his own state of mind to influence his choice of details; he merely selects those that contribute to a single main impression and neglects others. Sometimes, however, unity of tone is derived from the writer's attitude toward the object or from a mood or an emotion wholly independent of it. Poe's description of the " melancholy House of Usher " (see page 194) is a remarkable example of such consistency of effect. Another traveler looking upon the same " bleak walls," " vacant and eye-like windows," and " rank sedges " might have felt no such depression of soul and might even have discovered in the scene some details of life and color that would have destroyed the unity of Poe's somber picture.

77. Reality of Impression. The success of a description depends upon its power to create mental images. An accurate list of the parts of an object or of the details of a scene may be of value in exposition; but in description only those details are useful that stir the memory and the imagination. Reality of impression is an illusion of actual experience, a calling up in the reader's mind of sensations akin to those remembered by the writer. It cannot be achieved by a mere catalog of sensations, for, as we have seen, a catalog would not give the unity of effect that we get from experience. Reality must be obtained by the choice of a few details capable of vividly suggesting the whole.

Slow and weak as words are, when compared with the swift reality of the senses, description possesses certain advantages. A reader who is accustomed to think of the relations or the uses of things (like the London agent in Newman's " View of Attica ") rather than the look of them may be led to give to a description attention that he would not give to an actual scene. He may find, too, that details which he would have looked upon as insignificant are vitalized and interpreted by an imagination more vigorous than his own. It follows that successful description is the result of keen and sensitive observation. A writer who thinks in symbols or in vague shapes rather than in clear images will have difficulty in making words convey authentic sensations to others.

How to observe acutely and to seize upon the details that will best suggest reality is a matter that cannot be reduced to rules. The practice of successful writers, although it varies greatly, affords a few general principles which may be summed up as follows. They select:

1. Details that Appeal Directly to the Senses. It is much easier ordinarily to convey knowledge of a fact than to think of the exact and specific words that will suggest the sensations by means of which the knowledge was gained. Yet it is the sensation words that arouse interest and feeling. We have seen that in expressing abstract ideas we turn naturally to imaginative diction which pretends to use senses that are not actually used, as when we speak of *sparkling* wit or *heavy* cares. There is all the more need, then, when we describe things that really sparkle or are heavy that we should not throw away the advantage of a direct appeal to the senses. Such details should not be displaced by generalizations nor overweighted with comment. Your reader will learn the facts more effectively if you will let him see and hear for himself. In the following descriptions note the objectivity of the details.

It was about two hours before the soft murmur of voices in the parlor ceased, the outer door closed with a thud, and Paulina came into the room. She was blushing and smiling, but she could not look in anyone's face at first. — MARY E. WILKINS FREEMAN in *The Twelfth Guest.*

She rocked herself softly in the haircloth armchair, and addressed as father the old man who sat at one end of the table between the windows, and drubbed noiselessly upon it with his stubbed fingers, while his lips, puckered to a whistle, emitted no sound. His face had that distinctly fresh-shaven effect which once a week is the advantage of shaving no oftener: here and there, in the deeper wrinkles, a frosty stubble had escaped the razor. — W. D. HOWELLS in *The Lady of the Aroostook.*

2. Details Interpreted by the Writer. It is not always best to be objective. Sometimes your reader will wish not merely to see and hear for himself but also to know what the sensations that you report have suggested to others. In these selections the authors have mingled interpretation with concrete details.

It was a summer sunset, portending for the land a morrow of great heat. But cool airs crept along the water, and the ferry-boats, thrust shuttlewise back and forth between either shore, made a refreshing sound as they crushed a broad course to foam with their paddles. People were pulling about in small boats; from some the gay cries and laughter of young girls struck sharply along the tide. The noise of the quiescent city came off in a sort of dull moan. The lamps began to twinkle in the windows and the streets on shore; the lanterns of the ships at anchor in the stream showed redder and redder as the twilight fell. The homesickness began to mount from Lydia's heart in a choking lump to her throat; for one must be very happy to endure the sights and sounds of the summer evening anywhere. She had to shield her eyes from the brilliancy of the kerosene when she went below into the cabin. — W. D. HOWELLS in *The Lady of the Aroostook.* Used by permission of Houghton Mifflin Company.

Everything was looking at its brightest at this moment, for the sun shone right on the pewter dishes, and from their reflecting surfaces pleasant jets of light were thrown on mellow oak and bright brass; and on a still pleasanter object than these; for some of the rays fell on Dinah's finely-moulded cheek, and lit up her pale red hair to auburn, as she bent over the heavy household linen which she was mending for her aunt. No scene could have been more peaceful, if Mrs. Poyser, who was ironing a few things that still remained from the Monday's wash, had not been making a frequent clinking with her iron, and moving to and fro whenever she wanted it to cool; carrying the keen glance of her blue-gray eye from the kitchen to the dairy, where Hetty was making up the butter, and from the dairy to the back-kitchen, where Nancy was taking the pies out of the oven. Do not suppose, however, that Mrs. Poyser was elderly or shrewish in her appearance; she was a good-looking woman, not more than eight and thirty, of fair complexion and sandy hair, well shapen, light-footed: the most conspicuous article in her attire was an ample checkered linen apron, which almost covered her skirt; and nothing could be plainer or less noticeable than her cap and gown, for there was no weakness of which she was less tolerant than feminine vanity, and the preference of ornament to utility. — GEORGE ELIOT in *Adam Bede.*

3. A Summarizing Comparison. In the following selections, observe how details are generalized into single impressions and suggested by a striking likeness.

He was a chubby little boy with very pale eyes and hair, rather as if he had been boiled. — DE MORGAN.

Mrs. Whitefield, by the way, is a little woman, whose faded flaxen hair looks like straw on an egg. She has an expression of muddled shrewdness, a squeak of protest in her voice, and an odd air of continually elbowing away some larger person who is crushing her into a corner. — BERNARD SHAW.

The print faded before my eyes: in the second-hand bookshop it had suddenly grown dark. The old bookseller, pattering to the doorway, gazed out at the street, an old-fashioned, shabby little street in a part of town long unchanged — though with the ever-changing city pressing all about it — a part of town like one of those patches of smooth water, full of driftwood, that continue calm, one wonders how, in the midst of a swift current.

" Raining! " chirruped the bookseller, with an accent of intense interest. It was so: the pavements were mottled, in another moment they turned black and glistening, while the brick fronts of the houses opposite abruptly showed long, diagonal swaths of moisture. The rattle of the spring shower became resonant; spray leaped from the cobble stones; the gutters flooded.

" It'll be a good thing for the streets," commented the old man. And, with that well-worn remark, he came in, lit the gas, sat down in a broken chair, and smiled at me sociably.

His eyes, magnified by the thick lenses of his spectacles, appeared out of proportion to his small, gray-bearded, withered face, and with their look of watery gentleness, dominated all his other features, which were insignificant. The transparency of his bald temples, the length of his meager neck, the thinness of his constricted shoulders, his whole appearance of exceeding delicacy, made one think of the frailness of a new-hatched bird. And he was full, too, of birdlike movements — of that curious spryness without object which one sees sometimes in little old men whose lives have been spent ineffectually in trifling and timid bustle. — G. F. WHIT-MAN in " The Thread of Gold." Used by permission of *Collier's Weekly*.

4. Effects. The reality of sensations may sometimes be intensified by a report of their effect upon an observer. When the object is so complex or so vague as to be difficult to describe in detail or so horrible that details are undesirable, the use of effects may take the place of other methods.

She had no startling brilliancy of beauty, no pearly whiteness, no radiant carnation: she had not the majestic contour that rivets attention, demands instant wonder, and then disappoints by the coldness of its charms. You might pass Eleanor Harding in the street without notice, but you could hardly pass an evening with her and not lose your heart. — ANTHONY TROLLOPE in *Barchester Towers*.

Our American sunrise had ushered in a noble summer's day. There was not a cloud, the sunshine was baking; yet in the woody river valleys among which we wound our way the atmosphere preserved a sparkling freshness till late in the afternoon. It had an inland sweetness and variety to one newly from the sea; it smelt of woods, rivers, and the delved earth. These, though in so far a country, were airs from home. I stood on the platform by the hour; and as I saw, one after another, pleasant villages, carts upon the highway, and fishers by the stream, and heard cockcrows and cheery voices in the distance, and beheld the sun, no longer shining blankly on the plains of the ocean, but striking among shapely hills and his light dispersed and colored by a thousand accidents of form and surface, I began to exult with myself upon this rise in life like a man who had come into a rich estate. — STEVENSON in *Across the Plains*. Used by permission of Charles Scribner's Sons.

. . . When Rachel stepped upon the scene, not with the customary stage stride, but with a dignity and majestic grace all her own, there was first a spell of intense astonishment and then a burst of applause. She stood still for a moment, in the folds of her classic robe, like an antique statue fresh from the hand of Phidias. The mere sight of her sent a thrill through the audience: her face a long oval, her forehead, shadowed by black wavy hair, not remarkably high, but broad and strong; under her dark arched eyebrows a pair of wondrous eyes that glowed and blazed in their deep sockets like two black suns; a finely chiseled nose with open, quivering nostrils; above an energetic chin a mouth severe in its lines, with slightly lowered corners, such as we may imagine the mouth of the tragic Muse. Her stature, sometimes seeming tall, sometimes little, very slender, but the attitude betraying elastic strength; a hand with fine tapering fingers of rare beauty; the whole apparition exciting in the beholder a sensation of astonishment and intense expectancy. — CARL SCHURZ in *Reminiscences*. Used by permission of Doubleday, Page and Co.

5. Action.   Since moving objects claim and hold our interest better than still ones, use is sometimes made of the method, as old as Homer, of telling how a thing looks by recounting the action which produced or changed it.

That, however, which was certain and beyond doubt, was that St. George's father, old General Dorsey Temple, had purchased the property near the close of the preceding century; that he had, with his characteristic vehemence, pushed up the roof, thrust in two dormer windows, and smashed out the rear wall, thus enlarging the dining room and giving increased space for a glass-covered porch ending in a broad flight of wooden steps descending to a rose garden surrounded by a high brick wall; that thus encouraged he had widened the fireplaces, wainscotted the hall, built a new mahogany spider-web staircase leading to his library on the second floor, and had otherwise disported himself after the manner of a man who, having suddenly fallen heir to a big pot of money, had ever after continued oblivious to the fact that the more holes he punched in its bottom the less water would spill over its top. — F. HOPKINSON SMITH in *Kennedy Square*. Used by permission of Charles Scribner's Sons.

SPECIMENS OF DESCRIPTION

I

THE SPANISH ARMADA

The scene as the fleet passed out of the harbor must have been singularly beautiful. It was a treacherous interval of real summer. The early sun was lighting the long chain of Galician mountains, marking with shadows the cleft defiles, and shining softly on the white walls and vineyards of Coruna. The wind was light, and falling towards a calm; the great galleons drifted slowly with the tide on the purple water, the long streamers trailing from the trucks, the red crosses, the emblem of the crusade, showing bright upon the hanging sails. — FROUDE in *History of England*.

II

KEYPORT HARBOR

Below him lay Keyport Village, built about a rocky half-moon of a harbor, its old wharves piled high with rotting oil-barrels and flanked by empty warehouses, behind which crouched low, gray-roofed cabins, squatting in a tangle of streets, with here and there a white church spire tipped with a restless weather-vane. Higher, on the hills, were nestled some old homesteads with sloping roofs and wide porches, and away up on the crest of the heights, over-looking the sea, stood the more costly structures with well-shaved lawns spotted with homesick trees from a warmer clime, their arms stretched appealingly toward the sea.

At his feet lay the brimming harbor itself, dotted with motion-less yachts and various fishing-craft, all reflected upside down in the still sea, its glassy surface rippled now and then by the dipping buckets of men washing down the decks, or by the quick water-spider strokes of some lobster-fisherman, — the click of the row-locks pulsating in the breathless air.

On the near point of the half-moon stood Keyport Light, — an old-fashioned factory chimney of a Light, — built of brick, but painted snow-white with a black cigar band around its middle, its top surmounted by a copper lantern. This flashed red and white at night over a radius of twenty miles. Braced up against its base, for a better hold, was a little building hiding a great fog-horn, which on thick days and nights bellowed out its welcome to Key-port's best.

On the far point of the moon — the one opposite the Light, and some two miles away — stretched sea-meadows broken with clumps of rock and shelter-houses for cattle, and between these two points, almost athwart the mouth of the harbor, like a huge motionless whale, lay Crotch Island, its backbone knotted with summer cot-tages. Beyond the island away out under the white glare of the risen sun could be seen a speck of purplish-gray fringed with bright splashes glinting in the dazzling light. This was Shark's Ledge. — F. HOPKINSON SMITH in *Caleb West, Master Diver*. Used by permission of Houghton Mifflin Company.

III

ASHORE IN ENGLAND

Then the mail and trunks being off, and that boat having veered away, another and somewhat smaller one came alongside, and we first- and then the second-class passengers went aboard, and I watched the great ship growing less and less as we pulled away from it. It was immense from alongside, a vast skyscraper of a ship. At a hundred feet it seemed not so large, but exceedingly more graceful; at a thousand feet all its exquisite lines were perfect, its bulk not so great, but the pathos of its departing beauty wonderful; at two thousand feet it was still beautiful and large against the granite ring of the harbor; but, alas! it was moving. The captain was an almost indistinguishable spot upon the bridge. The stacks, in their way gorgeous, took on beautiful proportions. I thought, as we veered in near the pier and the ship turned within her length or thereabouts and steamed out, I had never seen a more beautiful sight. Her convoy of gulls was still about her. Her smoke-stacks flung back their graceful streamers. The propeller left a white trail of foam.

But finally the train was started, and we were off. The track was not so wide as ours, if I am not mistaken, and the little freight-cars were positively ridiculous, mere wheelbarrows by comparison with the American type. As for the passenger cars, when I came to examine them, they reminded me of some of our fine street-cars that run from, say, Schenectady to Gloversville. They were the first-class cars, too — the English Pullmans. The train started out briskly and you could feel that it did not have the powerful weight to it which the American train has. An American Pullman creaks significantly, just as a great ship does when it begins to move. An American engine begins to pull — slowly because it has something to pull — like a team with a heavy load. I didn't feel that I was in a train half so much as I did that I was in a string of baby carriages. — THEODORE DREISER in " The First Voyage Over." *The Century Magazine*, August, 1913. Used by permission.

WRITING

IV

The House of Usher

During the whole of a dull, dark, and soundless day in the autumn of the year, when the clouds hung oppressively low in the heavens, I had been passing alone, on horseback, through a singularly dreary tract of country; and at length I found myself, as the shades of evening drew on, within view of the melancholy House of Usher. I know not how it was — but, with the first glimpse of the building, a sense of insufferable gloom pervaded my spirit. I say insufferable; for the feeling was unrelieved by any of that half pleasurable, because poetic, sentiment, with which the mind usually receives even the sternest natural images of the desolate or terrible. I looked upon the scene before me — upon the mere house, and the simple landscape features of the domain — upon the bleak walls — upon the vacant and eye-like windows — upon a few rank sedges — and upon a few white trunks of decayed trees — with an utter depression of soul which I can compare to no earthly sensation more properly than to the afterdream of the reveler upon opium — the bitter lapse into everyday life — the hideous dropping off of the veil. There was an iciness, a sinking, a sickening of the heart — an unredeemed dreariness of thought which no goading of the imagination could torture into aught of the sublime. What was it — I paused to think — what was it that so unnerved me in the contemplation of the House of Usher? It was a mystery all insoluble; nor could I grapple with the shadowy fancies that crowded upon me as I pondered. I was forced to fall back upon the unsatisfactory conclusion, that while, beyond doubt, there *are* combinations of very simple natural objects which have the power of thus affecting us, still the analysis of this power lies among considerations beyond our depth. It was possible, I reflected, that a mere different arrangement of the particulars of the scene, of the details of the picture, would be sufficient to modify, or perhaps to annihilate, its capacity for sorrowful impression; and acting upon this idea, I reined my horse to the precipitous brink of a black and lurid tarn that lay in unruffled lustre by the dwelling, and gazed down — but with a shudder even more thrilling than before — upon the remodelled and inverted images of the gray sedge, and the ghastly tree stems, and the vacant and eye-like windows. — POE in *The Fall of the House of Usher.*

Exercises in Description

1. In the *New International Encyclopedia,* Volume 20, under *St. Gaudens,* study the picture of the Shaw Memorial, and write a brief description in which you try to suggest it in words.

2. In the same encyclopedia study the portrait of Marcus Aurelius, Shakespeare, Lord Bacon, or Napoleon, and attempt a description in words.

3. Write a paragraph beginning with the topic sentence — " It was a bitter cold morning," and make your details so objective that you can strike out the opening sentence without loss.

4. Describe the campus from two different points of view.

5. A student who is reading a letter at the post office is pleased, disappointed, puzzled, shocked, or angered by its contents. Make his state of mind obvious by concrete details.

6. Describe a scene in such a way as to make dominant the idea of its stillness, activity, monotony, or sadness.

7. Describe an oak tree and a beech tree so as to suggest their essential difference.

8. John Smith enters his living room after an absence and finds that it has been ransacked by burglars.

9. Find one of these objects and observe it keenly. Then try to give your reader a clear idea of the look of it. Do not offer him, except incidentally, information about the object. Do not merely enumerate parts. Avoid trite metaphors; for example, do not call a tree a lone sentinel or a locomotive a monster. It is often best to indicate the point of view from which you see the object. Be specific:

1. Oak tree	4. Church steeple
2. Old pump	5. Field of grain
3. Stretch of macadam road	6. Doorway

7. Tall chimney
8. Railroad signal tower
9. Canoe afloat
10. Tennis court
11. Freight locomotive at night
12. Factory smoke in early morning
13. Abandoned house
14. New-ploughed land
15. Seashore
16. Blacksmith's forge
17. The football kick-off
18. Waterfall
19. Fire-engine in motion
20. Steamship

10. *Dramatic incidents.* Although the emphasis is to be laid on description and narration, some analysis of the significance of the event is appropriate. Get your information from several sources. Realize the incident vividly for yourself before you try to write about it for others. Center attention upon the significant parts of the action, and above all avoid tedious beginnings. Beware of anachronisms.

1. The Death of Samson
2. Balboa discovers the Pacific
3. Luther at Worms
4. The Pilgrims land at Plymouth
5. Ethan Allen takes Ticonderoga
6. The Capture of Major André
7. Key writes the Star Spangled Banner
8. Grant and Lee meet at Appomattox
9. The Spanish Fleet comes out of Santiago Harbor
10. The Loss of the Titanic.

CHAPTER VIII

STRUCTURE AND STYLE IN NARRATION

NARRATIVE WRITING

78. As a Form of Discourse. Of all the forms of discourse, narrative writing is the most interesting and, in many respects, the most difficult. It is interesting because life is interesting, and narration strives to set forth events in succession with some of the reality of life. We are interested in such events partly because we wish to know what they will lead to and partly because we grow curious as to the reasons why they happen and the influence they have upon persons involved in them. It is sometimes possible to read on in the crudest narrative if we have got far enough into it to wonder what will happen next. And it is also possible to read with interest an account of very commonplace happenings if the persons to whom they happen become sufficiently real to us.

Narrative writing is difficult for much the same reasons that make description difficult. The unity of narrative is not that singleness of impression that is so hard to achieve in written portrayal; but it is no less troublesome. For events do not occur in a simple and uncomplicated series. Several different events happening at the same time combine to produce one situation and are necessary to an understanding of it. Several different persons, all of whom the reader must know something about, share in a single happening and are differently affected by it. Yet the written narrative must move forward with something like the unrelenting steadiness of experience and must be kept clear and convincing. Moreover, it must, like description, suggest a sense of reality. Narration can no more be content with a catalog of events in chronological order than can description with an itemized list of details. In order to be clear, narration necessarily makes incidental use of exposition; in order that events may be realized, there must be some description of the persons and things concerned in them.

79. As a Fine Art. There is a practical art of narration, used in business records, in science, and in reports of news. Such narrative is largely expository in purpose and in so far as it differs from pictorial narration does so by adopting the methods of exposition. It is as a fine art, rather, that narration concerns us. For narrative writing is the dominant type of prose literature. As exposition is indispensable to science and business as a means of recording human knowledge, narration, both true and fictitious, affords us the best means of preserving the spirit of past times and of expressing our sense of the significance of life.

The Elements of a Narrative

In every narrative three things are essential: action, that is, the events themselves; the characters, the persons or things to whom and by means of whom the events happen; and the setting, the place and the time of the events. Ordinarily action is the chief element; but any of the three may be made a source of special interest, and modern fiction has tended to emphasize the significance of both setting and characters.

80. Action. The nature of the events which are narrated may vary greatly. For convenience we may classify them as, (*a*) a simple sequence of events, (*b*) historical narrative, (*c*) plot or complicated narrative.

The first is narrative from one point of view, excluding parallel lines of events and actions that impede or change its progress. It is typified by the story of simple personal experience, as in the following:

I made my way steadily upward in a straight line, through a dense undergrowth of mountain laurel, until the trees began to have a scraggy and infernal look, as if contending with frost and goblins, and at length I reached the summit just as the sun was setting. Several acres here had been cleared, and were covered with rocks and stumps, and there was a rude observatory in the middle which overlooked the woods. I had one fair view of the country before the sun went down, but I was too thirsty to waste any light in viewing the prospect, and set out directly to find water. First, going down a well-beaten path for half a mile through the low scrubby wood, till I came to where the water stood in the tracks of the horses which had carried travelers up, I lay down flat, and drank these dry, one after another, a pure, cold, spring-like water, but yet I could not fill my dipper, though I contrived little siphons of grass-stems, and ingenious aqueducts on a small scale; it was too slow a process. Then, remembering that I had passed a moist place near the top on my way up, I returned to find it again, and here, with sharp stones and my hands, in the twilight, I made a well about two feet deep, which was soon filled with pure cold water, and the birds too came and drank at it. So I filled my dipper, and, making my way back to the observatory, collected some dry sticks, and made a fire on some flat stones which had been placed on the floor for that purpose, and so I cooked my supper of rice, having already whittled a wooden spoon to eat it with. — THOREAU in *A Week on the Concord and Merrimack Rivers*. By permission of Houghton Mifflin Company.

The interest of such simple narrative lies in the details themselves, usually because of their novelty or of the familiar associations which they arouse. The interest of historical narrative, though much of it may be the recounting of events in single file, is in the significance of the details and in their interrelations. Such narrative cannot move forward simply and directly but must from time to

time drop one thread of action and reach back to catch
up another.

As they sat at table, a courier entered, and handed to Arnold
the letter in which Colonel Jameson informed him that one John
Anderson had been taken with compromising documents in his
possession, which had been forwarded to the commander-in-chief.
With astonishing presence of mind, he folded the letter and put it
in his pocket, finished the remark which had been on his lips when
the courier entered, and then, rising, said that he was suddenly
called across the river to West Point, but would return to meet
Washington without delay; and he ordered his barge to be manned.
None of the officers observed anything unusual in his manner, but
the quick eye of his wife detected something wrong, and as he left
the room she excused herself and hurried after him. Going up to
their bedroom, he told her that he was a ruined man and must fly
for his life; and as she screamed and fainted in his arms, he laid
her upon the bed, called in the maid to attend her, stooped to kiss
his baby boy who was sleeping in the cradle, rushed down to the
yard, leaped on a horse that was standing there, and galloped down
a by-path to his barge. It had promptly occurred to his quick mind
that the *Vulture* would still be waiting for André somes miles down
stream, and he told the oarsmen to row him thither without delay,
as he must get back soon to meet Washington. A brisk row of
eighteen miles brought them to the *Vulture,* whose commander was
still wondering why André did not come back. From the cabin
of the *Vulture* Arnold sent a letter to Washington, assuring him of
Mrs. Arnold's innocence, and begging that she might be allowed to
return to her family in Philadelphia, or come to her husband, as
she might choose. Then the ill-omened ship weighed anchor, and
reached New York next morning.

Meanwhile, about noonday Washington came in for his breakfast, and, hearing that Arnold had crossed the river to West Point,
soon hurried off to meet him there, followed by all his suite except
Hamilton. As they were ferried across no salute of cannon greeted
them, and on landing they learned with astonishment that Arnold
had not been there that morning; but no one as yet had a glimmer
of suspicion. When they returned to the Robinson House, about
two o'clock, they found Hamilton walking up and down before the
door in great excitement. Jameson's courier had arrived, with
letters for Washington, which the aide had just opened and read.
The commander and his aide went alone into the house, and ex-

amined the papers, which, taken in connection with the traitor's flight, but too plainly told the story. From Mrs. Arnold, who was in hysterics, Washington could learn nothing. He privately sent Hamilton and another aide in pursuit of the fugitive; and coming out to meet Lafayette and Knox, his voice choking and tears rolling down his cheeks, he exclaimed, "Arnold is a traitor, and has fled to the British! Whom can we trust now?" — FISKE in *The American Revolution,* Chapter XIV. Used by permission of Houghton Mifflin Company.

The episode of Arnold's treachery includes the material for several simple narratives. It could be told as if it concerned Arnold alone, or André, or Washington. But no one of these stories would have been sufficient. It was necessary for the author to make clear to us at least three simultaneous actions: André's ill-fated journey and his capture, Washington's absence and his return, and Arnold's escape to the British. How to weave such parallel lines of action into a consecutive narrative, halting one to bring forward another, is one of the chief problems of the writer of history.

Complicated action, or plot, combines the qualities and difficulties of the other two types. It emphasizes one main line or series of events. But it does not ignore the happenings by which these events are shaped or hindered; and in order to make us aware of them it sometimes turns back to relate action simultaneous with what has already been told. The interest of such action is not in the events themselves but in the interrelations, and the narrative is not a single line or a number of parallel lines but rather a tangled skein, which it is the reader's interest to unravel.

It happened upon a November evening (when I was about fifteen years old, and out-growing my strength very rapidly, my sister Annie being turned thirteen, and a deal of rain having fallen, and all the troughs in the yard being flooded, and the bark from the woodricks washed down the gutters, and even our water-shoot going brown) that the ducks in the court made a terrible quacking, instead of marching off to their pen, one behind the other. Thereupon Annie and I ran out, to see what might be the sense of it. There were thirteen ducks, and ten lily-white (as the fashion then of ducks was), not I mean twenty-three in all, but ten white and three brown-striped ones; and without being nice about their color, they all quacked very movingly. They pushed their gold colored bills here and there (yet dirty, as gold is apt to be), and they jumped on the triangles of their feet, and sounded out of their nostrils; and some of the over-excited ones ran along low on the ground, quacking grievously, with their bills snapping and bending, and the roofs of their mouths exhibited.

Annie began to cry "dilly, dilly, einy, einy, ducksey," according to the burden of a tune they seem to have accepted as the national duck's anthem; but instead of being soothed by it, they only quacked three times as hard, and ran round, till we were giddy. And then they shook their tails all together, and looked grave, and went round and round again. Now I am uncommonly fond of ducks, whether roystering, roosting, or roasted; and it is a fine sight to behold them walk, poddling one after other, with their toes out, like soldiers drilling, and their little eyes cocked all ways at once, and the way that they dib with their bills, and dabble, and throw up their heads and enjoy something, and then tell the others about it. Therefore I knew at once, by the way they were carrying on, that there must be something or other gone wholly amiss in the duck-world. Sister Annie perceived it too, but with a greater quickness; for she counted them like a good duck-wife, and could only tell thirteen of them, when she knew there ought to be fourteen.

And so we began to search about, and the ducks ran to lead us aright, having come that far to fetch us; and when we got down to the foot of the court-yard where the two great ash-trees stand by the side of the little water, we found good reason for the urgence and melancholy of the duck-birds. Lo! the old white drake, the father of all, a bird of high manners and chivalry, always the last to help himself from the pan of barley-meal, and the first to show fight to a dog or a cock intruding upon his family, this fine fellow, and pillar of the state, was now in a sad predicament, yet quacking very stoutly. For the brook, wherewith he had been familiar from his callow childhood, and wherein he was wont to quest for water-newts, and tadpoles, and caddis-worms, and other game, this brook, which afforded him very often scanty space to dabble in, and sometimes starved the cresses, was now coming down in a great brown flood, as if the banks never belonged to it. The foaming of it, and the noise, and the cresting of the corners, and the up and down, like a wave of the sea, were enough to frighten any duck, though bred upon stormy waters, which our ducks never had been.

There is always a hurdle, nine feet long, and four and a half in depth, swung by a chain at either end from an oak laid across the channel. And the use of this hurdle is to keep our kine at milking time from straying away there drinking (for in truth they are very dainty) and to fence strange cattle, or Farmer Snowe's horses, from coming along the bed of the brook unknown, to steal our substance. But now this hurdle, which hung in the summer a foot above the trickle, would have been dipped more than two feet deep, but for the power against it. For the torrent came down so vehemently that the chains at full stretch were creaking, and the hurdle, buffeted almost flat, and thatched (so to say) with the drift-stuff, was going see-saw with a sulky splash on the dirty red comb of the water. But saddest to see was between two bars, where a fog was of rushes, and floodwood, and wild celery-haulm, and dead crowsfoot, who but our venerable mallard, jammed in by the joint of his shoulder, speaking aloud as he rose and fell, with his top-knot full of water, unable to comprehend it, with his tail washed far away from him, but often compelled to be silent, being ducked very harshly against his will by the choking fall-to of the hurdle.

For a moment I could scarce help laughing; because, being borne up high and dry by a tumult of the torrent, he gave me a look from his one little eye (having lost one in fight with the turkey-cock) a gaze of appealing sorrow, and then a loud quack to second it. But the quack came out of time, I suppose, for his throat got filled with water, as the hurdle carried him back again. And then there was scarcely the screw of his tail to be seen until he swung up again, and left small doubt by the way he spluttered, and failed to quack, and hung down his poor crest, but that drown he must in another minute, and frogs triumph over his body.

Annie was crying, and wringing her hands, and I was about to rush into the water, although I liked not the look of it, but hoped to hold on by the hurdle, when a man on horseback came suddenly round the corner of the great ash-hedge on the other side of the stream, and his horse's feet were in the water.

" Ho, there," he cried; " get thee back, boy. The flood will carry thee down like a straw. I will do it for thee, and no trouble."

With that he leaned forward and spoke to his mare — she was just of the tint of a strawberry, a young thing, very beautiful — and she arched up her neck, as misliking the job; yet, trusting him, would attempt it. She entered the flood, with her dainty fore-legs sloped further and further in front of her, and her delicate ears pricked forward, and the size of her great eyes increasing; but he kept her straight in the turbid rush by the pressure of his knee on her. Then she looked back, and wondered at him, as the force of the torrent grew stronger, but he bade her go on; and on she went, and it foamed up over her shoulders; and she tossed up her lip and scorned it, for now her courage was waking. Then as the rush of it swept her away, and she struck with her forefeet down the stream, he leaned from his saddle, in a manner which I never could have thought possible, and caught up old Tom with his left hand, and set him between his holsters, and smiled at his faint quack of gratitude. In a moment all three were carried down stream, and the rider lay flat on his horse, and tossed the hurdle clear from him, and made for the bend of smooth water.

They landed, some thirty or forty yards lower, in the midst of our kitchen-garden, where the winter cabbage was; but though Annie and I crept in through the hedge, and were full of our thanks, and admiring him, he would answer us never a word, until he had spoken in full to the mare, as if explaining the whole to her.

"Sweetheart, I know thou couldst have leaped it," he said, as he patted her cheek, being on the ground by this time, and she was nudging up to him, with the water pattering off from her; "but I had good reason, Winnie, dear, for making thee go through it."

She answered him very kindly with her soft eyes, and sniffed at him very lovingly, and they understood one another. Then he took from his waistcoat two pepper-corns, and made the old drake swallow them, and tried him softly upon his legs, where the leading gap in the hedge was. Old Tom stood up quite bravely, and clapped his wings, and shook off the wet from his tail feathers; and then away into the courtyard, and his family gathered around him, and they all made a noise in their throats, and stood up, and put their bills together, to thank God for this great deliverance. — BLACK-MORE in *Lorna Doone*, Chapter X.

In this selection from *Lorna Doone* the action is not merely personal experience of John Ridd. The ducks, the children, and Tom Faggus and his mare are all involved in a succession of events which grows more complex up to the point where it is said of the drake that "drown he must in another minute"; and which thereupon resolve themselves into a situation in which the characters are once more in equilibrium. What happens next to each of them is another story. What happens in this episode, however, is a story that they must inevitably share. The heavy rainfall, which produces the critical situation of the venerable drake, the commotion in the duck-yard, which excites the curiosity and sympathy of the children, the opportune arrival of the highwayman and his mare, are not separable actions. Our interest in the affairs of the duck-world is due to their complexity. When this is resolved the ducks pass out of the story; the plot has fulfilled its purpose.

81. Characters. The agents of the action may be persons or animals or even inanimate objects. In simple narratives they are sometimes mere types, like the lion and the mouse in the fable or the old witch in the fairy story, and properly so, for characterization is unnecessary. In other narratives the characters remain lifeless when they should be made real, like the typical sleuth in crude stories of adventure. In effective narration, even when the chief interest is in the events and their outcome, characters are sufficiently realized to enable us to image them as the action goes forward; and in much good fiction they are made so individual that they become interesting in themselves.

82. Setting. Places and objects concerned in the action but not the agents of it constitute the setting. In most narratives a carriage would be merely setting. In " The Deacon's Masterpiece " the one-hoss shay is one of the characters. Except in the simplest of tales, the reader will need a background against which he will conceive the events and the actors as placed. He will need also to be made aware of the time when the action happens and of the duration of periods of time. The setting as to time ranges from the vaguest designations, as in the " once upon a time stories," to precise periods and intervals.

THE QUALITIES OF NARRATION

The qualities that help to make narrative effective are many and various. In the selection from *Lorna Doone* cited above, for example, a quiet humor and a touch of the mock heroic make the incident delightful. There are, however, certain qualities which are to be expected in every good narrative. Among them are:

83. Unity. An effective narrative impresses the reader as one story. The action that it recounts must begin arbitrarily at a certain point in time, must exclude as it proceeds many parallel events related to it by cause and effect, and must end with many of its consequences untold. What shall be included is determined by various considerations.

1. *By the Dominance of a Main Character or Characters*. In nearly every successful narrative, events are selected because they concern one, or at most two, characters, whose story it really is, and in whom the reader's interest centers. Even history tends naturally to become the story of single men or groups of men. In a personal narrative of fact diverse happenings are held together by the identity of the main character and the sequence of time. Fiction is able to simplify the complexity of life only by limiting it from the point of view of one person. The chief test, therefore, of the relevance of a detail is its bearing, direct or indirect, upon the reader's interest in the hero of the action.

2. *By the Outcome of the Action*. A narrative is further limited in that it must lead up to a predetermined end.

A central character and a foreseen climax are enough to fix the fundamental idea out of which the structure of a narrative is to be developed. We can imagine Blackmore as saying to himself, " I will have the old drake, in peril of drowning, saved by the opportune appearance of Faggus." That unity of impression that critics so emphasize in discussing the short story is possible only when every detail of action or setting is made to contribute to the climax. In the more leisurely type of short story, like " Rip Van Winkle," the demands of the denouement are less insistent. In novels like *David Copperfield* and *Joseph Vance* they are still less so. But every good narrative is determined in part by the deliberate approach to a necessary and natural conclusion.

3. *By the Writer's Purpose.* A few narratives exist merely to make the reader aware of facts; others are intended to convey to his imagination some sense of the reality of interesting events; still others are designed to illustrate a principle, to plead for a cause, to give a picture of life or manners, or to present vividly the qualities of a character. These diverse aims greatly modify the requirements of unity.

84. Movement. Every narrative must move forward. A recital of events in the reverse of their time order would be explanation but not narrative. When a news story begins with a summary of a series of events, restates them in slightly greater detail, and then tells the whole story from the beginning, we have really a combination of exposition and narration. The success of a narrative depends largely upon the degree to which its movement suggests for us the forward march of actual events. It is not to be judged merely by the rapidity of movement. One can leap to the end at any time by turning to the last page of the book. Good movement is varied. It is made slower by description of setting, by delineation of character, by the recital of previous action which must be understood. It is accelerated by the omission of detail and by the suggestion of events rather than the telling of them. But it never stops and turns in a circle. Every situation must push forward the progress of the narrative towards its goal.

85. Interest. A narrative can have unity and movement, not to speak of other desirable qualities, and still be insupportably dull. And, since relatively little narration is read for information alone, dullness is a fatal defect. A story must win and hold attention — must be interesting — or it will not be read. The sources of interest differ widely in different narratives and are not always easily analyzed. Among them are:

1. *Concreteness.* Action is more interesting than explanation or comment, and action that is concretely and specifically portrayed is more interesting than action that is merely said to have taken place. Characters which we are permitted to infer from objective details are usually more convincing than characters expounded to us deliberately. And setting will be more serviceable as a background and more likely to interest for itself if it is presented concretely. Interest is not gained, of course, by the heaping up of minor details, however objective, but by the selection of details that will powerfully suggest others.

2. *Suspense.* Interest, when once aroused, is kept up and heightened by curiosity as to the outcome. Suspense occurs in single situations as well as in the unfolding of the main plot, in the development of character, and even in the forward movement of action carried on by characters with which we have come to feel acquainted. It is admirably illustrated in Stevenson's " The Sire de Malétroit's Door " and in Aldrich's *Marjorie Daw*.

3. *Emotion.* Incident that stirs in us those feelings com-

monly aroused by our concern for living creatures — sympathy, affection, pity, indignation — will give to a narrative what has come to be called human interest. It is this, along with the realism of the story, that makes Mrs. Freeman's *The Revolt of Mother* so successful. The same quality dominates Bret Harte's *The Luck of Roaring Camp* and " Tennessee's Partner."

4. *Humor.* From incidental touches that merely lighten the style or fix the tone to deliberate drollery of character and laughableness of incident, humor contributes in a great variety of ways to the success of narrative. It lies in the author's comments on his work, as in much of O. Henry; in the turn of his phrase, as not infrequently in Harte; and in frankly ludicrous incident, as in Stockton.

5. *Novelty.* Readers are always ready to hear some new thing. The writer who has ingenuity enough to conceive a new combination of incidents, or a new treatment of an age-old situation will find readers, unless his technic is distinctly forbidding. Mark Twain's *The Jumping Frog of Calaveras County* is humorously, though loosely, told; but it was the novelty of the incident rather than its humor that set the whole country laughing.

THE CONSTRUCTION OF A NARRATIVE

86. The Preparation for the Action. Every narrative is linked to its past. The period which it occupies is preceded by events some of which the reader must know. We may conceive a story as represented by this diagram:

A is the antecedent action, leading from an indefinite past up to the story that is to be told. *B* is the significant action. *C* is the subsequent action, which concerns us only because we have become interested in the fate of the characters who take part in *B*. How to make the reader aware of *A* without lessening his interest in *B* is a practical difficulty. It is solved in at least three different ways.

1. *By Deliberate Narration in Advance.* This is the logical method. What we need to know of the past is explained to us before any of the significant action begins. It has the disadvantage of a weak opening, since the antecedent action is less interesting than the story itself. Used skilfully, however, this beginning may be made to prepare for what follows and at the same time prove interesting for its own sake, as in " Rip Van Winkle," in " Tennessee's Partner," and in " David Swan."

2. *By an Inverted Opening.* Some stories begin with *B* and, after the interest of the reader has been enlisted, halt the narrative to bring in antecedent action. This gives a stronger beginning but at the expense of the movement. It is the method of Kipling's *William the Conqueror* and of Ibanez's *The Four Horsemen of the Apocalypse,* in which novel it is a serious structural defect.

3. *By an Absorbed Opening.* Other stories begin with *B,* so absorbing *A* in the significant action, that it is presented incidentally in dialog, in casual comment, or in such mechanical devices as letters or story within story. It is a common artistic device, neatly used by Stevenson in " The Sire de Malétroit's Door," by Mrs. Freeman in " A Gala Dress," and by O. Henry in " The Gift of the Magi."

87. The Report of the Action. The events constituting the significant action, whether true or fictitious, simple or complicated, require an actual narrator. Though the conventions of fiction are generous, they do not, as a rule, permit the detailed account of an experience out of which nobody survived to tell the tale, for the mood of all narrative is personal observation and report. The narrator may, however, recount the action in one of several ways.

1. In the first person, as the chief character. This method gives naturalness. It makes for unity, for the action centers about the speaker and what is beyond his point of view is presumably unimportant. It is subject to the defect that some action of which the hero is ignorant may need to be told, and that, moreover, what he knows and takes part in cannot be told objectively. If the hero magnifies his own deeds, his egotism offends us; if he minimizes them, the story loses vigor; and the assumption of modesty may be too obvious. In Stevenson's *Kidnapped* this difficulty is overcome by the use of Alan Breck Stewart as a foil for David Balfour, and in *Lorna Doone* by making John Ridd a man of simple character and the events which he recounts reminiscences of a remote past.

2. In the first person, as a secondary character. By this means the hero is spared the necessity of speaking for himself, and the narrator may even serve as a sort of chorus to point out to us his principal's daring or cleverness. It is most used in the detective story, in which Poe found the minor character a convenient person to whom the mystery could be explained. Frank Hopkinson Smith, in *Colonel Carter's Christmas,* employs the same device, and with less success. For we naturally wonder what " the major " really has to do with the action and why he could not have been dispensed with.

3. As an impersonal onlooker, accepting the point of view of the hero and reporting the action in the third person. This method attempts to keep the naturalness of the hero's point of view without his limitations. The narrator of " The Sire de Malétroit's Door " seems to accompany Denis throughout the action and sees and hears nothing that would not have been obvious to Denis himself; yet in such remarks as, " He would have done better

to remain beside the fire," and " There he sat, playing with the guard of his rapier " the point of view is independent of that of the hero.

4. As an omniscient onlooker. Such a narrator looks down upon the action as if from the sky. He has consequently so wide an angle of vision that he can convincingly recount events that happened at the same time in two different places and can readily shift from present to past time. He can report, not merely what an actual observer at each scene could have known, but also what passes through the minds of his characters, even describing mental processes of which they are not themselves conscious. The advantages of this method are obvious. For the unfolding of a highly complex plot, for a story in which description of setting seems desirable, for the study of character, it is the natural recourse. For these advantages, however, it must pay in a loss of vividness. The illusion of personal experience is not entirely consistent with omniscience. For this reason novels like *David Copperfield* and *Joseph Vance* are told in the first person, and stories of adventure frequently use the hero as narrator.

5. As the author, personally addressing his reader. This is a variation of the method just described, a device reminiscent of the essay, from which form the modern short story developed. In " David Swan " Hawthorne frankly takes the essayist's point of view. O. Henry uses it in " A Municipal Report " and in many other stories. Thackeray is one of the few novelists who have ventured to employ it in longer works. Except for humor, it is of doubtful value, for the interest of the reader should not be needlessly distracted from the action, even at the beginning of the narrative.

88. The Situations. A personal narrative is likely to unfold by successive units of time. Such, for example, is the structure of Dana's *Two Years Before the Mast,* Parkman's *Oregon Trail,* Thoreau's *Week,* Stevenson's *An Inland Voyage.* Most historical writing is analytical in method. A plot develops by situations. A situation is a single stage in the interaction of forces that creates and then solves the complication which makes a plot. In " Rip Van Winkle " the first situation is Rip's laziness, good nature, and domestic unhappiness. If Irving had been writing a Spectator essay he might have done no more than develop this topic. In a contemporary short story this first situation would have been regarded as antecedent action, and would have been presented objectively. The second situation is Rip's meeting with the ghostly crew of *The Half Moon.* The third is his return to the village and his recognition. With that event the problem is solved. What follows, told in the leisurely fashion of the opening, is subsequent action.

The situations composing " David Swan " and " The Sire de Malétroit's Door " may be analyzed as follows:

" DAVID SWAN "

Introduction: " The airy footsteps of the strange things that almost happen."

1. David Swan sleeps by the roadside.
2. A wealthy merchant and his wife think of waking him.
3. A pretty young girl brushes a bee from his face.
4. Two villains plan to rob him.
5. Unconscious of all these things, David wakes and boards the stage for Boston.

" THE SIRE DE MALETROIT'S DOOR "

1. Denis de Beaulieu, in escaping from the men-at-arms, finds himself locked in a strange house.
2. He has a puzzling interview with the Sire de Malétroit.
3. He meets Blanche and learns that he is expected to marry her.
4. He declines and learns the alternative.
5. He talks with Blanche till dawn.
6. He decides to live.

The office of a situation in a story may be:

1. *To begin the Action.* One or more of the situations making up a narrative may be required to set events in motion. Alone, situation 1 of "David Swan" would be a character sketch. It would serve equally well as the impulse for the action of several different stories, as Hawthorne hints when he mentions the widow and the temperance lecturer. The accident that places Denis within the locked door of a strange house promises adventure, but we cannot guess what it will be.

2. *To Complicate the Action.* Until there is a conflict of forces and two possible lines of action there can be no plot. After Denis has his interview with the Sire, puzzling as the encounter is, we recognize that two stubborn wills are in opposition.

3. *To Bring the Action to a Crisis.* In life some conflicts go on indefinitely. In a story, particularly in a short story, they demand a solution. The situations that bring Blanche's will into the struggle and offer Denis the unpalatable alternative draw toward the moment when Blanche says "Alas! what shall we say to my uncle when he returns?"

4. *To Bring the Action to an End.* The last situation should satisfy us with a solution of the problem, an untying of the knot created by the preceding situations. Will the old drake drown? Will Blanche and Denis yield to the will of Alain of Malétroit and how? When these questions are answered the significant action is completed.

89. The Subsequent Action. What happens after the denouement does not always interest the reader. In "The Sire de Malétroit's Door" the solution is so complete that the rest need not be told. In many other short stories the subsequent action is so easily inferred that it is unnecessary even to hint at it. This is true of "Markheim" and "The Necklace." In such short stories as require a hint, nothing more is permissible. As Kipling says at the end of " Cupid's Arrows," the rest isn't worth printing. Cable concludes " Posson Jone' " as follows:

In all Parson Jones's after life, amid the many painful reminiscences of his visit to the City of the Plain, the sweet knowledge was withheld from him that by the light of the Christian virtue that shone from him even in his great fall, Jules St.-Ange arose, and went to his father an honest man.

The Technic of Narrative

90. Characterization. The actors in a narrative may be of three kinds — types, individuals, and caricatures.

Action may be carried on — interesting action, at that — by actors that are not individualized at all but merely, like the giants, witches, and fairies of stories for children, and indeed, most of the knights and ladies of the early romances, made to represent the classes to which they belong. Some of the minor characters in an effective narrative may properly remain types, for there is no need that they shall become individuals. It is important, however, that the main characters shall not remain mere figures and that minor characters shall have enough reality to be convincing. In the crude narrative from which the following is taken Jack is throughout merely the type of boy hero, who is " in his element " in danger and who always fires " a well-aimed shot."

" . . . What must have been hours afterward, his faithful horse nosed him. Jack awoke in time to see shadows over near his camp fire. He had taken the precaution of lying down at some distance from his fire. Watching, he decided that the shadows were probably caused by Indians, and no doubt he did not wish to parley with any of them. He knew little of the tribes in that region. Quietly and with the speed of long practice he slipped the hobbles from his horse, saddled her, sprang upon her back, and dashed away in the darkness. After a ride of two long hours he dismounted, hobbled his horse, and laid (*sic*) down for needed rest. . . ."

Successful characterization gives such reality to an actor in a narrative that he becomes a real person. Thackeray, in one of the *Roundabout Papers,* " On a Peal of Bells," lists the characters in fiction that he loves best, quite as if he had known them all personally. Characterization is accomplished in two ways:

1. Directly, by analysis and description.

The old squire was an implacable man: he made resolutions in violent anger, but he was not to be moved from them after his anger had subsided — as fiery volcanic matters cool and harden into rock. — GEORGE ELIOT in *Silas Marner.*

He was smallish in stature, but well set and as nimble as a goat; his face was of a good open expression but sunburnt very dark, and heavily freckled and pitted with smallpox; his eyes were un- usually light and had a kind of dancing madness in them that was both engaging and alarming. . . . Altogether I thought of him, at the first sight, that here was a man I would rather call my friend than my enemy. — STEVENSON in *Kidnapped.*

2. Indirectly, by self-revelation through speech and ac- tion and by the comments and actions of other characters. The choice of a name is an important means of incidental characterization, ranging from the obviously allegorical Mr. Gathergold and Dr. Battleblast of Hawthorne to the more subtle contrasts in Stevenson's David Balfour and Alan Breck Stewart and Kipling's Kitty Beighton and Commissioner Barr-Saggott.

Young Cubbon on the left turned white and his Devil prompted Barr-Saggott to smile. Now horses used to shy when Barr-Saggott smiled. — KIPLING in *Cupid's Arrows.*

He was not yet in sight; and then her eyes crept back to the package, her thoughts seeming to run on what was inside it. At length she drew the parcel into her lap, and untied the paper covering; a small swing looking-glass was disclosed, in which she proceeded to survey herself attentively. Then she parted her lips and smiled. — THOMAS HARDY in *Far from the Madding Crowd.*

Caricature is the emphasis of a personal quality or a physical detail until the character is over-individualized and abnormal. Though sometimes useful for humor or satire, it is usually as undesirable as under-characterization.

As I came back, I saw Uriah Heep shutting up the office; and, feeling friendly toward everybody, went in and spoke to him, and at parting gave him my hand. But oh, what a clammy hand his was! as ghostly to the touch as to the sight! I rubbed mine afterwards, to warm it, *and to rub his off.* . . . I found Uriah Heep reading a great fat book, with such demonstrative attention that his lank forefinger followed up every line as he read, and made clammy tracks along the page (or so I fully believed) like a snail.

— DICKENS in *David Copperfield*.

91. Dialogue. Talk between the characters in a narrative heightens reality and interest, enables the actors to reveal themselves, and gives the reader, more neatly than by direct explanation, useful information about setting and antecedent action. It consists of two parts — speeches and stage directions. The speeches must be consistent, brief, and interesting. The " stage " directions should be subordinate, neither monotonous repetitions of " he said " nor fantastically varied ingenuities such as " thrilled she," " winced he." (For an amusing and valuable discussion of stage directions consult Mark Twain's essay on " Howells " in *Harper's Monthly,* Volume 103, page 674.).

SPECIMENS OF NARRATION

I

WE SIGHT SPAIN

When I came on deck at midnight of the third day out of Penzance we were running seven knots, rolling deeply, so that the boom trailed in the wave-tops with a spout of faintly phosphorescent spray; the sails were steady and quiet, every rope was taut, and the *Caltha's* long thin bow was cutting the water with a steady roar.

The port light, shining into the hollow of the spinnaker, made the sail glow ruby red; to starboard, under the boom, I could see the faint spectral green of the starboard light on the tumbling bow wave. We had a riding lantern lashed in the mizzen rigging, with a shield of tin on the forward side of it, and it lighted the quarter-deck. The dew had tightened the boat cover, and I drummed on it. Before me as I steered was the compass card, the most important point in the world, a yellow disk, floating in space. Beyond the ship was blue deep darkness; the sea was the color of the sky, and there was no horizon.

At two-thirty I was relieved, and went below. After the endless waves and the rush of the wind through space it was pleasant to stand for a moment in the saloon doorway and feel the security of the four protecting walls. The lamplight filled the room and glinted cheerfully on the panels. The swing table, with its brown cloth, dizzily balanced the chart and the Light List that lay upon it. The yellow oilskin coats were heaped in a corner of the sofa. After the chirp of blocks, far up in the dark, and the gnawing noise of the water beside the ship, the ticking of the saloon clock was a small, comforting, domestic sound.

In the cabin, the dim starlight, reflected from the mainsail, shone down through the skylight, showing the backs of the books in the shelves and the white pillows in the berths. It seemed very strange that there should be a bed here, in the very center of the sea, a warm bed, with a mile of cold sea water under it. The noise of the wind outside was like a faint memory of things that happened long ago, and could not happen now.

On the morning of the fourth day we saw a whale. He blew first at a distance, in the classic position of " Weather bow! " and later came close to look at us. He rolled his little eye out of the water; he seemed utterly unconscious of his own unimportance. We brought a rifle on deck and fired at him; the bullet struck the water near him; he left, and did not come back.

There is always something miraculous about a landfall. That a man should be able to find his way across the " trackless ocean " — about which one hears so much — when his guides are the Magnetic Pole, the Observatory at Greenwich, a pair of printed books, and the sun in the sky — all of which are fantastically remote from his immediate question — is nothing less than magical.

At the noon observation of the fourth day I marked our position on the chart with an arrogant cross. "Here we are," I said, trying to make it sound probable. "And Finisterre lies east southeast of us, distant twenty-six miles." Now there was nothing in sight to the east southeast, or anywhere else. And the only navigating I had ever done, before this, was in a book. We looked at one another, and went trooping solemnly up on deck, where Ball was steering.

"Put her east southeast," said Pat.

"East southeast, sir," Ball said, and hauled the tiller over.

This was at noon. At twenty minutes before two we made out a luminous cloud on the horizon ahead, and an hour later we saw the sun shining on a high red cliff. This was the northwest corner of Spain. It seemed incredible. Yet there it was.

None of us had ever seen Spain before, excepting Ball, who had been everywhere. But it looked exactly as we thought it should look: bare mountains, brown and dry, with jagged crests, rising up out of the sea; there was white surf at their feet, and lonely white houses clinging to their sides. We passed a fisherman — a long, lean, double-ended boat, carrying an enormous lateen sail set on a yard that bent like a whip. Ball cried, "*Buenos días, señor!*" as she went swooping past, and the man at the tiller raised his arm and shouted something in reply. There could no longer be any doubt of it. — ARTHUR STURGES HILDEBRAND in *Blue Water*. By permission of Harcourt, Brace and Company.

II

WE BUY A HORSE

Everything was talked over, ciphered over, and freely discussed by my wife and myself, except one matter, which I planned and worked out alone, doing most of the necessary calculations at the office, so as not to excite Euphemia's curiosity.

I had determined to buy a horse. This would be one of the most important events of our married life, and it demanded a great deal of thought, which I gave it.

The horse was chosen for me by a friend. He was an excellent beast (the horse), excelling, as my friend told me, in muscle and wit. Nothing better than this could be said about a horse. He was a sorrel animal, quite handsome, gentle enough for Euphemia to drive, and not too high-minded to do a little farm-work, if necessary. He was exactly the animal I needed.

The carriage was not quite such a success. The horse having cost a good deal more than I expected to pay, I found that I could only afford a second-hand carriage. I bought a good, serviceable vehicle, which would hold four persons, if necessary, and there was room enough to pack all sorts of parcels and baskets. It was with great satisfaction that I contemplated this feature of the carriage, which was a rather rusty-looking affair, although sound and strong enough. The harness was new, and set off the horse admirably.

On the afternoon when my purchases were completed, I did not come home by the train. I drove home in my own carriage, drawn by my own horse! The ten-mile drive was over a smooth road, and the sorrel traveled splendidly. If I had been a line of kings a mile long, all in their chariots of state, with gold and silver, and outriders, and music, and banners waving in the wind, I could not have been prouder than when I drew up in front of my house.

There was a wagon-gate at one side of the front fence which had never been used except by the men who brought coal, and I got out and opened this, very quietly, so as not to attract the attention of Euphemia. It was earlier than I usually returned, and she would not be expecting me. I was then about to lead the horse up a somewhat grass-grown carriage-way to the front door, but I reflected that Euphemia might be looking out of some of the windows and I had better drive up. So I got in and drove very slowly to the door.

However, she heard the unaccustomed noise of wheels, and looked out of the parlor window. She did not see me, but immediately came around to the door. I hurried out of the carriage so quickly that, not being familiar with the steps, I barely escaped tripping.

When she opened the front door she was surprised to see me standing by the horse.

"Have you hired a carriage?" she cried. "Are we going to ride?"

"My dear," said I, as I took her by the hand, "we are going to ride. But I have not hired a carriage. I have bought one. Do you see this horse? He is ours — our own horse."

If you could have seen the face that was turned up to me — all you other men in the world — you would have torn your hair in despair.

Afterward she went around and around that horse; she patted his smooth sides; she looked, with admiration, at his strong, well-formed legs; she stroked his head; she smoothed his mane; she was brimful of joy.

When I had brought the horse some water in a bucket — and what a pleasure it was to water one's own horse! — Euphemia rushed into the house and got her hat and cloak, and we took a little drive.

I doubt if any horse ever drew two happier people. Euphemia said but little about the carriage. That was a necessary adjunct, and it was good enough for the present. But the horse! How nobly and with what vigor he pulled us up the hills and how carefully and strongly he held the carriage back as we went down! How easily he trotted over the level road, caring nothing for the ten miles he had gone that afternoon! What a sensation of power it gave us to think that all that strength and speed and endurance was ours, that it would go where we wished, that it would wait for us as long as we chose, that it was at our service day and night, that it was a horse, and we owned it! — FRANK R. STOCKTON in *Rudder Grange*. Used by permission of Charles Scribner's Sons.

III

AFFAIRS OF THE MORGANS

"Hetty!" Miss Alice Morgan called her niece.

There was a note in her voice that was not there when the world went well with Miss Alice and when her charming heart was free from worry. Not that you could call it irritability or irascibility or tartness or acerbity or protervity or any of the other words in your thesaurus. It was simply that, for a certain reason, her nerves were taut. So far, no one in the house had noticed it except the fourteen-year-old Hetty, who, spending the summer in the country home, being tutored in trigonometry and Virgil, had plenty of time to notice everything.

It was curiosity as well as obedience that brought her so promptly to the room they always called "Aunt Alice's room" whether Aunt Alice happened to be visiting them or not.

Miss Alice Morgan sat at her desk with a box of her best note paper before her — creamy, smooth, delicious white. She held a sealed envelope, creamy and smooth, in nervous fingers. She was slim and dark and more beautiful than she had been at twenty — now she was thirty-four — and was likely to be even more beautiful at forty, since hers was the sort that is derived chiefly from the spirit within.

"Hetty," Miss Alice Morgan began, and then stopped suddenly and thoughtfully as if she had half a mind not to say it.

"Yes, darling?" Hetty encouraged her, for after all it would be a pity not to hear what it was.

"Hetty, this is the morning you go in town to the dentist, isn't it?"

Yes, it was.

"James going to drive you in?"

Yes, James was going to drive her in.

"Now, Hetty, your father and mother are away to-day. So I am taking all the responsibility of this myself. I will explain everything to them. You won't even need to mention the matter to them. If they want to blame anyone I am the one they are to blame."

She stopped again.

"Yes?" Hetty encouraged her again. This sounded good, whatever it might be. Very, very good, indeed!

"After you go to the dentist's will you please have James drive you around to my apartment: Mamie is there and she will give you your lunch. But before you have your lunch there will — probably a — a gentleman will come. And I want you to give him this letter and tell him I was ill and could not come. You understand. Hetty? And I *am* ill. You can see for yourself, Hetty, that I am ill to-day."

Hetty regarded her with cool interest. "It isn't an awfully showy kind of illness, Aunt Alice," she admitted. "But I'll take your word for it. I would take your word for almost anything."

"Well, I am," said Miss Alice Morgan firmly. "I *am* ill. That is why I am sending this note instead of going in person. And there isn't any other way of getting word to him because he will already have started from Boston. And when you have explained all this and have given him the note, you are to ask him very politely if he will stay to lunch. I know he won't — after he reads the note. But he will have come expecting to stay, so you must at least go through the form of asking him. Do you understand, Hetty?"

"Yes, Aunt Alice," said the calm Hetty. But to herself she added, "But just the same it would be nice to have him stay for lunch."

Then her Aunt Alice, after she had given her the note, made a motion as if to take it back again. And then, although she let it go, she put her hand over her eyes and said, " I don't know. I don't know. I just want to be let alone."

As Hetty drove into town with James she thought it all over with interest. "Aunt Alice has lost her nerve about something," she decided with conviction and curiosity.

After the dentist's James drove her to her aunt's apartment and reminded her that he had had instructions to come back for her at two-thirty.

" Yes, but a great deal could happen," she replied, apropos it would seem, of nothing at all, " between now and two-thirty."

It was July and it was hot in the city. But she could not remember ever before being in town in midsummer, which made it all the nicer, like an adventure, like being in a brand new place where she had never been before.

And Aunt Alice's flat was like that, too. It was lovely in winter, to be sure, so lovely that she never had enough of it on the occasional winter Saturday when she had come there to lunch; for it always seemed that no sooner was lunch over than they dashed off to the matinée or a concert or a charity fair. This time she would have a little while at least to get acquainted with it.

The elevator whisked her up to the sixth floor.

Up on the sixth floor the city was not hot, for a little breeze that refused to drop to street level played around the windows of her Aunt Alice's apartment.

Hetty turned on the electric fan, not because she needed it, but because it seemed a pity when it was there not to use it.

Mamie was not especially glad to see her, although she expected her, because Miss Alice had telephoned her the change of plan.

Mamie did not mind in the least coming in from her vacation on her married sister's farm to dust up the apartment and get in provisions and altogether upset the careful arrangements which had been made when the apartment was closed for the summer. It would have been all right if the lunch had been for Miss Alice herself, but she rather resented so much disturbance for the sake of feeding this chit of a thing.

Hetty didn't expect Mamie to be very glad to see her. It was well known that Mamie cared nothing for anyone but Aunt Alice. She had been Aunt Alice's nurse when Aunt Alice was a tiny thing and, as Aunt Alice was now thirty-four, that made Mamie — according to Hetty's arithmetic — somewhere in her fifties. And as

Hetty liked to be very gentle with the old, she gave Mamie a nice kiss on the cheek.

Mamie did not seem very appreciative.

Hetty looked about the kitchen to see what was being prepared for lunch. "Oh yummy, yum!" she cried. "Broilers! Mamie! And French pastries! Mamie, I adore you! Mamie, did you know I adored you?"

"You adore your stomach," said Mamie coldly.

Hetty turned that over thoughtfully. "Not that," she decided. "It isn't my stomach I adore. It is the things that go into my stomach."

Then she went over to the table and examined the pastries with joyful anticipation. "Oh, the white-cherry tart!" she exclaimed. "And this precious chocolate, *and* the pie-crusty, whipped-cream one!"

She put her arm about Mamie's waist, and this time the kiss she gave her was a resounding one. "Mamie," she told her, "you are my heart's treasure. You are my one love." She ignored the way Mamie shrugged her shoulders and went on shelling peas. And speaking of love, something else came into her mind. "You know, Mamie," she said, "I am going to tell you something I have never told anyone before: Mamie, do you know that I have never had a real affair in my life? Of course, there have been the boys one meets one place and another. All that sort of thing. But not an *affair*. Not a real affair!"

Mamie gave a faint sniff. "Miss Alice seem pretty well?" she wanted to know.

"Oh, she is well," Hetty assured her. "She is as well as anything."

She drifted back to the living room to taste again the flavor of its midsummer strangeness. She had never liked it so well as in its present wrappings. Chairs and desks and sofas and pictures were masked in covers of gray and green-striped crash. It made of it a delightfully strange and unfamiliar place. It made it into a stranger's room. It was also like being at a masquerade ball, trying to recognize all these masked forms. The writing desk and sofa, of course, one knew. And the Italian chair between two of the windows was not hard to guess. But which was this slim little fellow over by the door? And which the subtle nondescript beside it?

And the pictures! One could never penetrate through those green and gray stripes to see where hung the painting of the blooming plum tree, and where the sunny strip of road, or which was the black and white print that looked half a castle and half a boat. Then suddenly she found it amusing to see those squares of striped crash hanging on the wall as if they themselves were *objets d'art.*

She walked to one, holding up an imaginary lorgnette. "Wonderful!" she exclaimed. "Wonderful tones. Wonderful lighting." But she soon gave up that game because she kept thinking how much more fun it would be if there were two of them to play it.

One mirror was unswathed. But she gave only a casual glance at the large, solid-looking, fresh-colored girl of fourteen who, in spite of her length of limb and her hundred and twenty pounds, looked only an extraordinarily good-natured child. She was not enthusiastic about what she saw. "I must do something about that sometime," she reflected.

Then the bell rang and the man arrived.

Hetty Morgan fell in love with him the minute she saw him. He was not too old; he was nice and slim; his clothes were above reproach; and his manners made her feel at once the grown lady. But in spite of his grownupness there was a look in his eyes that made her think of her little brother when he was afraid the pup was going to be put out in the rain.

His look grew very worried when Hetty delivered her aunt's message and his reading of her letter was almost feverish. When he had finished Hetty saw that the hand that held it so tightly shook a little. And she thought no less of him for that. Her woman's intuition told her what had happened: he had been hoping to marry her Aunt Alice, and Aunt Alice, as he might have expected if he had really known her, had suddenly been afraid to go on with it. Aunt Alice was like that.

He picked up his hat to go. But having so pleasantly fallen in love with him, she did not at all want him to go; he was so lean and dark and handsome! He was so impressively grown — and at the same time so like her little brother!

"But you are to have lunch with me," she remonstrated. "My Aunt Alice spoke of it specially — told me to be sure to ask you to stay. And there are French pastries and broilers. And I should hate to eat all by myself."

He hesitated.

She permitted her eyes to mist appealingly — a gift that she had. That conquered him; he released his hat again.

She linked her arm within his and gave it a little squeeze.

"You are a perfect darling to stay," she said. "And I'll do something for you some day."

She led him to the wall to where the biggest painting hung, concealed by its green and gray crash.

"Isn't this a lovely thing!" she cried to him.

She had never before known any human being to take so promptly to "fooling." He stood back a little as if to see it the better. "Lovely!" he exclaimed, with a delightful awe in his voice. "Lovely!"

She drew him to another of those flat green and gray suspended packages.

"I don't care so much for this one," he announced promptly.

She drew away from him with a shocked little murmur. "My dear!" she reproached him. "Why, it is a superb thing. It has been exhibited and everything."

"I can't help it," he told her.

She cocked her head on one side as if to see it from his point of view. "Just what is it, dear?" she asked him, "that you don't like about it?"

He closed one eye and held his hand at arm's length before him, his palm almost against the crash—a most professional-looking gesture. "It is all in through there," he told her presently, waving his hand at one whole side of the picture. "Very crude. Very strangely crude."

She chuckled inwardly and led him to another square of green and gray.

"My dear girl!" he exclaimed enthusiastically. "This is you! This is a portrait of you! What an extraordinary likeness!"

She was convulsed. She turned so that her head was against his shoulder and shook with laughter.

Then a sudden resolve came to her. She knew definitely and finally what she wanted.

She drew him over to the sofa. She sat down beside him and linked her arm with his.

"Do you believe in love at first sight?" she asked him by way of a preliminary.

A troubled reminiscent look came into his eyes.

She began a long and intimate monologue: she told him the kind of man she intended to marry; she told him of her secret sins— how greedy she was over a candy box and how she hated to make her bed and hang up her clothes. She told him what sins she most hated in others: she hated other people to be greedy and she

hated shirkers. She gave him scandalous bits of autobiography —
how she had almost been suspended from school, how she and her
brother Dick had taken out the roadster before either of them had
properly learned to drive and of the disaster that had befallen
them and the car. She spared herself in no way. She gave herself
to him at her worst in the most humiliating and most sinful part
of her history.

He listened gravely and respectfully and if sometimes there was
the shadow of a smile about his mouth she did not mind.

" Now tell me about you," she begged.

He started a little. " Oh! Me? There is nothing about me
that is interesting at all. I am only a prosy old man."

" Oh, not so old! " she assured him. There was almost a query
in her voice — as if she were inquiring just how old.

She waited a little to see if he had any confessions to make or
any personal history to tell.

It seemed he had not.

" Of course, I am ready to take you on faith," she told him.

He gave her a startled look.

" I knew," she went on, " from the first minute you came into
that room that we were meant for each other."

His eyes opened wide in alarm. " Dear little girl," he began
protestingly.

" I am almost as tall as you are," she reminded him gently. " I
know I am only fourteen years old, but I think I am the sort that
would marry young. Say, seventeen or eighteen. I don't mind
waiting for you at all. And it would give you time," she added
delicately, " to get over — er — anything else."

" But that is just it," he told her bravely. " I am the sort of
fool who doesn't get over things. I have cared for only one
woman and I am not likely to care for another one."

" Isn't that very rare? " she inquired with interest.

" So rare," he replied, " as to be almost bad form."

Her heart ached for him and she adored him for his loyalty.
She admired that aunt, who in spite of her years, could amazingly
evoke constancy like this.

" I appreciate the honor very much," he was going on. " I feel
it more deeply than I can tell you and I shall count it always one
of my most precious memories."

She liked that immensely. It seemed to her at that moment
that there was nothing she would rather be than a most precious
memory. It set one up so, it gave one confidence and satisfaction.

"You are not going to take this to heart, I hope," he begged her. "You are young and you may in time come to care for some one else."

"I may," she said. "And besides there is something distinguished about being disappointed in love. It is something I've always rather craved."

"But not to brood over it and pine away," he begged.

"No-o," she assented thoughtfully, almost reluctantly. "That isn't being done nowadays, is it?"

"It is not considered the thing any more at all," he instructed her.

"I know," she admitted. "It is a sort of dashing heartless devil-may-care age."

"It is," he said. "It is, indeed."

Then Mamie announced lunch.

She had forgotten that Mamie's luncheons were so lovely. There were little lettuce sandwiches and tall glasses of iced tea with a cherry floating on top of each. She did not notice that Mamie put all five pastries on the table. She did not notice that while she ate three the gentleman ate but one. She only saw with self-approbation and a vague regret that one was left on the plate.

After lunch there was an hour before James would come.

"I want to ask you to let me do something for you," he begged her. "You have done something very wonderful for me: you have softened for me a bitter hour. And besides I cannot forget that I am the cause of your first disappointment in love. Isn't there some little souvenir you would like?"

She considered it thoughtfully.

"Shoes?" she suddenly suggested inspirationally. "I am crazy for a pair of sand-colored sports but mother thinks I don't need them. I should adore having you get me those."

Mamie did not know they were gone until they returned, each of them carrying a box that looked suspiciously like a shoe box.

The time came for saying good-by, and it was then that she had her inspiration. She caught him by the lapel of his coat to detain him.

"You know," she explained to him, "my Aunt Alice in some ways is the bravest lady I know, but she really is an awful coward."

He had winced a little at the name.

"You know," she went on, "once when Dick and I were out in the sail-boat with Aunt Alice and a man who was visiting us, the boat capsized and some one got Dick and me both to shore and when we got there we found it was Aunt Alice who had saved us and not the man. It was Aunt Alice."

" She would," he said simply.

" But she gets cold feet," her niece confessed for her. " Sometimes they ask her to speak at clubs and things, and she says she will, and then when the time comes near, she gets scared and tries to back out. If my father is there he won't let her, because if she doesn't back out she goes through it beautifully."

A strange sudden hope came into his eyes. " You think," he began with a sort of desperate eagerness.

" I am practically sure," she told him.

" Then what should I do? " he asked her humbly.

" James will be here in just a moment," she told him. " Why don't you come out with me and *make* her? "

His face was radiant now. " Would I have time," he begged her humbly, " to dash out and get a few flowers? "

" Certainly," she assured him. " It won't hurt James to wait. Or candy. We have oceans of flowers in our garden."

While he was on his errand she went out to Mamie in the kitchen. " Mamie," she said, " this has been a real day. I have been to the dentist and had my teeth cleaned and two small fillings put in. I saw a gentleman have his heart broken. In fact, I handed him the letter that broke his heart. I had lunch with a strange man. I offered him my hand and heart in marriage and was refused. A man that I never saw before to-day bought me two pairs of shoes, sports that I asked him for and dancing shoes that I didn't. I have brought — or I think I have — brought together two people who thought they had separated forever. I have changed their whole lives. Mamie, if you can think of anything I haven't done I wish you would tell me."

Said Mamie with asperity, " there is one pastry left that you didn't eat." — EVELYN GILL KLAHR in *Harper's Magazine,* October, 1923. By permission of the publisher and the author.

IV

THE SIRE DE MALÉTROIT'S DOOR

Denis de Beaulieu was not yet two-and-twenty, but he counted himself a grown man, and a very accomplished cavalier into the bargain. Lads were early formed in that rough, warfaring epoch; and when one has been in a pitched battle and a dozen raids, has killed one's man in an honorable fashion, and knows a thing or

two of strategy and mankind, a certain swagger in the gait is surely
to be pardoned. He had put up his horse with due care, and
supped with due deliberation; and then, in a very agreeable frame
of mind, went out to pay a visit in the gray of the evening. It
was not a very wise proceeding on the young man's part. He
would have done better to remain beside the fire or go decently
to bed. For the town was full of the troops of Burgundy and
England under a mixed command; and though Denis was there on
safe-conduct, his safe-conduct was like to serve him little on a
chance encounter.

It was September, 1429; the weather had fallen sharp; a flighty
piping wind, laden with showers, beat about the township; and the
dead leaves ran riot along the streets. Here and there a window
was already lighted up; and the noise of men-at-arms making merry
over supper within, came forth in fits and was swallowed up and
carried away by the wind. The night fell swiftly; the flag of
England, fluttering on the spire-top, grew ever fainter and fainter
against the flying clouds — a black speck like a swallow in the
tumultuous, leaden chaos of the sky. As the night fell the wind
rose, and began to hoot under archways and roar amid the tree-tops
in the valley below the town.

Denis de Beaulieu walked fast and was soon knocking at his
friend's door; but though he promised himself to stay only a little
while and make an early return, his welcome was so pleasant, and
he found so much to delay him, that it was already long past
midnight before he said good-bye upon the threshold. The wind
had fallen again in the meanwhile; the night was as black as the
grave; not a star, nor a glimmer of moonshine, slipped through the
canopy of cloud. Denis was ill-acquainted with the intricate lanes
of Château Landon; even by daylight he had found some trouble in
picking his way; and in this absolute darkness he soon lost it
altogether. He was certain of one thing only — to keep mounting
the hill; for his friend's house lay at the lower end, or tail, of
Château Landon, while the inn was up at the head, under the
great church spire. With this clue to go upon he stumbled and
groped forward, now breathing more freely in open places where
there was a good slice of sky overhead, now feeling along the wall
in stifling closes. It is an eerie and mysterious position to be thus
submerged in opaque blackness in an almost unknown town. The
silence is terrifying in its possibilities. The touch of cold window
bars to the exploring hand startles the man like the touch of a
toad; the inequalities of the pavement shake his heart into his

mouth; a piece of denser darkness threatens an ambuscade or a chasm in the pathway; and where the air is brighter, the houses put on strange and bewildering appearances, as if to lead him farther from his way. For Denis, who had to regain his inn without attracting notice, there was real danger as well as mere discomfort in the walk; and he went warily and boldly at once, and at every corner paused to make an observation.

He had been for some time threading a lane so narrow that he could touch a wall with either hand when it began to open out and go sharply downward. Plainly this lay no longer in the direction of his inn; but the hope of a little more light tempted him forward to reconnoitre. The lane ended in a terrace with a bartizan wall, which gave an outlook between high houses, as out of an embrasure, into the valley lying dark and formless several hundred feet below. Denis looked down, and could discern a few tree-tops waving and a single speck of brightness where the river ran across a weir. The weather was clearing up, and the sky had lightened, so as to show the outline of the heavier clouds and the dark margin of the hills. By the uncertain glimmer, the house on his left hand should be a place of some pretensions; it was surmounted by several pinnacles and turret-tops; the round stern of a chapel, with a fringe of flying buttresses, projected boldly from the main block; and the door was sheltered under a deep porch carved with figures and overhung by two long gargoyles. The windows of the chapel gleamed through their intricate tracery with a light as of many tapers, and threw out the buttresses and the peaked roof in a more intense blackness against the sky. It was plainly the hôtel of some great family of the neighborhood; and as it reminded Denis of a town house of his own at Bourges, he stood for some time gazing up at it and mentally gauging the skill of the architects and the consideration of the two families.

There seemed to be no issue to the terrace but the lane by which he had reached it; he could only retrace his steps, but he had gained some notion of his whereabouts, and hoped by this means to hit the main thoroughfare and speedily regain the inn. He was reckoning without that chapter of accidents which was to make this night memorable above all others in his career; for he had not gone back above a hundred yards before he saw a light coming to meet him, and heard loud voices speaking together in the echoing narrows of the lane. It was a party of men-at-arms going the night round with torches. Denis assured himself that they had all been making free with the wine-bowl, and were in no mood to be particular about safe-conducts or the niceties of chivalrous war. It was as like as not that they would kill him like a dog and leave him where he fell. The situation was inspiriting but nervous. Their own torches would conceal him from sight, he reflected; and he hoped that they would drown the noise of his footsteps with their own empty voices. If he were but fleet and silent, he might evade their notice altogether.

Unfortunately, as he turned to beat a retreat, his foot rolled upon a pebble; he fell against the wall with an ejaculation, and his sword rang loudly on the stones. Two or three voices demanded who went there — some in French, some in English; but Denis made no reply, and ran the faster down the lane. Once upon the terrace, he paused to look back. They still kept calling after him, and just then began to double the pace in pursuit, with a considerable clank of armor, and great tossing of the torchlight to and fro in the narrow jaws of the passage.

Denis cast a look around and darted into the porch. There he might escape observation, or — if that were too much to expect — was in a capital posture whether for parley or defence. So thinking, he drew his sword and tried to set his back against the door. To his surprise, it yielded behind his weight; and though he turned in a moment, continued to swing back on oiled and noiseless hinges, until it stood wide open on a black interior. When things fell out opportunely for the person concerned, he is not apt to be critical about the how or why, his own immediate personal convenience seeming a sufficient reason for the strangest oddities and revolutions in our sublunary things; and so Denis, without a moment's hesitation, stepped within and partly closed the door behind him to conceal his place of refuge. Nothing was further from his thoughts than to close it altogether; but for some inexplicable reason — perhaps by a spring or a weight — the ponderous mass of oak whipped itself out of his fingers and clanked to, with a formidable rumble and a noise like the falling of an automatic bar.

The round, at that very moment, debouched upon the terrace and proceeded to summon him with shouts and curses. He heard them ferreting in the dark corners; the stock of a lance even rattled along the outer surface of the door behind which he stood; but these gentlemen were in too high a humor to be long delayed, and soon made off down a corkscrew pathway which had escaped Denis's observation, and passed out of sight and hearing along the battlements of the town.

Denis breathed again. He gave them a few minutes' grace for fear of accidents, and then groped about for some means of opening the door and slipping forth again. The inner surface was quite smooth, not a handle, not a moulding, not a projection of any sort. He got his finger-nails round the edges and pulled, but the mass was immovable. He shook it, it was as firm as a rock. Denis de Beaulieu frowned and gave vent to a little noiseless whistle. What ailed the door? he wondered. Why was it open? How came it to shut so easily and so effectually after him? There was something obscure and underhand about all this, that was little to the young man's fancy. It looked like a snare; and yet who could suppose a snare in such a quiet by-street and in a house of so prosperous and even noble an exterior? And yet — snare or no snare, intentionally or unintentionally — here he was, prettily trapped; and for the life of him he could see no way out of it again. The darkness began to weigh upon him. He gave ear; all was silence without, but within and close by he seemed to catch a faint sighing, a faint sobbing rustle, a little stealthy creak — as though many persons were at his side, holding themselves quite still, and governing even their respiration with the extreme of slyness. The idea went to his vitals with a shock, and he faced about suddenly as if to defend his life. Then, for the first time, he became aware of a light about the level of his eyes and at some distance in the interior of the house — a vertical thread of light, widening towards the bottom, such as might escape between two wings of arras over a doorway. To see anything was a relief to Denis; it was like a piece of solid ground to a man laboring in a morass; his mind seized upon it with avidity; and he stood staring at it and trying to piece together some logical conception of his surroundings. Plainly there was a flight of steps ascending from his own level to that of this illuminated doorway; and indeed he thought he could make out another thread of light, as fine as a needle, and as faint as phosphorescence, which might very well be reflected along the polished wood of a handrail. Since he had begun to suspect that he was not alone, his heart had continued to beat with smothering violence, and an intolerable desire for action of any sort had possessed itself of his spirit. He was in deadly peril, he believed. What could be more natural than to mount the staircase, lift the curtain, and confront his difficulty at once? At least he would be dealing with something tangible; at least he would be no longer in the dark. He stepped slowly forward with outstretched hands, until his foot struck the bottom step; then he rapidly scaled the stairs, stood for a moment to compose his expression, lifted the arras and went in.

He found himself in a large apartment of polished stone. There were three doors; one on each of three sides; all similarly curtained with tapestry. The fourth side was occupied by two large windows and a great stone chimney-piece, carved with the arms of the Malétroits. Denis recognized the bearings, and was gratified to find himself in such good hands. The room was strongly illuminated; but it contained little furniture except a heavy table and a chair or two, the hearth was innocent of fire, and the pavement was but sparsely strewn with rushes clearly many days old.

On a high chair beside the chimney, and directly facing Denis as he entered, sat a little old gentleman in a fur tippet. He sat with his legs crossed and his hands folded, and a cup of spiced wine stood by his elbow on a bracket on the wall. His countenance had a strongly masculine cast; not properly human, but such as we see in the bull, the goat, or the domestic boar; something equivocal and wheedling, something greedy, brutal and dangerous. The upper lip was inordinately full, as though swollen by a blow or a toothache; and the smile, the peaked eyebrows, and the small, strong eyes were quaintly and almost comically evil in expression. Beautiful white hair hung straight all round his head, like a saint's, and fell in a single curl upon the tippet. His beard and moustache were the pink of venerable sweetness. Age, probably in consequence of inordinate precautions, had left no mark upon his hands; and the Malétroit hand was famous. It would be difficult to imagine anything at once so fleshy and so delicate in design; the taper, sensual fingers were like those of one of Leonardo's women; the fork of the thumb made a dimpled protuberance when closed; the nails were perfectly shaped, and of a dead, surprising whiteness. It rendered his aspect tenfold more redoubtable, that a man with hands like these should keep them devoutly folded like a virgin martyr — that a man with so intent and startling an expression of face should sit patiently on his seat and contemplate people with an unwinking stare, like a god, or a god's statue. His quiescence seemed ironical and treacherous, it fitted so poorly with his looks.

Such was Alain, Sire de Malétroit.

Denis and he looked silently at each other for a second or two.

"Pray step in," said the Sire de Malétroit. "I have been expecting you all the evening."

He had not risen, but he accompanied his words with a smile

and a slight but courteous inclination of the head. Partly from the smile, partly from the strange musical murmur with which the Sire prefaced his observation, Denis felt a strong shudder of disgust go through his marrow. And what with disgust and honest confusion of mind, he could scarcely get words together in reply.

"I fear," he said, "that this is a double accident. I am not the person you suppose me. It seems you were looking for a visit; but for my part, nothing was further from my thoughts — nothing could be more contrary to my wishes — than this intrusion."

"Well, well," replied the old gentleman indulgently, "here you are, which is the main point. Seat yourself, my friend, and put yourself entirely at your ease. We shall arrange our little affairs presently."

Denis perceived that the matter was still complicated with some misconception, and he hastened to continue his explanations.

"Your door . . ." he began.

"About my door?" asked the other raising his peaked eyebrows. "A little piece of ingenuity." And he shrugged his shoulders. "A hospitable fancy! By your own account, you were not desirous of making my acquaintance. We old people look for such reluctance now and then; when it touches our honor, we cast about until we find some way of overcoming it. You arrive uninvited, but believe me, very welcome."

"You persist in error, sir," said Denis. "There can be no question between you and me. I am a stranger in this countryside. My name is Denis, damoiseau de Beaulieu. If you see me in your house, it is only — "

"My young friend," interrupted the other, "you will permit me to have my own ideas on that subject. They probably differ from yours at the present moment," he added with a leer, "but time will show which of us is in the right."

Denis was convinced he had to do with a lunatic. He seated himself with a shrug, content to wait the upshot; and a pause ensued, during which he thought he could distinguish a hurried gabbling as of prayer from behind the arras immediately opposite him. Sometimes there seemed to be but one person engaged, sometimes two; and the vehemence of the voice, low as it was, seemed to indicate either great haste or an agony of spirit. It occurred to him that this piece of tapestry covered the entrance to the chapel he had noticed from without.

The old gentleman meanwhile surveyed Denis from head to foot with a smile, and from time to time emitted little noises like a bird or a mouse, which seemed to indicate a high degree of satisfaction. This state of matters became rapidly insupportable; and Denis, to put an end to it, remarked politely that the wind had gone down.

The old gentleman fell into a fit of silent laughter, so prolonged and violent that he became quite red in the face. Denis got upon his feet at once, and put on his hat with a flourish.

"Sir," he said, "if you are in your wits, you have affronted me grossly. If you are out of them, I flatter myself I can find better employment for my brains than to talk with lunatics. My conscience is clear; you have made a fool of me from the first moment; you have refused to hear my explanations; and now there is no power under God will make me stay here any longer; and if I cannot make my way out in a more decent fashion, I will hack your door to pieces with my sword."

The Sire de Malétroit raised his right hand and wagged it at Denis with the fore and little fingers extended.

"My dear nephew," he said, "sit down."

"Nephew!" retorted Denis, "you lie in your throat"; and he snapped his fingers in his face.

"Sit down, you rogue!" cried the old gentleman, in a sudden, harsh voice, like the barking of a dog. "Do you fancy," he went on, "that when I had made my little contrivance for the door I had stopped short with that? If you prefer to be bound hand and foot till your bones ache, rise and try to go away. If you choose to remain a free young buck, agreeably conversing with an old gentleman — why, sit where you are in peace, and God be with you."

"Do you mean I am a prisoner?" demanded Denis.

"I state the facts," replied the other. "I would rather leave the conclusion to yourself."

Denis sat down again. Externally he managed to keep pretty calm, but within, he was now boiling with anger, now chilled with apprehension. He no longer felt convinced that he was dealing with a madman. And if the old gentleman was sane, what, in God's name, had he to look for? What absurd or tragical adventure had befallen him? What countenance was he to assume?

While he was thus unpleasantly reflecting, the arras that overhung the chapel door was raised, and a tall priest in his robes came forth and, giving a long, keen stare at Denis, said something in an undertone to Sire de Malétroit.

"She is in a better frame of spirit?" asked the latter.

"She is more resigned, messire," replied the priest.

" Now the Lord help her, she is hard to please! " sneered the old gentleman. " A likely stripling — not ill-born — and of her own choosing, too? Why, what more would the jade have? "

" The situation is not usual for a young damsel," said the other, " and somewhat trying to her blushes."

" She should have thought of that before she began the dance? It was none of my choosing, God knows that: but since she is in it, by our Lady, she shall carry it to the end." And then addressing Denis, " Monsieur de Beaulieu," he asked, " may I present you to my niece? She has been waiting your arrival, I may say, with even greater impatience than myself."

Denis had resigned himself with a good grace — all he desired was to know the worst of it as speedily as possible; so he rose at once, and bowed in acquiescence. The Sire de Malétroit followed his example and limped, with the assistance of the chaplain's arm, towards the chapel-door. The priest pulled aside the arras, and all three entered. The building had considerable architectural pretensions. A light groining sprang from six stout columns, and hung down in two rich pendants from the center of the vault. The place terminated behind the altar in a round end, embossed and honey-combed with a superfluity of ornament in relief, and pierced by many little windows shaped like stars, trefoils, or wheels. These windows were imperfectly glazed, so that the night air circulated freely in the chapel. The tapers, of which there must have been half a hundred burning on the altar, were unmercifully blown about, and the light went through many different phases of brilliancy and semi-eclipse. On the steps in front of the altar knelt a young girl richly attired as a bride. A chill settled over Denis as he observed her costume; he fought with desperate energy against the conclusion that was being thrust upon his mind; it could not — it should not — be as he feared.

" Blanche," said the Sire, in his most flute-like tones, " I have brought a friend to see you, my little girl; turn round and give him your pretty hand. It is good to be devout; but it is necessary to be polite, my niece."

The girl rose to her feet and turned toward the newcomers. She moved all of a piece; and shame and exhaustion were expressed in every line of her fresh young body; and she held her head down and kept her eyes upon the pavement, as she came slowly forward. In the course of her advance, her eyes fell upon Denis de Beaulieu's feet — feet of which he was justly vain, be it remarked, and wore in the most elegant accoutrement even while travelling. She paused

— started, as if his yellow boots had conveyed some shocking meaning — and glanced suddenly up into the wearer's countenance. Their eyes met; shame gave place to horror and terror in her looks; the blood left her lips; with a piercing scream she covered her face with her hands and sank upon the chapel floor.

"That is not the man!" she cried. "My uncle, that is not the man!"

The Sire de Malétroit chirped agreeably. "Of course not," he said, "I expected as much. It was so unfortunate you could not remember his name."

"Indeed," she cried, "indeed, I have never seen this person till this moment — I have never so much as set eyes upon him — I never wish to see him again. Sir," she said, turning to Denis, "if you are a gentleman, you will bear me out. Have I ever seen you — have you ever seen me — before this accursed hour?"

"To speak for myself, I have never had that pleasure," answered the young man. "This is the first time, messire, that I have met with your engaging niece."

The old gentleman shrugged his shoulders.

"I am distressed to hear it," he said. "But it is never too late to begin. I had little more acquaintance with my own late lady ere I married her; which proves," he added, with a grimace, "that these impromptu marriages may often produce an excellent understanding in the long run. As the bridegroom is to have a voice in the matter, I will give him two hours to make up for lost time before we proceed with the ceremony." And he turned toward the door, followed by the clergyman.

The girl was on her feet in a moment. "My uncle, you cannot be in earnest," she said. "I declare before God I will stab myself rather than be forced on that young man. The heart rises at it; God forbids such marriages; you dishonor your white hair. Oh, my uncle, pity me! There is not a woman in all the world but would prefer death to such a nuptial. Is it possible," she added, faltering — "is it possible that you do not believe me — that you still think this" — and she pointed at Denis with a tremor of anger and contempt — "that you still think this to be the man?"

"Frankly," said the old gentleman, pausing on the threshold, "I do. But let me explain to you once for all, Blanche de Malétroit, my way of thinking about this affair. When you took it into your head to dishonor my family and the name that I have borne, in peace and war, for more than three-score years, you forfeited not only the right to question my designs, but that of looking me in the face. If your father had been alive, he would have spat on you and turned you out of doors. His was the hand of iron. You may bless your God you have only to deal with the hand of velvet, mademoiselle. It was my duty to get you married without delay. Out of pure good-will, I have tried to find your own gallant for you. And I believe I have succeeded. But before God and all the holy angels, Blanche de Malétroit, if I have not, I care not one jack-straw. So let me recommend you to be polite to our young friend; for upon my word, your next groom may be less appetizing."

And with that he went out, with the chaplain at his heels; and the arras fell behind the pair.

The girl turned upon Denis with flashing eyes.

"And what, sir," she demanded, "may be the meaning of all this?"

"God knows," returned Denis, gloomily. "I am a prisoner in this house, which seems full of mad people. More I know not; and nothing do I understand."

"And pray how came you here?" she asked.

He told her as briefly as he could. "For the rest," he added, "perhaps you will follow my example, and tell me the answer to all these riddles, and what, in God's name, is like to be the end of it."

She stood silent for a little, and he could see her lips tremble and her tearless eyes burn with a feverish lustre. Then she pressed her forehead in both hands.

"Alas, how my head aches!" she said wearily — "to say nothing of my poor heart! But it is due to you to know my story, unmaidenly as it may seem. I am called Blanche de Malétroit; I have been without father or mother for — oh! for as long as I can recollect, and indeed I have been most unhappy all my life. Three months ago a young captain began to stand near me every day in church. I could see that I pleased him; I am much to blame, but I was so glad that any one should love me; and when he passed me a letter, I took it home with me and read it with great pleasure. Since that time he has written many. He was so anxious to speak with me, poor fellow! and kept asking me to leave the door open some evening that we might have two words upon the stair. For he knew how much my uncle trusted me." She gave something like a sob at that, and it was a moment before she could go on. "My uncle is a hard man, but he is very shrewd," she said at last. "He has performed many feats in war, and was a great person at court, and much trusted by Queen Isabeau in old days. How he came to suspect me I cannot tell; but it is hard to keep anything from his knowledge; and this morning, as we came from mass, he took my hand into his, forced it open, and read my little billet, walking by my side all the while. When he finished, he gave it back to me with great politeness. It contained another request to have the door left open; and this has been the ruin of us all. My uncle kept me strictly in my room until evening, and then ordered me to dress myself as you see me — a hard mockery for a young girl, do you not think so? I suppose, when he could not prevail with me to tell him the young captain's name, he must have laid a trap for him: into which, alas! you have fallen in the anger of God. I looked for much confusion; for how could I tell whether he was willing to take me for his wife on these sharp terms? He might have been trifling with me from the first; or I might have made myself too cheap in his eyes. But truly I had not looked for such a shameful punishment as this! I could not think that God would let a girl be so disgraced before a young man. And now I tell you all; and I can scarcely hope that you will not despise me."

Denis made her a respectful inclination.

" Madam," he said, "you have honored me by your confidence. It remains for me to prove that I am not unworthy of the honor. Is Messire de Malétroit at hand? "

"I believe he is writing in the salle without," she answered.

" May I lead you thither, madam? " asked Denis, offering his hand with his most courtly bearing.

She accepted it; and the pair passed out of the chapel, Blanche in a very drooping and shamefast condition, but Denis strutting and ruffling in the consciousness of a mission, and the boyish certainty of accomplishing it with honor.

The Sire de Malétroit rose to meet them with an ironical obeisance.

" Sir," said Denis, with the grandest possible air, " I believe I am to have some say in the matter of this marriage; and let me tell you at once, I will be no party to forcing the inclination of this young lady. Had it been freely offered to me, I should have been proud to accept her hand, for I perceive she is as good as she is beautiful; but as things are, I have now the honor, messire, of refusing."

Blanche looked at him with gratitude in her eyes; but the old gentleman only smiled and smiled, until his smile grew positively sickening to Denis.

"I am afraid," he said, "Monsieur de Beaulieu, that you do not perfectly understand the choice I have offered you. Follow me, I beseech you, to this window." And he led the way to one of the large windows which stood open on the night. "You observe," he went on, "there is an iron ring in the upper masonry, and reeved through that, a very efficacious rope. Now, mark my words: if you should find your disinclination to my niece's person insurmountable, I shall have you hanged out of this window before sunrise. I shall only proceed to such an extremity with the greatest regret, you may believe me. For it is not at all your death that I desire, but my niece's establishment in life. At the same time, it must come to that if you prove obstinate. Your family, Monsieur de Beaulieu, is very well in its way; but if you sprang from Charlemagne, you should not refuse the hand of a Malétroit with impunity — not if she had been as common as the Paris road — not if she were as hideous as the gargoyle over my door. Neither my niece nor you, nor my own private feelings, move me at all in this matter. The honor of my house has been compromised; I believe you to be the guilty person, at least you are now in the secret; and you can hardly wonder if I request you to wipe out the stain. If you will not, your blood be on your own head! It will be no great satisfaction to me to have your interesting relics kicking their heels in the breeze below my windows, but half a loaf is better than no bread, and if I cannot cure the dishonor, I shall at least stop the scandal."

There was a pause.

"I believe there are other ways of settling such imbroglios among gentlemen," said Denis. "You wear a sword, and I hear you have used it with distinction."

The Sire de Malétroit made a signal to the chaplain, who crossed the room with long silent strides and raised the arras over the third of the three doors. It was only a moment before he let it fall again; but Denis had time to see a dusky passage full of armed men.

"When I was a little younger, I should have been delighted to honor you, Monsieur de Beaulieu," said Sire Alain; "but I am now too old. Faithful retainers are the sinews of age, and I must employ the strength I have. This is one of the hardest things to swallow as a man grows up in years; but with a little patience, even this becomes habitual. You and the lady seem to prefer the salle for what remains of your two hours; and as I have no desire to cross your preference, I shall resign it to your use with all the pleasure in the world. No haste!" he added, holding up his hand, as he saw a dangerous look come into Denis de Beaulieu's face. "If your mind revolt against hanging, it will be time enough two hours hence to throw yourself out of the window or upon the pikes of my retainers. Two hours of life are always two hours. A great many things may turn up in even as little a while as that. And, besides, if I understand her appearance, my niece has something to say to you. You will not disfigure your last hours by a want of politeness to a lady?"

Denis looked at Blanche, and she made him an imploring gesture.

It is likely that the old gentleman was hugely pleased at this symptom of an understanding; for he smiled on both, and added sweetly: "If you will give me your word of honor, Monsieur de Beaulieu, to await my return at the end of the two hours before attempting anything desperate, I shall withdraw my retainers, and let you speak with greater privacy with mademoiselle."

Denis again glanced at the girl, who seemed to beseech him to agree.

"I give you my word of honor," he said.

Messire de Malétroit bowed, and proceeded to limp about the apartment, clearing his throat the while with that odd musical chirp which had already grown so irritating in the ears of Denis de Beaulieu. He first possessed himself of some papers which lay upon the table; then he went to the mouth of the passage and appeared to give an order to the men behind the arras; and lastly he hobbled out through the door by which Denis had come in, turning upon the threshold to address a last smiling bow to the young couple, and followed by the chaplain with a hand-lamp.

No sooner were they alone than Blanche advanced toward Denis with her hands extended. Her face was flushed and excited, and her eyes shone with tears.

"You shall not die!" she cried, "you shall marry me after all."

"You seem to think, madam," replied Denis, "that I stand much in fear of death."

"Oh, no, no," she said, "I see you are no poltroon. It is for my own sake — I could not bear to have you slain for such a scruple."

"I am afraid," returned Denis, "that you underrate the difficulty, madam. What you may be too generous to refuse, I may be too proud to accept. In a moment of noble feeling towards me, you forgot what you perhaps owe to others."

He had the decency to keep his eyes on the floor as he said this, and after he had finished, so as not to spy upon her confusion. She stood silent for a moment, then walked suddenly away, and falling on her uncle's chair, fairly burst out sobbing. Denis was in the acme of embarrassment. He looked round, as if to seek for inspiration, and seeing a stool, plumped down upon it for something to do. There he sat playing with the guard of his rapier, and wishing himself dead a thousand times over, and buried in the nastiest kitchen-heap in France. His eyes wandered round the apartment, but found nothing to arrest them. There were such wide spaces between the furniture, the light fell so badly and cheerlessly over all, the dark outside air looked in so coldly through the windows, that he thought he had never seen a church so vast, nor a tomb so melancholy. The regular sobs of Blanche de Malétroit measured out the time like the ticking of a clock. He read the device upon the shield over and over again, until his eyes became obscured; he stared into shadowy corners until he imagined they were swarming with horrible animals; and every now and again he awoke with a start, to remember that his last two hours were running, and death was on the march.

Oftener and oftener, as the time went on, did his glance settle on the girl herself. Her face was bowed forward and covered with her hands, and she was shaken at intervals by the convulsive hiccup of grief. Even thus she was not an unpleasant object to dwell upon, so plump and yet so fine, with a warm brown skin, and the most beautiful hair, Denis thought, in the whole world of womankind. Her hands were like her uncle's; but they were more in place at the end of her young arms, and looked infinitely soft and caressing. He remembered how her blue eyes had shone upon him, full of anger, pity, and innocence. And the more he dwelt on her perfections, the uglier death looked, and the more deeply was he smitten with penitence at her continued tears. Now he felt that no man could have the courage to leave a world which contained so beautiful a creature; and now he would have given forty minutes of his last hour to have unsaid his cruel speech.

Suddenly a hoarse and ragged peal of cockcrow rose to their ears from the dark valley below the windows. And this shattering noise in the silence of all around was like a light in a dark place, and shook them both out of their reflections.

" Alas, can I do nothing to help you? " she said, looking up.

" Madam," replied Denis, with a fine irrelevancy, " if I have said anything to wound you, believe me, it was for your own sake and not for mine."

She thanked him with a tearful look.

" I feel your position cruelly," he went on. " The world has been bitter hard on you. Your uncle is a disgrace to mankind. Believe me, madam, there is no young gentleman in all France but would be glad of my opportunity, to die in doing you a momentary service."

" I know already that you can be very brave and generous," she answered. " What I want to know is whether I can serve you — now or afterwards," she added, with a quaver.

" Most certainly," he answered with a smile. " Let me sit beside you as if I were a friend, instead of a foolish intruder; try to forget how awkwardly we are placed to one another; make my last moments go pleasantly; and you will do me the chief service possible."

" You are very gallant," she added, with a yet deeper sadness . . . " very gallant . . . and it somehow pains me. But draw nearer, if you please; and if you find anything to say to me, you will at least make certain of a very friendly listener. Ah! Monsieur de Beaulieu," she broke forth — " ah! Monsieur de Beaulieu, how can I look you in the face? " And she fell to weeping again with a renewed effusion.

" Madam," said Denis, taking her hand in both of his, " reflect on the little time I have before me, and the great bitterness into which I am cast by the sight of your distress. Spare me, in my last moments, the spectacle of what I cannot cure even with the sacrifice of my life."

" I am very selfish," answered Blanche. " I will be braver, Monsieur de Beaulieu, for your sake. But think if I can do you no kindness in the future — if you have no friends to whom I could carry your adieux. Charge me as heavily as you can; every burden will lighten, by so little, the invaluable gratitude I owe you. Put it in my power to do something more for you than weep."

" My mother is married again, and has a young family to care for. My brother Guichard will inherit my fiefs; and if I am not in error, that will content him amply for my death. Life is a little vapor that passeth away, as we are told by those in holy orders. When a man is in a fair way and sees all life open in front of him, he seems to himself to make a very important figure in the world. His horse whinnies to him; the trumpets blow and the girls look out of window as he rides into town before his company; he receives many assurances of trust and regard — sometimes by express in a letter — sometimes face to face, with persons of great consequence falling on his neck. It is not wonderful if his head is turned for a time. But once he is dead, were he as brave as Hercules or as wise as Solomon, he is soon forgotten. It is not ten years since my father fell, with many other knights around him, in a very fierce encounter, and I do not think that any one of them, nor so much as the name of the fight, is now remembered. No, no, madam, the nearer you come to it, you see that death is a dark and dusty corner, where a man gets into his tomb and has the door shut after him till the judgment day. I have few friends just now, and once I am dead I shall have none."

"Ah, Monsieur de Beaulieu!" she exclaimed, "you forget Blanche de Malétroit."

"You have a sweet nature, madam, and you are pleased to estimate a little service far beyond its worth."

"It is not that," she answered. "You mistake me if you think I am easily touched by my own concerns. I say so, because you are the noblest man I have ever met; because I recognize in you a spirit that would have made even a common person famous in the land."

"And yet here I die in a mousetrap — with no more noise about it than my own squeaking," answered he.

A look of pain crossed her face, and she was silent for a little while. Then a light came into her eyes, and with a smile she spoke again.

"I cannot have my champion think meanly of himself. Anyone who gives his life for another will be met in Paradise by all the heralds and angels of the Lord God. And you have no such cause to hang your head. For . . . pray, do you think me beautiful?" she asked, with a deep flush.

"Indeed, madam, I do," he said.

"I am glad of that," she answered heartily. "Do you think there are many men in France who have been asked in marriage by a beautiful maiden — with her own lips — and who have refused her to her face? I know you men would half despise such a triumph; but believe me, we women know more of what is precious in love. There is nothing that should set a person higher in his own esteem; and we women would prize nothing more dearly."

"You are very good," he said; "but you cannot make me forget that I was asked in pity and not for love."

"I am not so sure of that," she replied, holding down her head. "Hear me to an end, Monsieur de Beaulieu. I know how you must despise me; I feel you are right to do so; I am too poor a creature to occupy one thought of your mind, although, alas! you must die for me this morning. But when I asked you to marry me, indeed, and indeed, it was because I respected and admired you, and loved you with my whole soul, from the very moment that you took my part against my uncle. If you had seen yourself, and how noble you looked, you would pity rather than despise me. And now," she went on, hurriedly checking him with her hand, "although I have laid aside all reserve and told you so much, remember that I know your sentiments towards me already. I would not, believe me, being nobly born, weary you with importunities into consent. I too have a pride of my own; and I declare before the holy mother of God, if you should now go back from your word already given, I would no more marry you than I would marry my uncle's groom."

Denis smiled a little bitterly.

"It is a small love," he said, "that shies at a little pride."

She made no answer, although she probably had her own thoughts.

"Come hither to the window," he said with a sigh. "Here is the dawn."

And indeed the dawn was already beginning. The hollow of the sky was full of essential daylight, colorless and clean; and the valley underneath was flooded with a gray reflection. A few thin vapors clung in the coves of the forest or lay along the winding course of the river. The scene disengaged a surprising effect of stillness, which was hardly interrupted when the cocks began once more to crow among the steadings. Perhaps the same fellow who had made so horrid a clangor in the darkness not half an hour before, now sent up the merriest cheer to greet the coming day. A little wind went bustling and eddying among the tree-tops underneath the windows. And still the daylight kept flooding insensibly out of the east, which was soon to grow incandescent and cast up that red-hot cannon-ball, the rising sun.

Denis looked out over all this with a bit of a shiver. He had taken her hand, and retained it in his almost unconsciously.

"Has the day begun already?" she said; and then, illogically enough: "the night has been so long! Alas! what shall we say to my uncle when he returns?"

"What you will," said Denis, and he pressed her fingers in his.

She was silent.

"Blanche," he said, with a swift, uncertain, passionate utterance, "you have seen whether I fear death. You must know well enough that I would as gladly leap out of that window into the empty air as to lay a finger on you without your free and full consent. But if you care for me at all, do not let me lose my life in a misapprehension; for I love you better than the whole world; and though I will die for you blithely, it would be like all the joys of Paradise to live on and spend my life in your service."

As he stopped speaking, a bell began to ring loudly in the interior of the house; and a clatter of armor in the corridor showed that the retainers were returning to their post, and the two hours were at an end.

"After all that you have heard?" she whispered, leaning towards him with her lips and eyes.

"I have heard nothing," he replied.

"The captain's name was Florimond de Champdivers," she said in his ear.

"I did not hear it," he answered, taking her supple body in his arms, and covering her wet face with kisses.

A melodious chirping was audible behind, followed by a beautiful chuckle, and the voice of Messire de Malétroit wished his new nephew a good morning. — ROBERT LOUIS STEVENSON in *The New Arabian Nights*. Used by special arrangement with Charles Scribner's Sons.

EXERCISES IN NARRATION

I

Tell the story of one of the following incidents reported in the newspapers. Realize the action for yourself; then report it so that the reader will see it happen. Invent detail; give names. Use the past tense.

1. A two-year-old child climbs out of an open second-story window in a department store while the mother's back is turned. A young man on the other side of the street sees the child on the window sill and runs across just in time to catch him in his hands like a ball.

2. A painter falls from a scaffold on a high building and catches the edge of a wire sign suspended high above the street. Fellow workmen on the roof rescue him as follows: One lies on the roof

and holds by the ankles a companion, who hangs head downward and grasps the painter by the wrists. The man on the roof pulls them both up safely.

3. A man who has been injured by an automobile dies in a New York hospital. The police are asked to notify his widow. By mistake they notify the wife of a man of a similar name. She hurries to the hospital and on the way meets her husband alive and well. The lodge to which he belongs goes forward with preparations for his burial, and the man himself dismisses the undertaker whom they send.

4. A woman sleeping on the third floor of a frame dwelling is waked by the shrill cries of a canary bird in a cage downstairs. She goes down and finds that the house is afire, and that in a few minutes the escape of the family will be cut off. She gives the alarm and all are saved, including the bird.

5. (In the first person.) You are in a school or college building after everybody else has left. As you are about to go out you smell smoke. You see a thin curl of smoke come from a closet and then a glow of flame. You remember a fire extinguisher at the head of the stairs and run to fetch it. When you get back the room is dense with smoke. You try to operate the extinguisher and the cock refuses to turn. The smoke chokes you. At last the cock yields, the spray flows, and you get the fire under control just as help comes.

6. A locomotive engineer, seventy years old, is about to be retired with a pension after more than forty years of service without a serious accident. On his last run something goes wrong with his engine, and while he attends to it he runs past a signal and crashes into a freight. The fireman jumps but the engineer sticks to his post. Nobody is injured. He expects, according to the rules of the company, to be discharged and to lose his pension. An officer of the company calls on him the next day, and after talking with him for a few moments tells him than an exception has been made of his case and that he is to have his pension.

II

Use one of the following suggestions for a short story. You cannot be expected to invent a wholly new type of plot for your story. It will be enough to put an old motive into a setting that is real to you and to provide characters that are true to your own observation. Do not imitate a particular story. Try rather to tell a story of a given type.

1. *The Ugly Duckling Type.* One member of a group of persons has acquired in some way a reputation for incompetence or cowardice. He is consequently neglected or even persecuted. In some crisis he proves that he has been misjudged, and having shown himself braver or more skillful than others, promptly comes into his own.

2. *Bread Upon the Waters.* You are on your way with a number of companions to engage in some form of pleasure. You see somebody in need or distress. Your companions all hurry on. If you stop and give help you may be left behind. You hesitate and finally stop and do a considerate act. You are left behind, miss the expected pleasure, and are tempted to reproach yourself with having been foolishly unselfish. Some time later you unexpectedly meet the person whom you helped, and your kindness is abundantly repaid.

3. *The Biter Bitten.* A designing or ill-natured person is caught in his own trap. For example, a practical joker plans an unkind or humiliating joke on somebody, and finds by a certain turn of events that he is himself the victim of it. An overshrewd business man plans to take advantage of an unsophisticated old couple in a real estate transaction. He overreaches himself and in the end proves a loser by his own designs.

4. *Who Laughs Last.* Two boys come in from a walk and report what they think is a great discovery — they think they have seen train robbers, for example. There is reason to think them mistaken and everybody ridicules their credulity. Investigation undertaken quietly shows that they were right and their former tormentors are silenced.

5. *Coals of Fire.* A selfish and self-reliant person refuses to grant a not unreasonable favor, and expresses scorn of sentimentality or weakness. By chance he finds himself helpless, and the person whom he has treated unkindly comes generously to his assistance. Remorseful and ashamed he strives to make up for his previous ill-nature.

REFERENCES

1. To Narratives Mentioned in the Text: *A Week on the Concord and Merrimack Rivers:* Thoreau, H. D. (Houghton Mifflin); *The American Revolution:* Fiske, John (Houghton Mifflin); *Lorna Doone:* Blackmore, R. D. (Oxford Press); *Marjorie Daw:* Aldrich, T. B. (Houghton Mifflin); *The Revolt of Mother:* Freeman, M. W., in *A New England Nun* (Harper); also in *Short Stories for High Schools:* Mikels, R. M. R. (Scribner) and *Century Readings in American Literature:* Pattee, F. L. (Century); *The Luck of Roaring Camp:* F. Bret Harte (Houghton Mifflin); *Tennessee's Partner,* in the same volume and in *Short Stories for High Schools; The Jumping Frog:* Mark Twain in Collected Works (Harper), Vol. 19, in *Short Stories for High Schools,* and in Century Readings in American Literature; *William the Conqueror:* Kipling, R., in *The Day's Work* (Scribner); *The Four Horsemen of the Apocalypse:* Ibanez, Blasco (Dutton); *A Gala Dress:* Freeman, M. W., in *A New England Nun;* also in *College Readings in English Prose:* Scott and Zeitlin, and *A Book of Short Stories:* Williams, B. C.; *The Gifts of the Magi:* O. Henry in *The Four Million* (Doubleday, Page); *A Municipal Report:* O. Henry in *Strictly Business;* (Doubleday, Page); *Two Years Before the Mast:* Dana, R. H. (Houghton Mifflin); *The Oregon Trail:* Parkman, F. (Little, Brown); *Posson Jone':* Cable, G. W., in *Old Creole Days* (Scribner).

2. To Text-books: *The Rhetorical Principles of Narration* by C. L. Maxcy (Houghton); *A Handbook of Short Story Writing* by B. C. Williams (Dodd, Mead); *Short Stories in the Making* by R. W. Neal (Oxford); *A Manual of the Art of Fiction* by Clayton Hamilton (Doubleday, Page); *A Study of Prose Fiction* by Bliss Perry (Houghton Mifflin); *The Technique of the Novel* by C. E. Horne (Harpers); *The Study of the Novel* by S. L. Whitcomb (Heath); *The Short Story* by E. M. Albright (Macmillan); *Narrative Technique* by Thomas H. Uzzell (Harcourt, Brace); *How to Write Stories* by Walter B. Pitkin (Harcourt, Brace).

3. To Collections: *A Book of Prose Narratives* by C. W. Wells (Ginn); *A Book of Narratives* by Campbell and Rice (Heath); *Representative Narratives* by C. L. Maxcy (Houghton Mifflin); *The Short Story* by Brander Matthews (American Book Co.); *Types of the Short Story* by B. A. Heydrick (Scott, Foresman); *Americans All* by B. A. Heydrick (Harcourt, Brace); *Short Stories of America* by R. L. Ramsay (Houghton Mifflin).

CHAPTER IX

STRUCTURE AND STYLE IN ARGUMENTATION

ARGUMENTATIVE WRITING

92. The Nature of Argumentation. As an explanation tries to make the truth known and available, an argument endeavors to get the truth believed and acted upon. Hence an illogical argument is a bad argument and argument and sophistry are two different things. Hence also an argument presupposes a practical purpose. Other forms of discourse may unfold ideas or impressions for their own interest; argument aims at a definite object. It is in daily use by many persons as a means of livelihood. The agents, salesmen, and advertisers who address you constantly in person or in letters and newspapers prosper in their business according to their skill in argumentation. And your success in the business of life requires that you shall be able to analyze and test the reasoning of others and to advance effective arguments of your own.

Argumentation is significant, also, because it is a great engine of social progress. Without the interchange of opinions that we call debate government would degenerate into despotism or anarchy. In modern society great masses of people, different in interests and prejudices, must discover and exercise a common will. Without that general discussion which all new ideas provoke this would be impossible. The necessity for arguments in legislative assemblies and in the directorates of business organizations is obvious enough. But the use of argumentation cannot be restricted to oral debate or left to editors and politicians.

We are ruled not by laws but by public opinion. We are well ruled only by such public opinion as grows out of thoughtful discussion. And such thoughtful discussion, in which every citizen should have at least a passive part, is the normal use of argumentation.

PROOF

93. Proof and Persuasion. Argumentation, as the term is commonly used, includes two processes — proof and persuasion. Proof secures intellectual assent to the truth of fact or opinion. An honest mind yields such assent, however disagreeable the conclusion, for proof is a kind of conquest and cannot be denied. Persuasion wins emotional assent, not by conquering one's reason, but by arousing feelings which will result in belief or action. These two processes are not necessarily or even usually kept apart in practice; most argumentation uses them both. But they should be studied separately because they differ strikingly in method. The methods of proof will be sufficient to convince a man that he has added a column of figures incorrectly or that his watch is fast. If he doubts that a field contains five acres, you can confidently offer him the surveyor's figures as to its size. But if you want him to go for an outing with you on the afternoon that he had planned to spend otherwise, or to give to a worthy cause the five dollars that he was going to pay for theater tickets, you need something different from proof. The assent that you hope for is not "I concede that you are right"; but rather "I am willing to do what you ask." If you want to sell him the field, you may need both proof and persuasion. You must win his interest in the field before you can convince him that it will increase in value and that the price is reasonable. And when you have proved these things, you must persuade him to sign a contract of sale. Proof and persuasion are commonly thus intermingled in effective argument.

94. The Method of Proof. Proof consists of a proposition and inferences that warrant its acceptance as true. There is no other method. Any subject worth arguing about can be phrased in an affirmative sentence that clearly expresses the point at issue. It may be desirable at times to keep the proposition to yourself until you have made some progress toward showing it to be true; but in any case you must know precisely what you want to prove before you begin. And nothing but an inference will make a proposition worthy of belief. Voluble and repeated assertion, willingness to bet, fluent comment on things in general — none of these will contribute to proof. An unwarranted inference or an inference as to the truth of a wholly unrelated proposition is equally useless. A valid inference is a judgment correctly based on the laws of cause and effect. The relation of cause and effect may not be understood; but it must be known to exist. Distrust an inference, however plausible, that like many old saws and modern superstitions can show no possibility of a causal connection.

95. The Sources of Proof. For proof that a proposition is true we look to various sources. Not all of these sources are available in every case nor are they of equal value. From some of them we get not proof but such a degree of probability as may point the way to proof. Frequently different kinds of proof support each other and so produce jointly a convincing conclusion. For grounds for belief in a proposition, then, look:

1. *To its reasonableness.* How does it bear the test of your general experience and the experience of the race? You reject instantly the suggestion that a certain white object seen in the moonlight is a ghost. You suspect a stranger who as a great favor to you offers to sell an article

at much less than its apparent value. In general you trust the collected wisdom of the past and feel that even though you lack positive proof that a thing is true your confidence that it "stands to reason" is not without weight.

2. *To the opinions of persons who ought to know.* Such persons we call authorities. The acceptance of their opinions as proof is a more specific use of the experience of the race. It is the natural method of children, who must begin the acquisition of knowledge by believing what their elders tell them. It was for many centuries the method of proof used by wise men, even in matters of natural science. And it is still often our only way of arriving at a judgment about questions too complex or too technical to permit us to draw our own inference from the facts.

3. *To its similarity to other propositions that are admitted or are more easily shown to be true.* This is a still more specific use of experience, for it makes concrete our confidence in the uniformity and consistency of natural laws. The Civil War in America was followed by a period of business depression. Many business men argued, apparently with justice, that a similar period was to be expected after the World War. Even so vague a similarity as is commonly termed analogy is of great value in argument, not because it is in itself convincing, but because it may clarify the principles involved and thus help us to find other sources of proof.

4. *To facts that support it.* Upon such facts, technically called evidence, all proof must ultimately rest. The facts may support the proposition directly, as silent mills, falling prices, and numbers of unemployed are evidences of business depression, or indirectly when they prove the existence of a set of similar circumstances in the past, attest the trustworthiness of an authority, or indicate the existence of a motive which might have prompted an alleged act. For every contention that is not admittted you must

find evidence. Evidence that is not accepted as true must be supported by other evidence until you are able to offer established facts and compelling inferences. The result is proof. It does not beg for acquiescence; it demands acceptance.

96. The Establishment of Evidence. With the exception of the few facts that you are able to observe for yourself you must secure evidence from the observation of others. Such persons are called witnesses, that is, those who know. Their report of the facts is called testimony. The facts obtained from testimony will be useless to you unless you are satisfied that they are true. These facts and those that you have observed for yourself must in the same way be accepted as true by any person whom you wish to convince. To establish the truth of the facts, then, we ask:

1. *Do they come from a trustworthy source?* A printed source may be unworthy of confidence because, like your grandmother's school atlas and dictionary or last summer's railway time-table, it is too old; or because, like an unsupported biography or history written many years after the events that it records, it is not old enough. The medical science to be gleaned from the pages of patent medicine almanacs may possibly be correct but a wise man will ask for a more reputable source of information. For an impartial estimate of the qualities of a man who has just been nominated for the presidency, you would not choose the speeches in the national convention of his party or the biography prepared by the managers of his campaign. In short, you will wish to know that a witness is both able and willing to tell the truth.

2. *Are they consistent?* The facts from one source sometimes contradict each other. If a text-book in one place represents a work as published in 1579 and in other places as published in 1597, you do not accept either date

until you have consulted another book. If a witness testi-
fies that he saw minute details at the moment of an accident and presently says that several minutes elapsed before
he reached the scene, you dismiss all of his evidence as
doubtful. Sometimes the facts are inconsistent with well
established experience. When an imposter announced that
he had discovered the North Pole, a veteran explorer examined his report of his journey and showed that with
the dog-teams and the supplies alleged to have been used
the trip was impossible.

3. *Are they borne out by other facts?* Evidence is
finally tested by other evidence. It is said that Lincoln,
appearing for the defense in a murder case, led on a witness
to a positive assertion that he had been able to see the
crime committed because the moon was shining. When he
produced an almanac and showed that on the night of the
crime the moon did not rise until several hours later, this
piece of evidence not only overthrew the first but also
elicited a new one, an involuntary confession from the per-
jurer. Conflicting testimony is not always so easily solved.
Until, however, it can be clearly shown that the weight
of the evidence is distinctly heavier on one side, it is not
possible to regard the facts as established or as justifying
an inference.

97. The Establishment of Authority. Authority differs
from evidence in that it offers us inferences already made
instead of facts from which to draw our own inferences.
Except when it is used merely to confirm the conclusions
which we have previously reached, the acceptance of authority implies a giving up of some of our own power to
reason about the matter at issue. It should not be resorted
to as a substitute for our own thinking, nor should it receive
more reverence than it merits. The need for authority
and its value depend, therefore, upon:

1. *The nature of the question.* There is no reason for

an appeal to authority in a case in which we are all able to judge for ourselves. What kinds of questions warrant a resort to authoritative opinion?

(*a*) Those in which the evidence is too varied or complex to be presented. Some of the evidence in the question, " Are the Filipinos now ready for full self-government? " could be known and tested only by long and intimate experience in Filipino affairs. The opinion of an observer who is broad-minded enough to consider this evidence judicially would outweigh our own interpretation of the few facts that could be offered to us.

(*b*) Those in which the evidence is too technical to be weighed by persons not specially trained to estimate it. Whether a set of chimes are in perfect tune, or a bridge subjected to heavier traffc than it was designed to bear is really safe are questions in which we defer to experts who are equipped to answer them.

(*c*) Those in which the evidence is so intangible as to be apprehended only by mature wisdom or cultivated tastes. Questions of policy often rest upon such evidence. Will a memorial erected according to these plans produce an artistic structure? Will this play succeed? Should a publisher accept this novel or that? The failure of wise men to answer such questions infallibly illustrates the fact that all argument from authority has to reckon with human frailty.

2. *The attitude of the audience.* An authority is valid only to those who respect it. It will make no difference how much you yourself reverence a source of opinion; if you cannot bring your audience to share your feeling you will gain nothing by citing it. The medieval attitude of credulous and eager acceptance of authorities has given way to a scientific spirit that demands assurance that its confidence is deserved. What kinds of opinion are audiences disposed to regard as authoritative?

(*a*) Those that are consecrated by antiquity. In the absence of disproof we are likely to assume that a reputation that has endured for a long time is not ill-founded. When Senator Douglas appealed to " our fathers who framed this government " as authority on the slavery question, Lincoln did not flout the wisdom of the fathers. He refuted the argument by showing that they really did not hold the views ascribed to them. In the same way contemporary writers who believe that the United States should abandon the policy of isolation yet recognize the authority of Washington and Jefferson in matters of statesmanship and show by the words and deeds of those great leaders that their opposition to " entangling alliances " has been popularly misconceived.

(*b*) Those that are dignified by official position. A judge of the Supreme Court, an officer of an important government bureau, or a teacher on the staff of a reputable university will be heard with respect in his own field of knowledge by persons who know nothing of his attainments. They assume that his fitness for the appointment that he holds has been carefully weighed by others competent to judge. It should be remembered that such a man's opinion outside of his own field is entitled to no special regard.

(*c*) Those whom you can show to have had special opportunities to know and to be well fitted to judge. Persons who had never heard of Lord Bryce might be ready, after hearing a brief account of his varied public service, to give considerable weight to his judgment as to whether the reports of atrocities said to have been committed in a war-wasted country which he had just visited were true or not. In general, however, it is best not to lean heavily upon authorities which will need great justification.

98. The Logic of Proof. No matter how carefully evidence has been sifted and established, it will not give us proof unless the facts are correctly interpreted. They can be interpreted correctly only in accordance with those laws of logic which for many centuries have been recognized as governing the reasoning of normal minds. Such reasoning is classified, traditionally, into two kinds — inductive and deductive.

1. *Inductive reasoning.* Inference by induction recognizes and trusts the uniformity of nature. There is a logic in things which permits us to think of them in classes and from our knowledge of particular members of a class to leap to knowledge of all the others. This method of acquiring new general knowledge is a process sometimes called generalization. It may be studied in three forms, differing according to the nature of the particulars from which it proceeds.

(*a*) From specific instances. Long before it occurred to men to analyze the reasoning process they made free use of the method of generalization. From observing the habits of a few animals they learned how to overcome or domesticate many others. By studying the phenomena of nature, often in absurd ignorance of their causes, they laid the foundations of modern science. Their experience among men they generalized into a knowledge of human nature, such as is summed up in proverbs like " Willful waste makes woeful want " or " Pride goeth before a fall." This same process, by which we turn specific instances into general principles merely by observing enough of them to give us confidence in our judgments, still gives us much of our knowledge in science as well as in everyday affairs.

(*b*) From parallel cases. Another type of reasoning from particulars — variously named and defined — is that which, instead of forming a general rule and applying it where it seems to fit, takes a short-cut from one particular to another. It assumes that if two things are similar in one respect they may be expected to be similar in others.

Obviously this is not a safe conclusion unless the two things are closely parallel, and in such a case the general rule which governs both can usually be discerned. If I argue that I can complete a four-year course in three years because B has done it, I shall probably be asked whether I am his equal in preparation and general capacity. If I can answer yes, it may still be well to inquire whether it is safe to assume from one case the rule, Students so equipped can reasonably expect to complete the work in three years; and this leads me back to the search for other specific instances. Yet the possibility of pointing to B has been of great value, for he makes the problem concrete. In this function of illuminating a question by exhibiting the principle under other circumstances, argument from parallels takes various forms. In fables, long used for purposes of instruction, the principle is all the clearer because the story is obviously unreal. In proverbs, which strive to concentrate wisdom and put it to homely uses, the principle is brought out sharply. The pitcher that goes to the well, the eggs counted before they are hatched, the stitch in time that saves nine have little value as proof but a great deal of force as means of giving form to a vaguely felt general law.

(c) From the relation of cause and effect. The phenomena about which we may have occasion to argue are bound together, not only by those laws of class and kind which, as we have seen, enable us to trust generalizations, but also by laws of cause and effect. The most valuable form of induction is that which leads to certainty about these laws. For our knowledge of a thing is imperfect so long as we are ignorant as to its cause or causes and its effects. We may imagine a medieval scientist interested in the phenomena of combustion. From specific instances he asserts that wood will burn and iron will not. From a parallel case — the behavior of fermented liquids — he perhaps concludes that since there is in wine a volatile fluid called spirit of wine that can be separated from it by distillation, there may very likely be in materials that will burn a similar spirit of fire. He gives this substance a name, phlogiston, and endeavors to isolate it. It is only when we begin to learn something as to the cause of burning that we see that both of his inductions are false — that under certain circumstances iron will burn as readily as wood and that the analogy between alcoholic fluids and combustibles is faulty. The methods by which induction as to cause and effect are made and tested are the following:

1. The method of agreement. If the circumstances which always precede a phenomenon agree in only one particular, that particular is probably its cause.

When A B C D E are present the effect X follows.
When A G H I J K " " " " " "
When A R S T U V " " " " " "

In this case we conclude that since the three circumstances agree in A, and only in A, there must be causal relation between A and X. If our scientist found that a substance would burn in each of several different gaseous compounds which agreed only in having oxygen as a constituent he would suspect that oxygen had something to do with the burning. A wedding supper at which raw oysters were served was followed by the illness from typhoid fever of seven of the guests. It was found that all of these seven had eaten raw oysters and that there was no other uncooked food which they had all taken. The conclusion that the oysters were infected was confirmed by an examination of their source.

2. The method of difference. If the circumstances under which a phenomenon occurs and those under which it is lacking differ regularly in only one particular, that particular is probably its cause.

When $A\ B\ C\ D\ E$ are present X follows.

When $O\ B\ C\ D\ E$ "   " X does not follow.

If it is invariably true that X fails to occur whenever A is absent, no matter what other letters appear, we feel certain that there is a causal relation between A and X. If our scientist found that a compound of gases which would support combustion when a certain quantity of oxygen was included in it would never support combustion when the oxygen was withdrawn, he would suspect causal relation between oxygen and combustion.

3. The joint method of agreement and difference. The two methods may be combined to give increased validity to the conclusion, if two or more instances in which the phenomenon occurs agree only in one particular and two or more instances in which it is lacking agree only in its absence.

When $A\ B\ C\ D\ E$ are present X follows.

   " $A\ M\ N\ O\ R$ "   " X "

   " $A\ S\ T\ U\ V$ "   " X "

and

When $B\ C\ D\ E$ are present X is wanting.

   " $H\ M\ J\ K\ L$ "   " X "   "

   " $S\ T\ U\ V\ R$ "   " X "   "

In these circumstances A is the cause, or the result, of X.

4. The method of residues. If several causes probably contribute to a single result, that part of the effect which is due to any one cause is found by subtracting all the other causes. If $A\ B\ C\ D$ have contributed to produce the effect ed and it can be shown that $A\ B\ C$ together are responsible for e we are certain that D is the cause of d. The census shows that a town has gained twenty-five per cent in population. The growth is due chiefly to three factors — the action of a railroad company in estab-

lishing division headquarters there, a campaign to bring new industries, and the normal increase in population. The number of families affected by the first is known, the third can be estimated by comparison with certain other towns; what remains is to be attributed to the industrial campaign.

5. The method of concomitant variations. If two sets of circumstances which we can measure are found to vary correspondingly, we are confident that a causal relation exists between them. If it is learned by experiment that a combination of gases will support combustion better or worse in the precise degree in which the percentage of oxygen is raised or lowered, we are doubly sure of a causal connection between the presence of oxygen and the phenomenon of burning.

2. *Deductive reasoning.* Inference by deduction is based upon the certainty of known classifications. Accumulated experience has given us many generalizations which have proved true. We trust them and use them in particular cases. Induction leads us in from particular circumstances to the general rule; deduction leads us out from a general rule to particulars that come under it. The general knowledge which we apply in deduction may exist in various forms — in definitions which we accept, as when we say, Mr. B is a successful man; in recognized qualities, as when we say, This is a good apple; in accepted laws of cause and effect, as when we say, Your room will soon be comfortable, for I have turned on the heat.

Most of our deductive reasoning is expressed informally, often without any clear recognition of the precise nature of the general knowledge from which we start. When it is desirable to exhibit or test the logic of a deduction, however, we put it into the form of a syllogism. A deductive syllogism is a two-fold classification — a bringing together of two propositions which when combined make certain the truth of a third. A typical syllogism is represented by the formula

All <i>A</i>'s are <i>B</i>'s
All <i>C</i>'s are <i>A</i>'s
All <i>C</i>'s are <i>B</i>'s

The three propositions contain three terms <i>A, B,</i> and <i>C.</i> Of these <i>B</i> is the major term (the larger class); <i>C</i> is the minor term (the smaller class); and <i>A</i> is the middle term (the class that serves as a medium and is not named in the conclusion). The first propostion, which contains the major term, is the major premise; the second, which contains the minor term, is the minor premise. Expressed in an argument this syllogism may be represented by

All *articles guaranteed by Jones* are *well-made articles.*
All *" Wing "* *bicycles* are *articles guaranteed by Jones.*
All *" Wing "* *bicycles* are *well-made articles.*

In ordinary use such reasoning would probably be incomplete, in what the logicians call an enthymeme; for example,

You will find those " Wing " bicycles well-made; Jones guarantees them; or
Get a " Wing " bicycle; everything that Jones guarantees is well-made.

The various forms of the syllogism are too complex for explanation here. The rules which determine its validity may be summarized as follows:

(*a*) There must be three and only three terms.

All <i>A</i>'s are <i>B</i>'s
All <i>B</i>'s are <i>A</i>'s (not valid)
Some <i>B</i>'s are <i>A</i>'s (valid but no addition to our knowledge).

All <i>A</i>'s are <i>B</i>'s
All <i>X</i>'s are <i>AR</i>'s
All <i>X</i>'s are <i>B</i>'s (not valid).

(*b*) There must be three propositions.

(*c*) The middle term must be distributed at least once; that is, an assertion about all members of the class must be made in at least one premise.

All *A*'s are *B*'s; i.e. are some of *B*'s
All *X*'s are *B*'s; i.e. are some of *B*'s
All *A*'s are *X*'s (not valid).

(*d*) A term may not be distributed in the conclusion unless it is distributed in one of the premises.

All *A*'s are *B*'s
Some *X*'s are *A*'s (*X* is not distributed)
Some *X*'s are *B*'s (valid, but all *X*'s are *B*'s is not valid).

All *A*'s are *B*'s (i.e. are some of *B*'s; *B* not distributed)
No *X*'s are *A*'s
No *X*'s are *B*'s (invalid for *B* is distributed by the negative).

(*e*) No conclusions may be drawn from two negative premises.

(*f*) If one premise is negative the conclusion must be negative.

All *A*'s are *B*'s	No *A*'s are *B*'s
No *X*'s are *B*'s	All *X*'s are *A*'s
No *X*'s are *A*'s (valid).	No *X*'s are *B*'s (valid).

PERSUASION

99. The Method of Persuasion. Proof is not dependent on a reader or hearer. A scientist reasoning out the significance of his experiments may prove his theory correct without thinking of his argument as addressed to any other mind than his own. When it is addressed to others his problem is the same as that of exposition — to make the matter clear. Your proof is none the less valid because a stubborn hearer refuses to admit its validity; but if your success depends on your influencing this stubborn hearer you have not necessarily succeeded when he admits your contention. He may still refuse to act as it prescribes. You must turn your attention, therefore, to the person whom your reasoning is designed to affect. The method of persuasion requires the discovery of means of winning and holding the attention of the person addressed and of inducing him to believe and to act as you desire. To do this three conditions are ordinarily essential:

1. *You must find common ground with him.* Before you undertake to change his attitude toward the matter at issue, it will be well to ask what are the things about which you and he already feel alike. As proof goes back ultimately to admitted propositions, persuasion goes back to a community of feeling and interest. A man who is wholly out of sympathy with your plans for a certain charity and who dislikes and distrusts the persons at the head of it probably shares with you your pity for suffering children. It is on that common ground only that you can hope to influence him. If a teacher wants to stir a feeling of patriotism in a boy who has been taught to hate the symbols of nationalism, and who ardently believes in the ideals of soviet government, she will be wise to ask herself what loyalties he has in which she can join.

2. *You must offer him a vital choice.* Unless the person to whom persuasion is addressed is free to act, appeal to him is futile. If the choice that is open to him is a matter of indifference, if it can be deferred without loss or evaded with ease, if the responsibility for not making it seems to him a trifling matter, you will not easily secure the kind of acquiescence that you want.

3. *You must discover a tangible motive.* He will act only in obedience to an impulse strong enough to overcome inertia and, if necessary, opposition. Before you undertake to set such an impulse in motion you will do well to

ask yourself what things he desires, what obligations he recognizes, whose good opinion he covets, and whose censure he fears. If you want a man to join your society, study the man as well as the inducement that you have to offer him.

Persuasion involves three processes, sufficiently distinct to deserve separate discussion. They are technically known as conciliation, enlistment, and excitation. In some speeches they seem to stand in the relation of introduction, body, and conclusion; but they are not merely structural elements. A speech may consist throughout of any one of three and when all are used they may be interrelated without reference to structure.

100. Conciliation. The purpose of conciliation is to secure a fair hearing. It is preliminary to an appeal to those motives that you have decided upon as most effective. Attention must first be won and whatever stands in the way of persuasion must be removed. The aims of conciliation, then, are:

1. *To Remove Prejudice.*

(*a*) Against the subject. Suppose that the person whom you wish to persuade is saying to himself, " I know what he wants and I am not going to do it! " If you try to browbeat him out of his opposition you may only increase it. If this hostility is really prejudice, it rests on an insecure foundation. You will ordinarily be wise, therefore, to turn aside from the precise point of his objection and seek broader ground. Men take pride in being open-minded and many prejudiced persons honestly believe that they are fair. Do not accuse them of prejudging your case; but show that it has other aspects than that which evokes their hostility and lead them gradually to a willingness to hear you.

(*b*) Against the speaker. The speaker is always in a sense on trial. He has been given the floor; what is he going to do with it? A speaker who is unknown may count on a certain aloofness even from an audience naturally well-disposed. It is necesssary for him to break the ice. When he faces an audience that distrusts him or the class to which he belongs, he must disarm their hostility before he can hope for a favorable hearing. He should be modest without truckling. An audience resents an assumption of superiority and instinctively recognizes and dislikes egotism. Yet it admires frankness and sincerity. The speaker should be scrupulously fair. Don't expect your hearers to give up their prejudice if you are obviously prejudiced yourself. Since it is your subject that you are really concerned about, turn the thoughts of the audience away from yourself as soon as you can and make them think of your cause instead. Webster, in the opening sentences of his speech in the White murder case, skilfully parries an attempt to use prejudice against him, and merges his identity in the prosecution of the crime.

2. *To Remove Apathy.* An audience that is indifferent must be stirred by a new interest. Such indifference may be counted on from persons who are tired or uncomfortable. An appeal that follows a number of other speeches or comes at the end of a day's work should be made with such freshness and vigor as to challenge attention. Force your audience to form mental images, that is, be concrete. If possible pique their curiosity, but be sure that you can satisfy it. In general remember that the pathway to attention is through feelings and that the avenue to feelings is through sensations.

101. Enlistment. Conciliation makes the hearer willing to listen and disposed to be fair with you. Enlistment is getting him on your side. Having won a hearing how shall you hold his attention until his feelings begin to be exerted in the direction that you suggest to him and he begins to wish to do what you advocate? The secret of doing this is not, of course, to be learned from rules; but a few general suggestions may be offered.

1. *For taking hold of interest.* The first element in enlistment is a subtle seizure of the interest of your hearer. He finds himself lost in the matter to the exclusion of other things. The choice that you hold out to him is no longer obscured by distractions, and possible objections do not easily obtrude themselves. For accomplishing this use:

(*a*) The familiar as a starting point. Give him the pleasure of recognition, of feeling that he belongs. When he says " That's right! I know that! " you have made a beginning in enlistment. A classic example of this device is Paul's most famous speech, which begins with an allusion to an altar that must have been familiar to every one present (Acts XVII, 23).

(*b*) The concrete before the abstract. The order of explanation is sometimes the reverse. But enlistment will go best from what is tangible to what must be grasped only by the mind. When Charles Dickens has an appeal to make for the support of a hospital for sick children, he begins with one sick child. A successful salesman realizes the value of getting a difficult customer to agree with him about a concrete object before he talks with him about such articles in general.

(*c*) The striking or unexpected turn of thought. Interest is stimulated by an unforeseen assault upon the attention. It is well to begin with the familiar; but you will want to pass beyond it and to make your hearer say, " True, I never thought of that! " This is sometimes effectively done by turning a familiar phrase into an unexpected meaning, as Paine does in showing that the remark " Give me peace in my day " is an unfatherly expression.

2. *For stirring emotion.* As has already been made

clear, the core of persuasion is the successful appeal to
feeling. When I begin to want something, to pity somebody, to be angry about something, I have enlisted among
those who will do what such feelings dictate. To reach
the emotions of a reader or hearer, you may use:

(*a*) The typical specific case. Generalizations do not
make us feel keenly. Actual suffering will arouse more
pity than a description of suffering. A description of a
single case of distress will, in much the same way, stir us
far more than the general statement that such and such
misery exists. As Dickens uses the single child and Paine
the incident of the inn-keeper and his little son, you can
give effectiveness by the use of specific examples in preference to abstractions.

(*b*) Authority. We have seen that the value of authority as a means of proof is necessarily limited. As a
source of persuasion it is often far more forcible. For the
reverence which supports an authority is a favorable mood
for persuasion. The personality of " our fathers who
founded this government " reinforces the logical strength
of their position.

(*c*) Contrast. A marked contrast heightens reality, and
reality is the clue to feeling. Paradox may easily be overdone; but within its limits it illustrates the stimulus which
can be given to the imagination by the sudden bringing
together of extremes.

102. Excitation. The final test of persuasion is its
power to take advantage of what it has won. Excitation
is the lash that drives into action. Its place is naturally
at the climax of an appeal and its style is necessarily swift
and vivid. The skilled speaker knows when to stop; he
does not endanger his success by wearying his hearers but
drives home his final point and leaves his words free to
produce their effect. The subject-matter of excitation is
not necessarily different from that of enlistment. It differs

rather in mood, and makes use of various devices for heightening emotional effect. Some of these devices are:

1. *Irony.* Like any other play upon the meaning of words irony stimulates attention. Effectively employed it does more, for it challenges feeling. " You're a fine representative of the chapter!" you may say to a lazy and indifferent chum; " It is a splendid advertisment for a team to have a reputation for not keeping their word! " you argue in a discussion on an athletic policy; and the sarcastic phrases sting.

2. *Question.* The direct question is useful to bring an issue home. It forces the choice upon the attention of a hearer as no amount of assertion can do. For excitation, however, the rhetorical question is more valuable. It is a vivid form of assertion that compels an emotional response. " Do you want to be the only member of the chapter who hasn't done something worth while? " you ask a student. " Are we indifferent to our reputation abroad? " you ask an audience. In either case you set in motion the impulse to answer no.

3. *Iteration.* A word or phrase persistently repeated burns its way into our thought and persists. The repetition gains also the effect of climax. In fact, if it doesn't produce a climax it may grow wearisome and defeat its purpose. Modern advertising is full of instances of the effective repetition of names and phrases.

4. *Command.* A sudden turn to direct command is often a valuable means of excitation. " Go! " carries more force than " You ought to go! " The vocative must not be overdone, however; if you exhort constantly exhortation will cease to have any meaning.

Specimens of Argumentation

I

Democracy and Peace

A steadfast concert for peace can never be maintained except by a partnership of democratic nations. No autocratic government could be trusted to keep faith within it or observe its covenants. It must be a league of honor, a partnership of opinion. Intrigue would eat its vitals away; the plottings of inner circles who could plan what they would and render account to no one would be a corruption seated at its very heart. Only free peoples can hold their purpose and their honor steady to a common end and prefer the interests of mankind to any narrow interests of their own.

— Woodrow Wilson.

II

Was it a Thief?

Was it a thief who had taken the bags? or was it a cruel power that no hands could reach, which had delighted in making him a second time desolate? He shrank from this vaguer dread, and fixed his mind with struggling effort on the robber with hands, who could be reached by hands. His thoughts glanced at all the neighbors who had made any remarks, or asked any questions which he might now regard as a ground of suspicion. There was Jem Rodney, a known poacher, and otherwise disreputable: he had often met Marner in his journeys across the fields, and had said something jestingly about the weaver's money; nay, he had once irritated Marner, by lingering at the fire when he called to light his pipe, instead of going about his business. Jem Rodney was the man. — George Eliot in *Silas Marner*.

III

Cats and Pansies

I am tempted to give one more instance showing how plants and animals remote in the scale of nature are bound together by a web of complex relations. . . . Nearly all our orchidaceous plants absolutely require the visits of insects to remove their pollen-masses and thus to fertilize them. I find from experiment that humble-bees are almost indispensable to the fertilization of the heartsease (Viola tricolor), for other bees do not visit this flower. I have also found that the visits of bees are necessary for the fertilization of some kinds of clover. . . . Humble-bees alone visit red clover, as other bees cannot reach the nectar. . . . Hence we may infer as highly probable that, if the whole genus of bumble-bees became extinct or very rare in England, the heartsease and red clover would become very rare, or wholly disappear. The number of bumble-bees in any district depends in a great measure on the number of field-mice, which destroy their combs and nests; and Col. Newman, who has long attended to the habits of bumble-bees, believes that "more than two-thirds of them are thus destroyed all over England." Now, the number of mice is largely dependent, as every one knows, on the number of cats; and Col. Newman says: "Near villages and small towns I have found the nests of bumble-bees more numerous than elsewhere, which I attribute to the number of cats that destroy the mice." Hence it is quite credible that the presence of a feline animal in large numbers in a district might determine, through the intervention first of mice and then of bees, the frequency of certain flowers in that district. — CHARLES DARWIN in *The Origin of Species,* 1859.

IV

THE WINDOWS IN THE RUE MORGUE

The murderers *did* escape from one of these windows. This being so, they could not have refastened the sashes from the inside, as they were found fastened; — the consideration which put a stop, through its obviousness, to the scrutiny of the police in this quarter. Yet the sashes *were* fastened. They *must,* then, have the power of fastening themselves. There was no escape from this conclusion. I stepped to the unobstructed casement, withdrew the nail with some difficulty, and attempted to raise the sash. It resisted all my efforts, as I had anticipated. A concealed spring must, I now knew, exist; and this corroboration of my idea convinced me that my premises, at least, were correct, however mysterious still appeared the circumstances attending the nails. A careful search soon brought to light the hidden spring. I pressed it, and, satisfied with the discovery, forebore to upraise the sash. I now replaced the nail and regarded it attentively. A person passing out through this window might have reclosed it, and the spring would have caught — but the nail could not have been replaced. The conclusion was plain, and again narrowed in the field of my investigations. The assassins *must* have escaped through the other window. — EDGAR ALLAN POE in *The Murders in the Rue Morgue.*

V

TO THE JURY

I am little accustomed, Gentlemen, to the part which I am now attempting to perform. Hardly more than once or twice has it happened to me to be concerned on the side of the government in any criminal prosecution whatever; and never, until the present occasion, in any case affecting life.

But I very much regret that it should have been thought necessary to suggest to you that I was brought here to "hurry you against the law and beyond the evidence." I hope I have too much regard for justice, and too much respect for my own character, to attempt either; and were I to make such attempt, I am sure that in this court nothing can be carried against the law, and that gentlemen, as intelligent and just as you are, are not, by any power, to be hurried beyond the evidence. Though I could well have wished to shun this occasion, I have not felt at liberty to withhold my professional assistance, when it is supposed that I may be in some degree useful in investigating and discovering the truth respecting this most extraordinary murder. It has seemed a duty incumbent on me, as on every other citizen, to do my best and my utmost to bring to light the perpetrators of this crime. Against the prisoner at the bar, as an individual, I cannot have the slightest prejudice. I would not do him the slightest injustice or injury. But I do not affect to be indifferent to the discovery and the punishment of this deep guilt. I cheerfully share in the opprobrium, how great soever it may be, which is cast upon those who feel and manifest an anxious concern that all who had a part in the planning, or a hand in executing, this deed of midnight assassination, may be brought to answer for their enormous crime at the bar of public justice. — DANIEL WEBSTER in his address to the jury in *The Knapp Murder Trial.*

VI

PEACE IN MY DAY!

I once felt that kind of anger, which a man ought to feel, against the mean principles that are held by the Tories; a noted one, who kept a tavern at Amboy, was standing at his door, with as pretty a child in his hand, about eight or nine years old, as ever I saw, and after speaking his mind as freely as he thought was prudent, finished with this unfatherly expression, " Well! give me peace in my day."   Not a man lives on the continent but fully believes that a separation must some time or other finally take place, and a generous parent should have said, " If there must be trouble, let it be in my day, that my child may have peace "; and this single reflection, well applied, is sufficient to waken every man to his duty. Not a place upon earth might be so happy as America.   Her situation is remote from all the wrangling world, and she has nothing to do but to trade with them.   A man can distinguish himself between temper and principle, and I am as confident as I am that God governs the world that America will never be happy till she gets clear of this foreign dominion.   Wars without ceasing will break out till that period arrives, and the continent must in the end be conqueror, for though the flame of liberty may sometimes ceases to shine, the coal can never expire. — THOMAS PAINE in *The Crisis.*

VII

THE MURDERERS OF LOVEJOY

A comparison has been drawn between the events of the Revolution and the tragedy at Alton.   We have heard it asserted here, in Faneuil Hall, that Great Britain had a right to tax the colonies, and we have heard the mob at Alton, the drunken murderers of Lovejoy, compared to those patriot fathers who threw the tea overboard!   Fellow citizens, is this Faneuil Hall doctrine?   The mob at Alton were met to wrest from a citizen his just rights, — met to resist the laws.   We have been told that our fathers did the same; and the glorious mantle of Revolutionary precedent has been thrown over the mobs of our day.   To make out their title to such defence, the gentleman says that the British Parliament had a right to tax these Colonies.   It is manifest that, without this, his parallel falls to the ground, for Lovejoy had stationed himself within con-

stitutional bulwarks. He was not only defending the freedom of
the press, but he was under his own roof, in arms with the sanction
of the civil authority. The men who assailed him went against and
over the laws; the *mob*, as the gentleman terms it, mob, forsooth!
certainly we sons of the tea-spillers are a marvelously patient
generation! the orderly mob which assembled in the Old South
to destroy the tea were met to resist, not the laws, but illegal
exactions. Shame on the American who calls the tea-tax and the
stamp-act *laws!* Our fathers resisted, not the King's prerogative,
but the King's usurpation. To find any other account, you must
read our Revolutionary archives upside down. Our State Archives
are loaded with arguments of John Adams to prove the taxes laid
by the British Parliament unconstitutional — beyond its power.
It was not till this was made out that the men of New England
rushed to arms. The arguments of the Council Chamber and the
House of Representatives preceded and sanctioned the contest. To
draw the conduct of our ancestors into a precedent for mobs, for
a right to resist laws we ourselves have enacted, is an insult to
their memory. The difference between the excitements of those
days and our own, which the gentleman in kindness to the latter
has overlooked, is simply this: the men of that day went for the
right as secured by the laws. They were the people rising to sustain the laws and constitution of the Province. The rioters of
our day go for their own wills, right or wrong. Sir, when I heard
the gentleman lay down principles which place the murderers of
Alton side by side with Otis and Hancock, with Quincy and Adams,
I thought those pictured lips [*pointing to portraits in the hall*]
would have broken into voice to rebuke that recreant American,
the slanderer of the dead. The gentleman said he should sink into
insignificance if he dared to gainsay the principles of these resolutions. Sir, for the sentiments he has uttered, on soil consecrated
by the prayers of Puritans and the blood of patriots, the earth
should have yawned and swallowed him up. — WENDELL PHILLIPS
in *The Murder of Lovejoy*.

VIII

A SICK CHILD

Some years ago, being in Scotland, I went with one of the most
humane members of the humane medical profession, on a morning
tour among some of the worst-lodged inhabitants of the old town

of Edinburgh. In the closes and wynds of that picturesque place
— I am sorry to remind you what fast friends picturesqueness and
typhus often are — we saw more poverty and sickness in an hour
than many people would believe in a life. Our way lay from one
to another of the most wretched dwellings, reeking with horrible
odors, shut out from the sky, shut out from the air, mere pits and
dens. In a room in one of these places, where there was an empty
porridge pot on the cold hearth, with a ragged woman and some
ragged children crouching on the bare ground near it — where, I
remember, — as I speak, that the very light, refracted from a high,
damp-stained and time-stained house wall, came trembling in, as
if the fever which had shaken everything else there had shaken
even it — there lay, in an old egg-box which the mother had begged
from a shop, a little, feeble, wasted, wan, sick child, with his little
wasted face, and his little hot, worn hands folded over his breast,
and his little bright, attentive eyes looking steadily at us. I can
see him now, as I have seen him for several years: there he lay
in his little frail box which was not at all a bad emblem of the
little body from which he was slowly parting — there he lay, quite
quiet, quite patient, saying never a word. He seldom cried, the
mother said; he seldom complained; " he lay there, seemin' to
woonder what it was a' aboot." God knows, I thought, as I stood
looking at him, he had his reasons for wondering — reasons for
wondering how it could possibly come to be that he lay there, left
alone, feeble and full of pain, when he ought to have been as bright
and as brisk as the birds that never got near him — reasons for
wondering how he came to be left there, a little decrepit old man
pining to death, quite a thing of course, as if there were no crowds
of healthy and happy children playing on the grass under the summer's sun within a stone's throw of him; as if there were no bright
moving sea on the other side of the great hill overhanging the city;
as if there were no great clouds rushing over it; as if there were
no life, and no movement, and vigor anywhere in the world —
nothing but stoppage and decay. There he lay looking at us, saying, in his silence, more pathetically than I have ever heard anything said by any orator in my life, " Will you please to tell me
what this means, strange man? and if you can give me any good
reason why I should be so soon so far advanced on my way to Him
who said that children were to come into His presence, and were
not to be forbidden, but who scarcely meant, I think, that they
should come by this hard road by which I am travelling; pray give
that reason to me, for I seek it very earnestly; and wonder about

it very much "; and to my mind he has been wondering about it ever since. Many a poor child, sick and neglected, I have seen since that time in London; many a poor sick child I have seen most affectionately and kindly tended by poor people, in an unwholesome house and under untoward circumstances, wherein its recovery was quite impossible; but at all such times I have seen my poor little drooping friend in his egg-box, and he has always addressed his dumb speech to me, and I have always found him wondering what it meant, and why, in the name of a gracious God, such things should be! — CHARLES DICKENS in a speech in behalf of a hospital for children. Reprinted in full in Knapp and French: *The Speech for Special Occasions.*

EXERCISES IN ARGUMENTATION

1. Suppose that, like Rip Van Winkle, you had just waked from a long sleep and had returned to the campus. From what evidence, as you looked about, could you draw an inference as to the season of the year?

2. Is a voter who has declared his affiliation with a political party and has voted in its primary election under any moral obligation to support that party in the general election? To what sources can you turn for arguments on this question? Test it by asking the opinions of three persons and noting their reasons.

3. Find in this argument examples of deductive and inductive reasoning. Frame two deductive syllogisms. Comment on the validity of the reasoning.

It would be profitable for the baseball clubs engaged in the world's championship series to make the contests as nearly even as possible so that all or nearly all of the seven games would have to be played, for the gate receipts would thus be increased. Do they thus manipulate the games? They obviously do not. Out of nineteen such contests only two reached a tie of 3 to 3, and only one other was won by a margin of one game. Exclusive of these three contests, the total number of games won by the losers of the series was only 23 against 79 won by the final champions. Why do they not? Because it wouldn't pay. So many persons would have to be included in the plot to "throw" the games that it would be sure to leak out. Once known it would destroy all interest in the series. The magnates are too shrewd to kill the goose that lays the golden egg.

4. Estimate the relative value of the facts reported below and give reasons for your conclusion.

A reputable merchant was accused of attempted arson. It was shown at the trial that he was heavily insured, and that his creditors were pressing him for money. A and B testified, their evidence agreeing in every detail, that they actually saw him apply the torch. A pile of charred rags was afterwards discovered in a corner of the building. The fire marshal testified that a blaze arising at that point could only have been of incendiary origin.

The defence showed that A was a discharged employe of the merchant, and that B was known to harbor a grudge against him, and had a bad record. An oil-can found in the alley after the fire was identified as A's property. On cross-examination A gave an unsatisfactory account of his actions previous to the breaking out of the fire.

5. Make a simple outline of this speech, arranging the arguments in the order that seems to you best.

A disinterested speaker addresses a body of miners who are about to strike for better wages. He believes the strike to be unwise, and wishes to overcome a strong feeling in favor of it. He appeals to them not to strike, for as cold weather is coming on loss of work will cause much misery. "Half a loaf," he says, "is better than no bread." Moreover, the strike will fail, for the operators have a good supply of coal on hand, too few miners are involved, and non-union workers will take their places. He reminds them that a similar strike two years previous proved disastrous — and points out that the operators, having wealth and power on their side, can afford to starve their opponents out by waiting.

6. Write the following speech.

What should Tom do? He is eighteen and about to graduate from high school. His mother is a widow, not dependent on him for support but unable to help him. He has inherited $2000 from an aunt. He is offered a $20-a-week job. He is in love with

Marjorie. You think him well-fitted for the profession that you are preparing for. Persuade him to make the sacrifices necessary to permit him to come to college and lay the foundation for professional work.

7. Reproduce the following in dialogue form.

Your roommate played football in high school with marked success but refuses to come out for the college team because his mother has asked him not to play. Her fear that he may be injured is based upon the fact that an untrained lad, too light for the sport, was permanently crippled by a football accident in her neighborhood. The coach asks you to endeavor to persuade her to withdraw her objection.

REFERENCES

1. To Text-books: *The Making of Arguments* by J. H. Gardiner (Ginn); *The Art of Debate* by R. M. Alden (Holt); *Argumentation* by G. K. Pattee (Century); *Argumentation and Debate* by Laycock and Scales (Macmillan); *Argumentation and Debating* by W. T. Foster (Houghton Mifflin); *The Art of Debate* by W. C. Shaw (Allyn and Bacon).

2. To Specimens: *Specimens of Exposition and Argument* by Percival and Jelliffe (Macmillan); *Argumentation and Debate* by J. V. Denny and Others (American Book Co.); *Masterpieces of Modern Oratory* by E. D. Shurter (Ginn); *The Lincoln and Douglas Debates* by A. L. Bouton (Holt).

PART TWO

USAGE

CHAPTER X

USAGE IN GRAMMAR AND IDIOM

103. The Value of Grammar. A college student should know English grammar in an orderly and systematic way, not because he cannot avoid errors without it, but because grammar makes him a more competent critic of his own work. His knowledge of English grammar helps him to translate foreign tongues, to comprehend and appreciate English poetry, to read aloud, and to analyze swiftly and accurately his own thought and the thought of others. He should not be content with that vague sense of grammatical relations which everybody who can read and write must possess, for a dull feeling for syntax is likely to go hand in hand with slow and clumsy reading and with feeble, though not necessarily incorrect, writing.

To provide means for such a rapid review as many college students need and to supply a set of terms to be employed in the correction of themes, this chapter takes the form of an outline of English grammar in which the forms recommended by the Committee on Grammatical Nomenclature have been adopted. A student who finds a survey of the subject inadequate should study one of the text-books of grammar mentioned among the references.

104. The Parts of Speech. Every word belongs to one of eight classes called parts of speech, namely, nouns, verbs, adjectives, adverbs, pronouns, prepositions, conjunctions, and interjections. These classes represent not so much kinds of words as kinds of functions in connected writing. It will be noticed that they fall into two groups — idea words, which present to the mind concepts of their own, and are used for what they themselves mean; and relation words, which exist to enable us to build other words into coherent speech.

IDEA WORDS

Nouns: naming words (Latin *nomen*, a name).

Verbs: asserting or asking words (*verbum*, a word).

Adjectives: attributing words (*ad + jectum*, thrown at).

Adverbs: qualifying words, used to modify verbs, adjectives, and adverbs (*ad + verbum*).

Interjections: words expressing sudden emotion (*inter + jectum*, thrown in between).

These idea words are the pictorial element of one's vocabulary, the substantial material of speech. Their functions of naming, asserting, and qualifying are readily passed from one part of speech to another, so that English usage does not hesitate to make verbs of nouns, nouns of verbs, or either out of adjectives and adverbs. The same functions are given to groups of words; phrases and clauses perform in a sentence the parts of nouns, adjectives, or adverbs.

RELATION WORDS

Pronouns: words that name relatively or as substitutes (*pro + nomen*).

Prepositions: connectives that relate part to part (*praepositum*, placed before).

Conjunctions: connectives that link part and part (*conjugum*, a yoking together).

Relation words furnish the analytic element in our vocabulary. Note the part that they play in the words made famous by Lincoln: " that government of the people, by the people, for the people, shall not perish from the earth." What does government *of the people* mean? Is it merely objective, meaning that the people are governed, or does the preposition make the two idea words mean a government springing from the people, natural to them and not alien, devised by them and not forced upon them?

Nouns

Distinguish a common noun, which names any member of a class, *city,* and a proper noun, which names an individual specifically, *Baltimore,* because proper nouns (and groups of words constituting proper names) are capitalized. Remember that a collective noun, *crowd,* may be either singular or plural. Nouns, pronouns, and any words or groups of words used in a sentence to serve as nouns are called substantives.

Verbs

To use a verb correctly you must know those forms, important because from them all other forms can be inferred, known as its principal parts: present tense, past tense, past participle. Verbs and verb-forms are classified as follows:

1. As to conjugation: Weak verbs, those having the past tense and past participle alike and formed by adding -ed, -d, or -t: *walk, walked, walked; send, sent, sent.*

Strong verbs, those having the past tense formed by a vowel variation and not by an inflectional ending: *ride, rode, ridden; drink, drank, drunk.* Notice that the vowel of the past tense always differs from that of the present.

The strong verbs, once as numerous as weak verbs, are now a limited class. They are nearly all of native, that is, old English origin and are chiefly monosyllabic. Newly coined or borrowed verbs are weak. You must know the principal parts of the strong verbs. The dictionary will always supply them.

All verbs in either conjugation are (*a*) transitive, taking an object or (*b*) intransitive, taking no object. A few verbs, having no personal subject, are called impersonal verbs; for example, It *is raining*. Do as *seems* best. A verb form is singular or plural. The verb is in the active voice if the subject acts (I *helped* a friend); it is in the passive voice if the subject is acted upon (I *was helped* by a friend). In mood a verb form is (*a*) indicative, expressing unqualified assertion (I *was sure*), (*b*) imperative, expressing a command or entreaty (Be *sure*), or (*c*) subjunctive, expressing doubt (If I *were sure* . . .).

2. As to predication.

Finite: all verb forms that are able to show variations in mood or to serve as the predicate of a sentence. Hence all verb forms except those known as, non-modal, not finite:

Infinitive: to *know*. I dare *say*.

Gerund: a verbal noun sharing the functions of both noun and verb. The joy of *knowing* the truth.

Participle: a verbal adjective, able to govern an object and to modify a substantive. We, *knowing* the truth of the matter, could not be deceived.

3. As to tense:

Present, I *know*. He *knows*.

Past, I *knew*.

Future, I *shall know*. He *will know*.

Present Perfect, I *have known*.

Past Perfect, I *had known*.

Future Perfect, I *shall have known*. He *will have known*.

Past Future, I *should know*. He *would know*.

Past Future Perfect, I *should have known*. He *would have known*.

Adjectives

1. As to function: Adjectives are descriptive or limiting. A descriptive adjective attributes a quality or a condition to the substantive to which it belongs. Such an adjective is, like a noun, either common or proper, and a proper adjective is capitalized. A limiting adjective does not describe, but rather identifies or limits, the term to which it is applied.

Limiting adjectives are,

Articles: definite, *the;* indefinite, *a,* or *an.* Use *an* before a vowel sound or an unaccented initial syllable beginning with h. *An* historical novel. *A* history.

Pronominal (also called adjective pronouns):
  Possessive: such as *my* friend, *his* house.
  Demonstrative: *this* man (plural *these*), *that* house (plural *those*).

Interrogative: *What* man? *Which* house? *Whose* book?

Indefinite: *some* persons; *any* man.

Intensive: the *very* house.

Identifying: the *same* house.

Numeral:
  Cardinal, *one, two* . . . ; ordinal, *first, second.* . . .

2. As to degree (comparison):
Positive: *fast, thin, careful.*
Comparative: *faster, thinner, more careful.*
Superlative: *fastest, thinnest, most careful.*
Relative: Jones is the *most careful* driver here.
Absolute: Jones is *most careful.*

3. As to position in the sentence:
Adherent (clinging to its substantive): a *tall* man.
  A man *blind* from his youth.

Appositive (set over against its substantive): This man, *blind* from his youth, can understand (note the comma).

Predicate (made a part of the verb phrase): The man is *tall*. He appears *blind*.

Adverbs

1. As to form: ending normally in -ly (from Old English -lic meaning like). A few formed by dropping an Old English inflectional -e have no ending: soon, fast.

2. As to degree: compared like adjectives; soon, sooner, soonest; truly, more truly, most truly.

3. As to special uses:

Relative: used to introduce clauses or infinitive phrases. I know *how* to go home. I know *where* it is.

Interrogative: used to introduce questions. *Where* is he?

Interjections

Expressions of sudden emotion thrust into the structure of the sentence and independent of it: *Oh! Alas! Ouch!* Remember to set them off by commas or exclamation marks.

Pronouns

Personal: *I, he, they, she, you,* etc.

Possessive: *Mine, his, yours,* etc. This book is *his*.

Demonstrative: *This, these, that, those.* I will take *these*.

Relative: *Who, which, what, that, whoever,* etc.

Indefinite: *One, none, each, everybody,* etc.

Reflexive: *Myself, himself,* etc. I hurt *myself*.

Reciprocal: *one another, each other.* Love *one another*.

Intensive: *Myself, yourself,* etc. You *yourself* said it.

Prepositions

Simple: *Of, for, by,* etc.

Compound: *According to, in spite of,* etc.

Participial: *Considering* his youth, he does well.

A prepositional phrase: *at home.*

Prepositions and adverbs are closely related. The same word may, in many cases, be used as an adverb or as a preposition.

Conjunctions

Coördinating, joining words, phrases, or clauses of equal rank.

Structural: *And, but, or, nor, for.*

Logical: *Hence, therefore, however, so,* etc.

The logical conjunctions do not so clearly link elements of structure as they do ideas. They are much like adverbs modifying the whole of the clause which they introduce, and on this account are sometimes called conjunctive adverbs. Distinguish them because of an important difference in punctuation.

Subordinating, introducing a dependent clause.

Simple: *If, as, unless, except,* etc.

Compound: *As soon as, in order that,* etc.

Correlative, used in pairs: *both . . . and; not only . . . but also; either . . . or; neither . . . nor; so . . . as; so . . . that; such . . . that.*

Expletives

The pronoun *it* and the adverb *there* are sometimes used merely to fill out the expression and when so used are called expletives; e.g., *It* is not reasonable to expect more. *There* is no book here.

105. Misuse of the Parts of Speech. In order to know how to use a word, you must know what part of speech

it is. Although English idiom permits considerable freedom in the adaptation of parts of speech — especially nouns
and verbs — to other than their original functions, usage
does not tolerate indiscriminate coinages. The noun *motor*
gives the forms *to motor* and *motor efficiency;* the word
suicide has not been accepted as a verb. When you are
in doubt as to usage consult a good dictionary.

1. *Adjectives and Adverbs.* Adjectives modify only substantives; adverbs only verbs, adjectives, other adverbs, and
in a few instances prepositions. Do not confuse them.

Distinguish:

This material looks *good* (good is an adjective).
This material looks *well* (well is an adverb).
Looks good means " looks like good material "; *looks well* means
" *makes* a good appearance."
She dresses tastefully (adverb) and looks lovely (adjective).

Say:

I feel *bad.* (Not I feel badly. Note the meanings of bad.)
The sap tastes *sweet* (not *sweetly*).

Avoid:

They live *good* in that camp (say live *well*). I *sure* will write
real soon (say *surely* will, *really* soon). Something is wrong *some
place* (say *somewhere*).

2. *Verb-Forms.* Do not confuse the past tense and past
participle of strong verbs.

Past	Past Participle	Past	Past Participle
Drank	having drunk	Rode	having ridden
Began	having begun	Lay	having lain
Ran	having run	Froze	having frozen
Came	having come	Swore	having sworn

Distinguish the present *choose* and the past *chose.* Remember that such forms as *bursted, busted, drownded, skun*
(skinned), *drinked* are not in good use.

106. Syntax. That part of grammar which is known as syntax has to do with the relations that words bear to one another in connected discourse. These relations, rather than the origin or the history of a word, determine what part of speech it shall be in a particular sentence. Thus in the sentence, His love for home and the home circle never left him and brought him after all his wanderings home to his father's house, the word *home* is first a noun, then an adjective, and finally an adverb. To show what part of speech a word is and how it is related to other words, we have, besides the meaning, three devices: the relation of words already described, the order of the words, and changes in form called inflection. In the sentence cited above, the syntax of *love for home* is clear because of a preposition; of *the home circle* and *brought him . . . home,* because of word order; and of *him, his,* and *father's* because of inflections.

CASE

1. *Case Forms.* The most important changes of form in nouns and pronouns are changes of case. The term *case* is used to mean both a form of a word and the relation which that form has come to indicate. It is derived from a Latin word which means a falling. The nominative (*nomen*) was known by the Latin grammarians as the upright case (*casus rectus*), and the others were termed, as we still call them, oblique cases. Hence the orderly recital of the cases of a word is called its declension.

In Old English there were five cases — Nominative, Accusative, Genitive, Dative, Instrumental. In Modern English only two distinct case-forms of nouns survive — a common form for the Old English Nominative, Accusative, and Dative, sometimes called the Common Case, and the Genitive; e.g., *man* and *man's.* Pronouns in Modern English have three distinct case-forms — Nominative, Accusative-Dative, and Genitive; e.g., *I, me, my.*

2. *Case Uses.* Since the relations formerly indicated by distinct case forms persist, though the forms themselves have been lost, some constructions can be explained only by reference to case. It is only in the use of pronouns that errors in case are likely to occur. For this reason the case uses are illustrated here, so far as possible, by pronouns.

The nominative case is used as,

Subject, *I* know him; *he* will pay the debt.
Predicate, It is *he* who paid.
Nominative of address, *John,* pay the chauffeur.
Nominative of exclamation, *He!* I expected Henry.
Nominative absolute, *He* being down, they fled.

The accusative case is used as,

Direct object, I paid *him.*
Secondary object, I taught him a *lesson.*
Retained object, I was taught a valuable *lesson* by him.
Cognate accusative, He sleeps the *sleep* of death.
Adjunct accusative, I appointed him *executor.*
Subject of infinitive, I expect *him* to be executor.
Predicate of infinitive, I knew it to be *him.*
Accusative of exclamation, O unhappy *me!*
Adverbial accusative, I lived there a *year.*
Accusative with a preposition, He is far above *me.*

The dative case is used as,

Indirect object, I paid *him* the money.
Dative of reference or concern, Do *me* a favor.

The genitive case is used as,

Genitive of possession, My *father's* house.
Genitive of connection, The *war's* delay.
Subjective genitive, *Tom's* choice pleased.
(Tom chose)
Objective genitive, *Tom's* election pleased.
(Tom was elected)

107. The Misuse of Cases. English has so few inflections that not many errors in case forms are possible. Avoid all the more carefully such as do occur.

1. Accusative Misused for Nominative.

1. As subject of a predicate not recognized.

Incorrect: I see a man *whom* I know will help you. Tell *whomever* asks for me I'm busy. Report all *whom* you have cause to believe were involved.

Right: I see a man who I know will help you (*Who* is the subject of *will help*). Tell whoever asks for me that I am busy (*Whoever* is the subject of *asks*. *Whoever asks for me* is a substantive, the object of *tell*). Report all who you have cause to believe were involved (*Who* is the subject of *were involved*).

2. As subject of a predicate not expressed.

Incorrect: He is younger than *me*. You are not so self-assured as *her*.

Right: He is younger than I (Than *I am* is implied). You are not so self-assured as she (is).

3. As part of the predicate.

Incorrect: The object of his attack is really *me*. If the applicants had been *him* and *me*, the request would have been refused.

Right: The object of his attack is really I. If the applicants had been he and I, the request would have been refused.

2. Nominative Misused for Accusative.

1. With a preposition.

Incorrect: This is between *you* and *I*. It is useless for *we* girls to try.

Right: This is between you and me (not to be confused with You and I are). It is useless for us girls to try (But, we girls couldn't succeed).

2. With the verb *to be*.

Incorrect: Instantly I knew it to be *he*. *Who* did you take him to be. He helped *whoever* he knew to be in want.

Right: Instantly I knew it to be him. Whom did you take him to be. He helped whomever he knew to be in want (But, he helped whoever he knew was in want).

3. *Genitive of Possession.*

1. Avoid the indiscriminate use of the possessive genitive of nouns not implying personality.

Faulty: The house's roof. That *farm's* area. (Prefer in such expressions the prepositional phrase; e.g., the roof of the house. The area of that farm.)
Right: The company's charter. The Government's intention. Do not doubt Love's power in the world.
Permitted by usage: The day's work, an hour's delay, and a few similar expressions involving periods of time.

2. Use the possessive genitive, not the accusative, of pronouns to modify a gerund.

Incorrect: The fear of *him* getting angry deters them. We have no record of *you* paying the premium.
Right: The fear of his getting angry deters them. We have no record of your paying the premium.

In these sentences *getting* and *paying* are gerunds or verbal nouns. Consequently *his* and *your* are as necessary as if the phrases had been *of his anger* and *of your payment.*. The rule applies somewhat less strictly to nouns. A few writers, when the possessive of a noun would be awkward, frankly give it up and use the accusative. It is better to recast the sentence.

Awkward: He gave assurance of the first battery of artillery's standing firm.
Undesirable: . . . of the first battery artillery standing firm.
Better: . . . that the first battery of artillery would stand firm.

4. *Cases in Apposition.*

Be sure that pronouns in apposition take the case of the substantive with which they agree.

Incorrect: He told us two, Tom and *I*, to come to his room. We two were late, Tom and *me*.

Right: He told us two, Tom and me, to come to his room. We two were late, Tom and I.

108. Agreement and Reference. Besides case, inflection serves to indicate other relations, namely, number, person, and gender. In English grammar such relations are not artificial but natural, and the agreement and interrelation of inflected forms is consequently much simpler than in many other languages. Such distinctions as English does require should be all the more carefully observed.

1. *Subject and Predicate.* A verb agrees with its subject in person and number. A singular subject takes a singular verb. Such a verb is not made plural (*a*) by additions to the subject by means of such expressions as *with, as well as, accompanied by;* (*b*) by two singular subjects correlated by such connectives as *either, or;* (*c*) by distributives such as *each, every, nobody.*

Right: The cause of all the sounds and movements *was* clear.

The captain, as well as the mate and three of the crew, *was* rescued.

Either the atlas or the text-book *is* wrong.

Each of the large number of boys in the camp *is* fond of him.

The predicate of a collective noun is singular or plural according to the sense.

Right: The majority *is* determined to enforce its will. The majority *are* familiar with farm problems.

Do not shift the agreement from one number to the other in the same sentence.

Wrong: The mob that *was* so unruly on Monday *were* docile as sheep on Tuesday.

A compound subject requires a plural verb unless the parts are felt as expressing one idea.

Right: Noise and loud talking *are* forbidden. There *are* to be a concert and a dance.

Also right: There *was* clatter and confusion. Bread and butter *is* wholesome.

2. *Pronoun and Antecedent.* A pronoun agrees with its antecedent — the substantive for which it stands — in gender and number. The distributives *each, every, nobody* consequently serve as pronouns in the singular. A collective antecedent, like a collective subject, may be regarded as singular or plural. An antecedent which includes persons of both sexes may take a masculine pronoun. The alternative forms *his or her* may be used in such a case, but are awkward and can usually be avoided by revision.

Right: Every pupil will invite *his* (not their) parents.
Also right: Every pupil will invite *his or her* parents.
Better: The pupils will invite their parents.

A pronoun does not agree with its antecedent in case, but takes the form demanded by the construction.

Right: I took my watch to a *jeweler who* I knew was reliable. He had an *employe whom* I knew to be careless. Which is the *man whom* they thought to be you?

The antecedent to which a pronoun refers should be (*a*) explicit and not merely implied, (*b*) exact, not vague, (*c*) specific, not ambiguous.

Wrong: (*a*) As his father and grandfather were *lawyers,* it is not strange that he was attached to the study of that subject. (*b*) He thought he had caught a *muskrat, which* are common in those waters. (*c*) I don't like to have *him* harness the horse, for *he* is not very gentle.

The reference of a pronoun to the general thought of a clause, though not impossible, is usually awkward and vague. For the same reason reference to an antecedent in the possessive case is undesirable.

Faulty: I could no longer see the lighthouse, which increased my fear.

This coat is Mary's, who came in a few minutes ago.

Better: I could no longer see the lighthouse, a fact which increased my fear; or . . . and this fact increased my fear.

This coat belongs to Mary, who came in a few minutes ago.

3. *Appositives.* Words or phrases in apposition, that is, used in the same construction and as names for the same thing, must agree logically as well as grammatically.

Wrong: Cornelia, the name of the mother, was listening to the boastful words of a friend. (*Correct:* Cornelia, as the mother was called, was listening.)

Probably no two of the transcendentalists, originally a nickname for the idealists of New England, held the same opinions.

4. *Participles.* A participle, being part adjective, should refer clearly to some substantive to which it is related in thought. This substantive should be expressed, not merely understood or implied, and should ordinarily be near to the participle and prominent enough to be instantly associated with it.

Wrong: Walking farther down the lane, the barn is visible.

Burdened with all these cares, life seemed too hard for her to bear.

Our camp was pitched near the large lake, thus *putting* us in reach of supplies.

Right: Walking farther down the lane, one can see the barn.

Burdened with all these cares, she thought life too hard to bear.

We pitched our camp near the large lake, thus putting ourselves in reach of supplies.

5. *The Gerund Phrase.* A gerund phrase that begins a sentence should ordinarily refer specifically to the subject of the clause or sentence of which it is a part.

Wrong: By *ordering* your seats early, there is no danger of being disappointed. *In exploding* a blast, it left him blind.

Right: By ordering your seats early, you will avoid being disappointed. In exploding a blast, he was made blind.

6. *Suspended Modifiers.* In general avoid loose and illogical reference in modifiers that begin the sentence. If the subject is implied in the modifier, supply it in the sentence, or else make it explicit in the modifier.

Wrong: About to cry out, the horror of it made me speechless.
When ready to make my report, the office was closed.
Due to his aggressive manner, I was prejudiced against him.
Right: About to cry out, I was made speechless by the horror.
I was about to cry out, but the horror of it made me speechless.
When ready to make my report, I found the office closed.
When I was ready to report, the office was closed.
Because of his aggressive manner, I was prejudiced against him.
(Avoid *due to* at the beginning of a sentence. Let it refer to a substantive, as in, I noticed a slight tremor, due to the passing train.)

7. *The Harmony of Tenses.* The tense of a verb in a subordinate clause or of an infinitive or a participle is determined with reference to the time of the principal verb. The dependent form may not express a time that is logically inconsistent with the tense of its principal.

Right: I trust that he *is* (*was, has been, will be, will have been*) here.

I trusted that he *was* (*would be, had been*) here.

I knew that it *pays* to be careful. (*Pays* is a general truth and consequently need not harmonize with knew.)

I *moved* because I *shall* be more comfortable here. (The subordinate refers to an entirely different period of time, and hence need not harmonize with *moved*.)

Wrong: It was a long time since I *saw* my home. (Say I *had seen*.)

Let us strive that we *might* succeed. (Say *may* succeed.)

I brought an excuse because I *have been late* last Tuesday. (Say *was late*.) I should have liked *to have gone*. (Say should have liked *to go*.) I had left, being called home. (Say *having been* called home.)

109. The Sentence. Two parts are essential to a sentence, a substantive and a predication. The substantive is the subject; the predication, an assertion or inquiry about the subject made by a form of the verb. Such a verb form, which must be finite, that is, limited as to time, person, and number, and hence able to adapt itself to various subjects, constitutes with its adjuncts the predicate of the sentence. A group of words making part of a sentence and having a subject and predicate of its own is called a clause. Such a group of words containing no predication is called a phrase.

Sentences are,

1. Affirmative or negative. This simple distinction is sometimes confused.

Incorrect: Prohibit throwing anything out, *not even* a scrap of paper.

Right: Prohibit throwing anything out, even a scrap of paper.

2. Declarative or interrogative. Note the difference in inflection of the voice between " yes and no " questions and questions of detail.

Are you going to the game? When are you going to the game?

3. Exclamatory and non-exclamatory.

How beautiful it is! It is beautiful.

4. Simple, compound, or complex.

Simple: one subject and one predicate. Either or both may be compound and may be modified by many adjuncts.

The attack came at last. The attack and the desertion of the scouts made the situation desperate.

Compound: two or more clauses logically related yet capable of standing alone.

The attack came, and we resisted stoutly.

Complex: a principal clause, capable of standing alone, and one or more clauses dependent upon it and incapable of standing alone.

The attack, which had been long expected, came in the morning.

The dependent clause is said to be subordinate.

Subordinate clauses are,

(1) Declarative: *which had been expected.*

(2) Interrogative: Tell me *whether you can come.*

(3) Assumptive: *Though he slay me,* I will trust him.

In function a clause may be,

(1) Substantive: *That he is wise* is true.

(2) Adjectival: One *who is wise* is happy.

(3) Adverbial: Men are wise *when they are old.*

Adjectival clauses are,

Descriptive: Two *who came late* were not admitted.

Determinative: Those *who came late* were not admitted.

In relation to its context a clause is,

Essential: So modifying or restricting the meaning of its principal as to alter it essentially if left out. Blind are those *who will not see.* The house *that Jack built.* Such men *as are competent.*

Non-essential: Adding to the meaning of its principal or so qualifying it as not to restrict its application. Test such a clause by leaving it out. A tall man, *who stood near,* called me. This house, *which Jack built for himself,* is now for sale. Experienced men, *as they have had an opportunity to prove their competence,* are preferred to beginners (note the difference in punctuation).

Conditional complex sentences, that is, sentences composed of a condition (the subordinate clause) and a conclusion (the principal clause) are,

1. Present in time,

(*a*) Neutral as to the present fact. *If that is true,* I must return. (It may or may not be true. I do not commit myself.)

(*b*) Doubtful as to the present fact: *If that be true,* I must return. (I commit myself to doubt about it and hence use the subjunctive.)

(*c*) Contrary to the present fact: *If that were true,* I should have to return. (I am convinced that it isn't true.)

2. Past in time,

(*a*) Neutral as to past fact: *If that was* true, my decision was wise. (Perhaps it was true; perhaps not.)

(*b*) Contrary to past fact: *If that had been true,* my decision would have been wise. (It was not true.)

3. Future in time,

(*a*) More vivid as to probable fact: *If that shall prove true,* my decision will be justified.

(*b*) Still more vivid: *If that proves true,* my decision will be justified.

(*c*) Less vivid: *If that should prove true,* my decision would be justified.

110. Coördination and Subordination. To know what a sentence means you must be certain as to the relative rank of its parts. To write a sentence that will say precisely what you mean you must know how to indicate their relative rank clearly. Skill in subordination is one of the most striking differences between a juvenile style and a mature style.

Words or groups of words of the same rank in the sentence are coördinate. Two subordinate clauses may be coördinate with each other as in, I often come here, *where I was born,* and *where I spent my childhood;* or one may depend on the other as in, It occurred to me *while he was asking where I spent my childhood.*

1. *Coördinate relations.*

1. Addition. Indicated structurally by *and,* a very old word having the same form in Old English, and *nor* (and not). " Come *and* see us " is a disputed idiom, established colloquially.

Logical conjunctions: *also, moreover, besides, likewise, too,* etc.

2. Contrast or opposition. *But,* the adversative con-

junction, developed from an old phrase meaning without.

Logical conjunctions: *however, nevertheless, notwithstanding, still,* etc.

3. Alternation. *Or, nor,* kindred in origin with *whether.* Distinguish alternative or (Come rain or shine) and appositive or (These are sonant, or voiced, sounds).

Logical conjunctions: *else, otherwise.*

4. Cause or consequence. *For,* formerly a preposition, cognate with Latin *pro;* unlike *and, but,* and *or* in not being able to link words and phrases.

Logical conjunctions: *accordingly, consequently, hence, so then, therefore,* etc.

2. *Subordinate relations.*

1. Time. *When, whenever, while, after, before, until, till, since, as soon as, now, once,* etc. Distinguish *when,* a point in time, and *while,* duration in time. It is best not to use *while* to mean whereas. Never use it merely to coördinate.

2. Place. *Where, wherever, whence, whencesoever, whither,* etc.

3. Reason. *Because, since, as,* etc. Do not regard these as exact synonyms. *Because* (once *by cause*) implies definite causal relation: Because my horse was lame, I walked home. *Since* implies a condition preceding in time: Since you have come for me, I will go, though I had not intended to. *As* implies a more causal or even accidental relation. Not: As I like Henry, I will do this for him; but: As we are here, we might as well go in. Prefer the initial position for *since* and *as* clauses.

4. Purpose. *That, in order that, so that, lest,* etc.

5. Result. *So that, so — that, such — that.*

6. Concession. *Though, although, even if,* etc. An assumption takes the subjunctive: Though this *were* my last day on earth, I would say the same. An admitted fact does not: Though it *is* a holiday, many shops are open.

7. Condition. *If, unless, on condition that, provided,* etc.

8. Comparison. *As, than, as — as, as if, not so — as, such — as,* etc. *As if* takes the subjunctive: He treats me as if I *were* a child.

9. Indirect quotation. *That,* introducing a substantive clause. Note that such a clause does not begin with a capital letter and is not included in quotes: He said *that he expected to be late.*

111. The Misuse of Conjunctions. In coördination and subordination avoid the following errors:

1. The coördination of parts of a sentence not of equal grammatical rank.

Incorrect: We studied English a year but spending most of our time on literature. (The clause and the phrase are not coördinate. Omit *but.*)

He is an old resident and who will be able to tell us. (The noun and the relative clause are not of the same rank. Omit *and* and remove the coördination, or omit *who* and coördinate *is* and *will.*)

2. The coördination of clauses which are not logically of equal rank.

Faulty: The night grew dark and made me afraid to go on. (This obviously means, so dark that I was afraid. . . .)

He has had the book a month and has not read it yet. (The relation is probably concessive. Though he has had the book a month, he has not read it yet.)

3. The use of the colloquial *so* as a structural conjunction.

Crude: We were tired, *so* we sat down to rest. (*And so* we sat down to rest is better. Better still, make the first clause subordinate to the second. As we were tired, we sat down . . . or Being tired, we sat down to rest.)

4. The use of *while* to indicate coördination.

Incorrect: I am secretary to the Board *while* he is assistant to the president. (Say *and.*)

5. Certain common errors in subordination.

(1) The use of *like* as a conjunction.

Incorrect: Do *like* they do in France. (Say *as* they do or *like the French.*)

(2) The use of *how* or *where* instead of *that.*

Incorrect: They told me *how* it was impossible to cross. I see in the paper *where* a man was hurt at the factory.

(3) The use of *immediately, directly, without* as conjunctions.

Incorrect: I can't go *without* you go along (say *unless you go*). *Immediately* he comes in, I will call you (say *as soon as*). *Directly* I entered I saw something was wrong (say *as soon as*).

112. The Uses of *Shall* and *Will*. Distinguish *shall* and *will, should* and *would* as follows:

1. Express futurity (prediction, confidence, expectation) by I shall (should), thou wilt (wouldst), he will (would), we shall (should), you will (would), they will (would).

I shall miss my train. You will succeed. They will arrive in time. We shall probably come.

2. Express volition (determination, threat, promise) by I will (would), thou shalt (shouldst), he shall (should), we will (would), you shall (should), they shall (should).

I will be heard; you shall listen. We will pay the debt. They shall suffer for this deed; I will punish them.

3. In questions: Shall (should) I? Shall (should) we? (Except when repeating a question addressed to the speaker). In the second and third persons determine the form from the corresponding declarative form or the expected answer. Shall I be too late? (I shall.) Shall we come in? (You shall come in.) Shall you go to the

dinner? (Expects prophecy, I think I shall.) Will you go to the dinner? (Expects promise, I will.) Shall these articles be sold? (Yes, i.e., they shall.) Will these be sold? (I hope so.)

4. In subordinate clauses expressing an indirect quotation (the thought of the subject of the principal clause), use the form that would be required if the subordinate clause were independent. I fear I shall be late. (I shall be late!) You hope you shall escape. (We shall escape.) They say they shall be refused admission. (We shall be refused.) I admit that I will decline. (I will decline.) You knew that you would not serve. (We would not serve.) They say that they will have a hearing. (We will have a hearing.)

5. In other subordinate clauses use shall (should) unless expression of independent volition on the part of the subject of the subordinate clause requires will (would). If I (you, he) should be late, do not be alarmed. I intend that they shall know the truth. Though you should fail me, I shall win. Whenever you shall call on me, I will respond. Take care lest he should hear you.

But: They will go if I *will* join them. You can work when you *will*. We hope that you *will* try. Whoever will study, *will* succeed.

113. The Uses of the Non-Finite Verb Forms. The infinitive, the gerund, and the participle have a variety of uses. Employ them as follows:

1. *The Infinitive,* used as,

Substantive: *To cross* the river is difficult. It is difficult *to cross* the river. Our plan is *to cross* the river. I like *to cross* the river by ferry. *To cross* by airplane! I should like that. Your plan, *to cross* by the bridge, is safer. There is no way but *to cross* here.

Adjective: I want a chance *to win.* This house is *to let.*

Adverb: I have come *to talk* with you. He is worthy *to be trusted*. I am grieved *to hear* of your misfortune.

Predicate: Though the infinitive is a non-predicative form, in one construction — known as the accusative with the infinitive construction or as the infinitive clause — it becomes equivalent in effect to a finite verb.

I advised him *to sell* the house. It is too high for a child *to reach*. I took it *to be* her who called.

In all these sentences the substantive preceding the infinitive is in the accusative case. It is known as the subject of the infinitive. In the first example, *house* is the object of *to sell* and the construction is much the same as, I advised that he sell the house. A substantive following the form to be, as in the third example, is in the accusative case, and is known as the predicate of the infinitive. Distinguish

It is *she* who called (both forms nominative).
I took *it* to be *her* (both forms accusative).

2. *The Gerund.*

In its function as a noun, in substantive constructions: *Crossing* the river is interesting. You prefer *crossing* by ferry. We can save time by *crossing* here.

In its function as a verb: *Crossing the river* daily becomes monotonous.

By extension of these uses as an adjective: This is the *smoking* car. Where is my *walking* stick?

3. *The Participle.*

As adjective, it modifies a substantive: A small *boat, crossing* the river in a fog, was run down. *He* is *winning* success.

As verb, it may take an object and modifiers: There was the steamer, *slowly crossing the river*.

Combined with a substantive, it may be used absolutely:

The *river having been crossed safely,* they pressed on. His *funds exhausted,* he was forced to beg.

This construction is known as the nominative absolute, the substantive being in the nominative case. In Old English the absolute construction was in the dative.

114. Idiom. The rules of grammar are based on principles which are much the same in all languages and which may be applied to one expression after another. An idiom is a peculiarity of usage, based entirely on well-established custom and not applicable to other expressions. A phrase which seems to violate a rule of grammar may yet be correct because it has become, through long usage, accepted as idiomatic. Thus the word *many* is a plural form, yet idiom justifies its combination with a singular substantive in the expression *many a year.* It is incorrect to say *all the farther* I read and quite correct to say *all the more eager.* Obviously, since idiom is based on custom it is to be mastered, not by the study of rules, but by careful attention to the usage of persons who write and speak correctly.

As correct idiom is partly a matter of the choice of words, a further discussion of the topic will be found in the chapter on Usage in Diction (p. 344).

1. *Prepositions with Other Parts of Speech.* Idiom rather than grammar determines what preposition is to be used with certain words. The dictionary sometimes indicates the correct usage.

acquit *of* (not from) an accusation
addicted *to* (not of) a habit
adhere *to* (not with) an object
adjacent *to* (not by) a place
averse *to* (not from) a plan
compare *with* to measure; *to* to indicate resemblance
deal *in* commodities; *with* subjects
different *from* (not to)

divest *of* (not from)
dissuade *from*
estrange *from*
expert *in* or *at* (not of)
expostulate *with* (not at or to)
frightened *at* or *by* (not of or toward)
ill *of* (not from) a disease
listen *to* (not at)
meet *with* (not up with)
minister *to* (not administer to)
opposed *to* (not against)
persevere *in* (not at)
recover *from*
scarcely *when* (not than)
sensible *of*
speak *with* or *to*
treat *of* (not on) a topic
versed *in* (not of)
zest *for* (not of)

2. *Confused Idioms.* Avoid the incorrect blending of two correct idioms.

among one another (among themselves or with one another).
cannot help but see (cannot help seeing or cannot but see).
couldn't scarcely see (couldn't see or could scarcely see).
different than (different from or other than).
equally as good as (equally good or as good as).
like they do (like them or as they do).
off of (a piece off or a piece of).
seldom or ever see (seldom see or seldom or never see).
such persons who see (persons who or such persons as).
those kind (those or that kind).
used to could (used to or once could).

EXERCISES IN GRAMMAR

Sentences for Analysis

1. By waiting here ten minutes I can see the soldiers marching by as well as if I were in the reviewing stand, for Tom has brought me a box to stand on.

In this sentence, distinguish and describe (*a*) the clauses, (*b*) the phrases, (*c*) a gerund and a participle, (*d*) an indirect object, (*e*) an adverbial accusative. Account for the form *I were*.

2. It is said that the right of suffrage is not valued when it is indiscriminately bestowed, and there may be some truth in this, for I have observed that what men prize most is a privilege; even if it be that of chief mourner at a funeral.

Explain (*a*) the construction of each pronoun, (*b*) the subject of each predication, (*c*) the mood of each verb. What verbs are strong and what are weak? What is the function of *there?*

3. Love and Death enter boarding-houses without asking the price of board, or whether there is room for them.

(*a*) What type of sentence? (*b*) The construction of *price?* (*c*) The mood of *is?*

4. Taking the old man to be a beggar, the tourist dropped a coin into his hat, and was astonished to see him fling the money away and stride off indignantly.

(*a*) Point out all the infinitives in the sentence. (*b*) Tell the construction of *old man* and *beggar*. (*c*) Of the verbs represented, tell whether they are transitive or intransitive, active or passive, and give the principal parts of each.

Write the following sentences, inserting either *shall* or *will* as the context may require:

1. I have decided that I . . . . vote for Jones; I am convinced that he . . . . be a good mayor.
2. Don't expect me. I . . . . come if I can; but I . . . . almost certainly be detained at the office.
3. I fear we . . . . be too late. We . . . . find missing our train no joke.
4. Thank you. I . . . . be much pleased to come.

5. He hopes he . . . . have an opportunity to see you again. If he comes . . . . you be glad to see him?

6. Yes, we . . . . accept your terms, if you . . . . put the agreement in writing.

7. He says you . . . .go, whether you wish to or not. When . . . . you be able to return?

8. I have decided that I . . . . invite Mary. . . . . you go if she goes? Please do.

9. When . . . . we see you again? . . . . it be long? I know I . . . . miss you dreadfully.

10. They hope they . . . . find the gate open, but they . . . . probably be mistaken. The keeper . . . . surely have locked it by this time. I . . . . never forget the time I was locked out. . . . . you?

Choose the correct form:

1. You must secure a guide (whom, who) you know is familiar with the country.

2. She has two invitations and (don't, doesn't) know which to accept.

3. This was intended only for you and perhaps (I, me) to use.

4. She has talent, but her sister sketches better than (she, her).

5. They are pleasant fellows, but I like Tom's brother better than (he, him).

6. A kit of first-aid articles (are, is) taken along.

7. The president expects you and (her, she) to be faithful workers.

8. There (have, has) been a succession of charming days.

9. I don't care for (that, those) kind of songs.

10. He was angry on account of (us, our) walking on his lawn.

11. When they had money they lived (good, well).

12. They have the finest spring water you ever (drunk, drank).

13. As soon as he (come, came) in, I knew she was (real, really) glad to see him.

14. When I had (swum, swam) a mile, I (begun, began) to tire.

15. It is important that the president (is, be) a good speaker.

Faulty Sentences for Correction

I

1. They have sent John and myself an invitation to the party.
2. This, of course, is between you and I.
3. The low standard of honor and ideals are the causes of the failures of those students in after life.
4. That is the way with persons addicted to the spending habit; they spend it because they have it.
5. The trainer knows that to get the very best out of his horse he must be in the best of condition.
6. We will borrow Smith's car, who was talking with me as you came out of the house.
7. When I go away on a visit, as soon as I get there I mail a post card to my mother.
8. As I have always been interested in a blacksmith I always linger at their shops whenever I pass them.
9. So it seems to me that anybody who will use a weak-minded person to do their bidding are quite more guilty than the one who performs them.
10. The question of American football as a game has been widely discussed by the people of our land for a various number of years, and by some colleges it has been entirely dispensed with.
11. Instead of a cushion of sand there is a binder of asphalt and limestone two inches thick on which is laid the wearing surface both of which are rolled.
12. He graduated in June 1829 in a class noted for its high character, and which then and for many years afterward made Holmes the center of their yearly reunion, which he often celebrated in verse.
13. I start toward the cellar. If there is any company, I take it with me. The cellar is as cool as an ice box and I have placed a bench that will hold three persons in a nice corner. I get a piece of ice out of the refrigerator as I pass it and break it up with a hammer.
14. In eleven years of fighting Caesar conquered the most powerful nations without sustaining a defeat and gained the supremacy at Rome, which is certainly an ample proof that he was a wonderful military genius, and that it is generally thought he would have conquered the whole of the known world.

II

1. Some students come to college not to develop their minds but their bodies.

2. I could not tell the damsel of my noble birth or on telling her she would not have believed.

3. In forming the plot it gives unity when one incident naturally follows the next.

4. I shall give the pocket book to whoever it belongs to.

5. A series of ventilators keeps the car cool in summer while it is warmed by electric heaters in winter.

6. The water is pumped out, thereby lowering the ship until the keel rests on supports which are placed on the bottom.

7. The Smith dry-dock is the largest of any dock south of New York, from which it can be seen that it is a big factor in the shipping of southern states.

8. Being made in biscuit form, you can prepare a delicious luncheon from this cereal.

9. Yours is one of the best trade papers that reaches us.

10. The man in public life whom I think most worthy of admiration is Mr. Wilson. The reason why I think so is because he is so sincere.

11. Being always a good student, I have not the slightest fear of him being unable to pass the examination.

12. The Indian chief was much surprised to know that New York was bigger than any city in the United States.

13. To rightly enjoy your recitations in this subject everybody must prepare their lessons carefully.

14. The conductor, as well as the motorman and the driver, were all frightened.

15. We made the platform of the best timber and very strong, so it lasted for over two years, but it began to creak when the wind blew the trees, so we decided to take it down.

16. Immediately he came in I told him I had talked with the president and he said he wanted to see him.

17. The information has been collected for three years and the report isn't ready for publication yet. It is an abuse of our confidence and something ought to be done about it.

18. The day previous was a rainy one as a heavy storm had come up from the west and if the storm center had passed out to sea as had been calculated on, the following day should have been a clear one.

III

1. The play was altogether different than I expected. She don't act the part at all like Julia Marlowe did.

2. Neither the letter nor the telegram have made us real sure that the accident was not serious.

3. The front seats are full, but there is plenty room enough in the back for anybody whom you are sure don't mind the jolting.

4. I had intended to have insisted on a settlement to-day, but I find that I will have to see another party first.

5. He has the ability of becoming a useful employe but those sort of men are out of place in a railroad office.

6. If any scout were to violate his promises he may be expelled from the camp by the scout-master.

7. Since I have seen you last I have changed my mind.

8. Improper lubrication means shortening the life of the bearing surfaces due to excessive wear and overheating.

9. Being engaged after school hours and in the evening rushing to prepare myself for class on the morrow, it naturally gives very little time for reading outside of the books prescribed in the course.

10. After writing a sentence it must be read over to see that it is a unit in matter, that is that it has one view-point and that view-point must occupy the prominent position, everything else must be subordinate.

REFERENCES

An Advanced English Syntax by C. T. Onions (Macmillan); *An Advanced English Grammar* by Kittredge and Farley (Ginn); *Report of the Joint Committee on Grammatical Nomenclature* (University of Chicago Press); *The King's English* by Fowler and Fowler (Oxford); *English Grammar* by Henry Sweet (Oxford).

CHAPTER XI

USAGE IN PUNCTUATION

115. The Purpose of Punctuation. Usage in punctuation has changed greatly during the past century. The older pointing was largely phrasal, designed to indicate the pauses made in reading. Thus George Washington wrote:

One method of assault may be to effect, in the forms of the constitution, alterations, which will impair the energy of the system, and thus to undermine what cannot be directly overthrown.

Punctuation of this sort is now obsolete. The purpose of modern punctuation is partly grammatical, to make instantly clear the construction of a sentence, and partly rhetorical, to prevent possible ambiguity or to heighten the emphasis. A modern writer would omit all the commas in Washington's sentence, unless for rhetorical effect he wished to give greater distinction to the phrase " in the forms of the constitution " by enclosing it in commas. The tendency to use fewer commas does not mean that all punctuation has come to be regarded as less important; in fact modern punctuation, by being more closely related to grammatical structure, has been made both more uniform and more significant.

Modern Punctuation. Punctuation to indicate structure will ordinarily be required for one of two reasons: (*a*) because a part of the sentence has been placed in a context to which it is not integrally related; (*b*) because two parts independent of each other and much more closely related to a third part are placed side by side. What is needed in the first case is enclosing marks, which will set the remotely related part off from its context. Such marks will be used in pairs, unless the element to be enclosed chances to come at the beginning or the end of the sentence. What is required in the other is separating marks, used singly since it is their office to push apart elements that might be understood to be closely related. Besides marks that enclose and marks that separate, there are marks used to terminate units of structure and still others to distinguish words and groups of words.

Punctuation for rhetorical effect consists of the occasional use of the structural marks to produce an added effect of emphasis or distinction and the routine use of certain terminal marks which indicate the mood or the intensity of an expression. When Dr. Eliot says, " There is one indispensable foundation for the satisfaction of life — health," he has used the dash to give added emphasis to the word *health*. When Kenneth Grahame wishes to intensify the wonder of a small boy at the obtuseness of his elders, he accomplishes his purpose by a heightening of the punctuation: " They were unaware of Indians, nor recked they anything of bisons or of pirates (with pistols!), though the whole place swarmed with such portents." To give precise rules for the rhetorical use of punctuation is impossible. It is a refinement of style which requires, in addition to taste and skill, a thorough mastery of the art of grammatical punctuation.

PUNCTUATION TO ENCLOSE

For enclosing parts of a sentence pairs of commas, of dashes, of parentheses, or of brackets may be employed. The commas, which indicate the slightest degree of distinction from the context, are the most frequently used. Dashes set off with greater emphasis, parentheses indicate still greater separation, and brackets are usually reserved for additions or comments by another than the author of the text. Unless the effect which you desire requires other marks, be satisfied with commas, remembering to use two.

116. Non-Essential Clauses. One of the most important rules of modern punctuation is that which requires that non-essential clauses (sometimes also called additive or non-restrictive clauses) shall always be enclosed by marks of punctuation. The nature of these clauses is indicated by the various names applied to them. They add something to the sense of the verb or substantive which they modify; they do not limit or restrict its meaning and hence are not essential to that meaning.

(*a*) Pitiful is the case of the blind, who cannot read the face; pitiful that of the deaf, who cannot follow the changes of the voice.

(*b*) A thing was worth buying then, when we felt the money we paid for it.

(*c*) When he does this — if he does it — we shall consider his proposal.

(*d*) The little boy (who is now ancient and not little) read this book in the summer-house of his great-grandmamma.

The distinction between non-essential clauses and essential clauses, which are not enclosed by marks, must be clearly understood. Until it is mastered, there can be no intelligent use of the principles of modern punctuation. Those who find the matter difficult may profitably study the following correctly punctuated sentences.

Essential Clauses

Do not enter the room while a class is in session.

He was surprised when I told him how anxious we had been.

You will find the bee-tree where the two lines meet in the woods.

When in this condition the bees will not sting unless they are taken hold of.

He will not accept the gift if he suspects that it was inspired by pity.

There is another lesson of great value which has been learned by the young man whom I am designating to you as a future bank president. He has learned to use the time which is available outside of his regular work.

Non-essential Clauses

Just now, while there is a class in session, the room is not open to visitors.

Next day, when I told him how anxious we had been, he was surprised.

The swarm was in an oak tree, where the two lines met in the woods.

A bee in that condition will not sting, unless, of course, it is taken hold of.

A gift from you, if he comprehends your motive in giving it, he will certainly accept.

This young man, whom I designate as a future bank president, has learned another lesson, of great value. Two hours daily, which are available outside of his regular work, he employs in acquiring more knowledge about the business of banking.

117. Non-essential Words and Phrases. Like clauses, words and phrases may be non-essential modifiers, adding to the idea to which they belong but not restricting or defining it. If they are omitted, the original meaning of that idea is not destroyed. Unless very brief and simple, such modifiers are enclosed by commas.

(*a*) Unbroken by hatred, unshaken by scorn, he worked and suffered for the people.

(*b*) In the gallery the few visitors rose, putting on coats and wraps.

(*c*) Night is a dead monotonous period under a roof; but in the open world it passes lightly, with its stars and dews and perfumes, and the hours are marked by the changes in the face of nature.

118. Suspended Clauses. An adverbial clause that precedes the predicate which it modifies must be held in suspense until the meaning of the principal clause is grasped. Such suspended clauses, essential as well as non-essential, are usually set off by commas. A clause that is the subject of the sentence in which it occurs is not so set off.

(*a*) If the powers continue their rivalry in armaments, war is inevitable.

(*b*) War is inevitable if the powers continue their rivalry in armaments. (No comma required.)

(*c*) Where the next meeting shall be held is yet to be determined. (No comma required.)

119. Directive Expressions. Words, phrases, and brief clauses interpolated into the structure of a sentence to indicate the turn of the thought, its relation to what precedes or follows, or the attitude of the writer at that particular point in the discourse are enclosed in commas. Directive expressions include sentence-adverbs, such as *however, still, indeed, now, truly, finally;* such phrases as *in the first place, to be sure, on the other hand, on the contrary;* such clauses as *as it were, so we are told, so it seems;* and the explanatory words that precede or follow direct quotations.

(*a*) Weeds are great travelers; they are, indeed, the tramps of the vegetable world.

(*b*) For instance, if you let go your grasp of an article you may have in your hand, it will immediately fall to the ground.

(*c*) Lastly, the school should teach every child, by precept, by example, and by every illustration its reading can supply, that the supreme attainment for any individual is vigor and loveliness of character.

(*d*) In others words, the guide board was not there.

(*e*) The reading habit is to be acquired, and with it the habit of discrimination in reading, or I might almost say, the habit of neglecting to read.

(*f*) " He delighted," says one of his courtiers, " in a bewitching kind of pleasure called sauntering."

NOTE. *Yes* and *no* are directive expressions and are regularly set off by commas. For greater distinction they may be followed by the semicolon or the period.

Yes, I am sure you are right.
Shall you vote for Smith?
Yes; and I hope to see him succeed. Or,
Yes. I hope to see him succeed.

120. Appositive Expressions. Words, phrases, or clauses that repeat an idea in other words for the sake of clearness, list beside a general term the specific elements which it includes, or fulfil the promise of such directive expressions as *these, the following, for example,* are grammatically in apposition to the expressions to which they are equivalent. The second of two such opposed expressions, unless very brief and closely related, is enclosed by commas or by dashes.

(*a*) Wolf, the critic of Homer, was of this opinion.

(*b*) In Kirkville, or Kenwood, as it is now called, he lived ten years.

(*c*) He had a set of friends in what we might call the other world, the world of working people, a world into which few of us actually penetrate except by proxy.

(*d*) The statement made a moment ago, that it is characteristic of our speech to hurry over unstressed syllables rapidly, suggests the converse, that it is also our tendency to linger on syllables strongly stressed.

(*e*) Advancement in life means becoming conspicuous in life — obtaining a position which shall be acknowledged by others to be respectable or honorable.

121. Contrasted Expressions. When two expressions are thrown into sharp contrast, the second is usually enclosed by commas.

(*a*) What the worthy unemployed ask is work, not charity.

(*b*) Responsibility for the high price must be laid, not upon the farmer, but upon the middlemen.

122. Direct Address. Vocative expressions are set off from their context by commas.

(*a*) I am honored, gentlemen, by your confidence.
(*b*) You may be sure, Mr. Brown, that I value your advice.
(*c*) This, sir, is your room.
(*d*) O mighty master, how potent is your art!

123. Absolute Expressions. The nominative absolute is regularly set off by commas. Participial phrases not in the absolute construction are also set off if they chance to be non-essential modifiers. Essential phrases are not enclosed by commas.

(*a*) Our protests being useless, we kept silent.
(*b*) The next day, his purpose having been accomplished, he returned to New York.
(*c*) He returned happy, having sold his quota of stock. (Not an absolute phrase. Comma required because the modifier is non-essential.)
(*d*) The prize will be given to the agent having sold the largest amount. (No comma required.)

124. Interjections. As the term implies, interjections are thrust into the context in which they occur, and should be enclosed in commas. An exclamation point used after an interjection replaces a comma.

(*a*) America, alas, has declined to aid.
(*b*) America, alas! has declined to aid.
(*c*) Ouch, this is hot! Oh, please hold it.

NOTE. When an interjection follows *and* or *but,* the first comma may be omitted.

(*a*) And oh, the difference it makes.
(*b*) I would go; but alas, it is too late.

Remember that O, though always the sign of direct address, is not an interjection. It is regularly capitalized, and is not followed by a mark of punctuation, though the expression of which it is a part is always set off by marks. On the other hand, *oh* is capitalized only when it begins a sentence or line of verse.

125. *Namely, that is, for example, for instance,* and sim-ilar expressions introducing explanatory or illustrative matter are both preceded and followed by (*a*) a comma. For greater distinction the preceding comma may be raised (*b*) to the semicolon, (*c*) the dash, or (*d*) the colon.

(*a*) In the study, for example, of western music, art and litera-ture, time would seem to have been simply wasted.

(*b*) Outsiders can be expected to judge a nation only by the amount that it has contributed to the civilization of the world; that is, by the amount that can be handled.

(*c*) In the execution the artist invariably loses his ideal — that is, falls short of it or fails to express it.

(*d*) Their plan is open to serious objections: for instance, it requires an amendment to the constitution.

Such as introducing an example or series of examples is preceded, ordinarily, by a comma, and is followed without punctuation by the example or examples, which are en-closed by a terminal comma.

Even men of brilliant talent, such as Edward Everett, were by no means free from this straining after effect.

126. Quoted Expressions. A word, phrase, or sentence directly quoted from another speaker is (*a*) always enclosed in commas, unless (*b*) it is grammatically inseparable from its context. A quotation within a quotation is (*c*) enclosed in single quotes. A speech of two or more sentences is (*d*) included in one pair of quotes. If such a speech is in more than one paragraph, the quotation marks are used at the beginning only of the paragraphs preceding the last para-graph and at the close of the last.

(*a*) "You don't believe in me," said the Ghost.

(*b*) Here I was "at ease in mine inn" and disposed to enact the experienced traveler.

(*c*) We receive passively the impressions of books without thought, without judgment, without any effort of "what we are pleased to call ' our minds.'"

(*d*) Rushing up he said breathlessly, "I am very sorry. We have had an accident. Nell is slightly hurt." I looked at him stupidly.

PUNCTUATION TO SEPARATE

For separating parts of sentences the comma, the semi-colon, and the colon, used singly, are regularly employed. The dash used alone is not so much structural as rhetorical, serving to indicate an abrupt break or to give emphasis to a separation normally expressed by the comma. The following elements of the sentence require separation.

127. Independent Clauses. The normal separation between independent clauses is the semicolon, which is, as Professor Genung says, "the mark of the added clause." As a general rule, the semicolon is used between clauses only when a period could be substituted without a change in the structure of either. Three cases may be kept in mind in which the semicolon is to be used regularly: (*a*) when the clauses are not linked by a connective; (*b*) when they are linked by an adverbial connective, such as *so, therefore, then, hence;* (*c*) when either clause requires a comma in its own structure.

(*a*) Poetry is the breath and finer spirit of all knowledge; it is the impassioned expression which is in the countenance of all science.

(*b*) I have always found his judgment correct; so I shall follow his advice.

(*c*) To know is comparatively easy; but to have our knowledge always ready to use, to apply it in every sentence we frame, whether we have time to be careful or not, is far from easy.

Lighter punctuation between independent clauses, by means of a comma instead of a semicolon, is preferred (*a*) often between clauses joined by a structural connective — *and, but, nor, for* — when the clauses are neither long nor complicated; (*b*) almost invariably when the two clauses, though structurally capable of independent expression, have subject or predicate or both in common. Sometimes (c) between very simple or very closely connected clauses no point is used.

(a) His portraits of men have a sort of similarity; but it is the similarity, not of a painting, but of a bas relief. It suggests a resemblance, but it does not produce an illusion. (Note the distinction between the two sentences.)

(b) Our disquiet comes of what nurses and other experienced persons call growing pains, and need not seriously alarm us.

They all had that distaste for innovation which belonged to their race, and many of them a distrust of human nature derived from their creed.

(c) We heedless and unintending speakers, under no exigency of rhyme or reason, say what we mean but seldom and still more seldom mean what we say

128. Dependent Clauses in a Series. Between two or more clauses which, though independent of each other, yet depend in common upon a principal clause, the normal mark of punctuation is a comma. This is true whether the clauses are used (a) without connectives or (b) with coördinating connectives, and (c) even if they are essential clauses, the first of which is not separated from the principal clause.

(a) When all was over, when he had left office, when his party was out of power and the fury of party execration on him was spent, his position was stronger than ever.

(b) One side of the garden wall is formed by the ancient wall of the city, which Cromwell's artillery battered, and which still retains its pristine height and strength.

(c) I remembered people who had to go to the Alps to learn the divine silence of snow, who must run to Italy to see the miracle of sunset, and who could not see among their own maples what a painter autumn is.

Simple and closely-linked clauses require no separation.

I told him that I agreed with him and that I would attend the meeting.

Longer and more significant dependent clauses, particularly those that are themselves subdivided by commas, may be separated by semicolons.

(*a*) A man is loyal when, first, he has some cause to which he is loyal; when, secondly, he willingly and thoroughly devotes himself to this cause; and when, thirdly, he expresses his devotion in some sustained and practical way by acting steadily in the service of his cause.

(*b*) The small colleges will be fortunate if they appreciate their own advantages; if they do not fall into the naturalistic fallacy of confusing growth in the human sense with mere expansion; if they do not allow themselves to be overawed by size and quantity.

129. Phrases in a Series. Phrases that stand side by side modifying the same element of the sentence and not depending on each other are kept apart (*a*) by commas or, exceptionally, (*b*) by semicolons. Between phrases linked by a coördinating conjunction (*c*) a comma is unnecessary except (*d*) when the last two only of a series are linked by a conjunction which indicates the relation of the whole series.

(*a*) I am thrilled by the perfume of the bursting sod, of the mold under the leaves, of the fresh furrows.

(*b*) The real advantage lies in the point and polish of the swordsman's weapon; in the trained eye quick to spy out the weakness of the adversary; in the ready hand prompt to follow it on the instant.

(*c*) No man is less likely to be deceived by fallacies or by exaggerated statements. (No comma needed.)

(*d*) The constructive imagination finds play in literature, in history, in theology, in anthropology, and in the whole field of physical and biological research.

A succession of phrases that depend on each other, producing a cumulative effect, does not constitute a series and requires no separation.

He is captain of the first company of the regiment of volunteers that occupied the village.

130. Words in a Series. Coördinate words that are linked by a conjunction (*a*) are obviously independent and need no separation. If the conjunction is lacking (*b*), the words are kept apart by a comma. When the conjunction is present the comma is used also in the following cases: (*c*) when one word has a modifier that applies to it exclusively, (*d*) when the words of a series are to be understood as related in groups, and (*e*) when to indicate the nature of the coördination in a series the conjunction is supplied between the last two only.

(*a*) The girls were flashing hither and thither over the grass in a flutter of saffron and green and crimson.

(*b*) It was an eloquent, sharp, ugly, earthly countenance.

(*c*) The boys clumped about the stoves in their cowhide boots and laughed and buzzed and ate apples and peanuts and giggled, and grew suddenly solemn when the grave men and women looked at them.

(*d*) It was wit and wisdom, and hard sense and poetry, and scholarship and music.

(*e*) The accuracy, promptness, versatility, and force of mental action may be steadily increased.

Note. The punctuation of a series of words in the form *A, B,* and *C,* illustrated above, is subject to some variation. In the names of business establishments, such as Brown, Smith and Company, the comma before *and* is always omitted. Business and journalistic usage permits its omission in letters and newspapers. The usage of books and periodicals requires the comma.

Remember that mere succession does not indicate a coördinate series, for a sequence of adjectives may be cumulative in effect. Such words should not be separated by commas.

Its flowers are a *deep violet blue,* the stamens projected beyond the mouth of the corolla with *showy red* anthers.

Test this distinction by observing whether *and* could be introduced between two words without changing the sense. In this sentence *deep and violet blue* would change the meaning, for *deep* modifies, not *blue,* but *violet blue.*

131. Anticipatory Expressions. Between an anticipating expression and the statement or list of particulars which it introduces a colon is the usual mark of separation. A colon is used (*a*) before specific instances or examples, (*b*) before an appositive word, phrase, or clause, (*c*) between the formal introduction to quoted matter and the quotation, (*d*) between the parts of titles, references, and numerals, (*e*) after the salutation in a letter.

(*a*) The sources of lasting satisfaction in life are these: health, intellectual power, and personal honor.

(*b*) He repeated an ancient bit of advice: First tell them what you are going to say, then say it, and then tell them what you have said.

(*c*) Pausing a moment he said sadly: "If our educated men had done their duty we should not now be in the condition which we bewail."

(*d*) Poetry: A Metrical Essay.
    Harper's Magazine, 103:279.
    Train 441 at 2:29 P.M.

(*e*) Dear Sir: Gentlemen: Dear Frank:

132. Omitted Words. When an omitted word is to be supplied from its previous use in the sentence the place of its omission (*a*) may be marked by a comma. When a number of words are omitted from a citation as not necessary for the immediate purpose, (*b*) their place is indicated by three periods in succession.

(*a*) One student worked spasmodically and brilliantly and the other, with quiet patience.

(*b*) "Consequently," he added, "to the presence of dust . . . we owe the formation of mists, clouds, and gentle, beneficial rains."

133. Possible Ambiguity or Awkwardness. Words that require no separation on other grounds may yet need (*a*) to be kept apart by a comma to avoid ambiguity or an awkward effect. When two Arabic numbers come together, the sentence should be recast or (*b*) the numbers should be separated by a comma. Long Arabic numerals are similarly (*c*) divided into threes by a comma.

(*a*) On the campus, walks an old man with feeble step. For many, a year abroad would be useless. Whatever is, is right.
(*b*) In May 1919, 137 boxes were shipped.
(*c*) Their progeny would number 19,000,000 in a few years.

PUNCTUATION TO TERMINATE

The terminal marks are the period, the interrogation point, the exclamation point, and the dash. In connected discourse every wholly self-dependent element must be followed by one of these marks.

134. The End of a Sentence. A complete sentence, or elliptical expression treated as a sentence, is followed by (*a*) a period if it is a declarative or imperative statement, (*b*) an exclamation point if it is an exclamatory statement, (*c*) an interrogation point if it asks a direct question.

(*a*) If you wish, I will call him.
　　 By all means. Certainly.
(*b*) What a wonderful view!
(*c*) Will you come over at once?
　　 What, to-day? In these clothes?

135. Parts of a Sentence. A direct question or an exclamation occurring within a declarative sentence should be followed by the appropriate mark, which then replaces any other mark that would normally be used at the same point.

When we have answered the question, Ought we to go? it will be time to ask, Which is the way?

This gentleman, save the mark! looked out for his own safety.

136. Fragmentary Sentences. Abrupt breaks in structure within a sentence or at the end are indicated by the dash.

If you think you can bully me —

Your ignoble views — we tried to think them funny.

137. Terminal Marks and Quotations. A final mark that belongs exclusively to a direct quotation is (*a*) placed within the second pair of quotes; an exclamation point or a question mark that applies to the whole sentence and not solely to the quotation (*b*) follows the quotes.

(*a*) They instantly raised the cry, "Stop thief!"
    He will ask innocently, "Where have you been?"
(*b*) Shall we also "have a previous engagement"?
    How good it seemed to hear himself called "Bud"!

A period or a comma following a quoted word is (*a*) always placed before the quote; a colon or a semicolon follows (*b*) the quote, unless (*c*) belonging exclusively to the quotation.

(*a*) "Yes, indeed," she asserted, "it would be splendid."
(*b*) He announced, "Briggs is elected"; so we all cheered.
    He had what he called "rock-ribbed convictions": hatred
      for war and faith in the League of Nations.
(*c*) Having written "My dear Sir:" he paused.

PUNCTUATION TO DISTINGUISH

Various mechanical devices are used, not to indicate structure, but to distinguish the words or groups of words to which they are applied. In regard to some of these marks the practice of writers varies considerably. In such matters a writer should be careful to follow consistently the method which he chooses to adopt.

138. Contractions. The apostrophe is essentially the sign of an omission in a word. Use it in contractions to mark the place of the omitted letter or letters.

Can't, don't, ne'er, I've, it's (it is), won't, rec'd, dep't, '24, in the 'nineties, five o'clock.

139. Possessive Genitives. The possessive singular of nouns is formed by adding (*a*) the apostrophe and *s* to the nominative; the possessive plural, by adding the (*b*) apostrophe if the plural ends in *s*, (*c*) the apostrophe and *s* if the plural is not so formed.

(*a*) Man's estate, Charles's book.
(*b*) Boys' books, our fathers' hearthstones.
(*c*) Men's deeds, the children's hour.

The formation of the possessive singular by means of the apostrophe alone has become idiomatic in certain combinations in which there would be a heaping up of sibilants.

For conscience' sake, Jesus' sufferings.

Some writers drop the *s* in the formation of the possessive singular of the proper names ending in *s*, writing Dickens' novels, Keats' poems. The weight of usage, however, is in favor of the full form, which usually is in accord with the pronunciation.

Dickens's novels, Keats's poems, Collins's odes, Furness's "Variorum."

Avoid the blunder of writing Dicken's, Keat's. Remember that the possessive of personal pronouns (*a*) is not formed by the apostrophe, though the possessive of indefinite pronouns (*b*) is so formed.

(*a*) Its, yours, theirs, ours, hers.
(*b*) One's, each other's, one another's, somebody's.

The possessive of a substantive of more than one word is formed by adding the apostrophe and *s* to the last word.

Somebody else's, Brown and Jones's store, Smith and Company's sale.

140. Plurals of Letters and Figures. Use the apostrophe and *s* to form the plurals of letters of the alphabet, numbers, and combinations of letters whose plural in *s* alone would be obscure or awkward.

Cross your t's and dot your i's. The 6's and 7's are indistinct. (But: "Things were at sixes and sevens.") Observe the *ly's* closely. His *and's* are hard to decipher.

CAPITAL LETTERS

141. Initial Capitalization. The use of capitals is initial when the capital letter marks the beginning of an element of style; or it is verbal, when the capital merely distinguishes the word to which it is applied. Initial capitalization is required at the beginning (*a*) of a new sentence, (*b*) of a verse in poetry, and (*c*) of a direct quotation having its own subject and predicate. It is not required (*c*), when a quotation is continued after an interpolation, nor (*d*) when the quotation is an integral part of the sentence in which it occurs.

(*a*)   Anger is like
    A full-hot horse, who being allowed his way,
    Self-mettle tires him.
(*b*) He smiled and said, "You have formed a very favorable idea of the abbey."
(*c*) "The first thing," said the third, "is to find out how to do it."
(*d*) When nature is "so careless of the single life," why should we coddle ourselves into the fancy that our own is of exceptional importance?

Initial capitalization is often used to mark the beginning of especially significant phraseology: (*a*) a subject propounded by the author for discussion, a watchword or phrase generally recognized as distinctive, or (*b*) the clause of a resolution, following an introductory *Whereas* or *Resolved*.

(*a*) The secret of public address to-day is then: Have something to say, something you wish to say; something you wish to say so that those who hear you shall understand, and act as you desire.

(*b*) Resolved, That immigration should be further restricted.

142. Verbal Capitalization. The use of capital letters to distinguish the word capitalized and not the element of which that word is the first, is peculiarly the sign of the proper name. It is applied in general to all words which serve as names of particular things. Accordingly the following classes of words should be capitalized:

1. All names of specific persons, races, and nationalities and all verbs and adjectives distinctly felt as derivatives of such names.

John, Henry V, Russian, Indian, Slav, Indo-Germanic, Aryan, to Americanize, Ciceronian, Martian.

BUT: gypsy, negro, to anglicize, welsh rabbit, the pasteurization of milk, harveyized steel, russia leather, knickerbockers.

2. Names of towns, countries, and, in general, recognized political and geographical divisions.

America, New England, the South, the Far East, the Orient, the East Side, the Mississippi River, the River Rhone, Cook County, Boston, Bostonians, Southern States, the State of Oregon, the State, Charles Street.

BUT: a state, to go west, the southern part of Georgia, the down-town wards. In certain publications, Charles street, the Mississippi river, New York bay.

3. Titles of persons when used with their names, and when standing alone, if the title is recognized as naming a particular person.

President Lincoln, the President, General Grant, Secretary of State Hay, the Secretary of State, Dr. Welch, C. W. Eliot, LL.D., John Jones, Ph.D., King Edward, Prince Henry, the King, the Crown, Chairman Brown, the Chair, the Postmaster-General.

BUT: the president of the society, the professor of Latin, the chairman of the meeting. The coroner was summoned.

4. Days of the week, months, recognized civil and ecclesiastical holidays, historical periods and movements, notable events that have become distinctively named.

Tuesday after the first Monday in November, the Fourth of July, the Fourth, Arbor Day, Defender's Day, New Year's Day, Easter, the Colonial Era, the Middle Age, the Renaissance, the Civil War, the Treaty of Paris, the Louisiana Purchase, Advent.

BUT: spring, winter, autumn, fall, the fifth of the month, lent, the dog days.

5. Names of the Deity, including adjectives used as names, and pronouns not preceded by their antecedent.

The Lord, the Almighty, the Ruler of the Universe, the Creator, Providence. And He that doth the ravens feed. God loves those whom he permits to suffer pain.

6. Names of legislative, judicial, administrative bodies, governmental departments, ecclesiastical courts.

Congress, the Fifty-second Congress, the New York Legislature, the Senate, the House, the Supreme Court, the Circuit Court, the Cabinet, the Department of the Interior, the Board of Health, the Electrical Commission, the Forestry Bureau, the General Assembly, the Conference, the Committee on Rules, The Lords, Parliament.

7. The names of societies and organizations, churches, educational and charitable institutions, corporations, trade unions, when called by their official titles or alluded to specifically by a title commonly accepted.

The Gridiron Club, Tammany Hall, Harvard College, Rockefeller Institute, the Carnegie Library, the Christian Endeavor Society, the Brick Church, Old North Church, The Brotherhood of Locomotive Engineers (the Brotherhood), The Standard Oil Company, The Sugar Trust, The University, The Phi Beta Kappa Society. The League of Nations. The League.

8. Personified Abstracts, when the personification is recognized.

Those who take honors in Nature's University are the really great and successful men in this world.

> Fair Science frowned not on his humble birth,
> And Melancholy marked him for her own.

9. The important words in the titles of books and papers, in the headings of chapters, and in the names of organizations. Usage varies slightly and is influenced by the effect in each case. Capitalize all nouns, pronouns, adjectives, verbs (except *be* and *is* when not final), and adverbs. Prepositions, articles, and conjunctions are ordinarily not capitalized. Capitalize both members of a compound noun, *Word-Formation*, the first member only of a compound adjective, *Twenty-five*.

NOTE. Usage does not warrant the capitalization of the traditional names of college classes, such as, freshman, sophomore; the names of school and college studies, such as grammar, history, mathematics, literature (except for emphasis in announcements); the names of sciences, such as paleography, comparative psychology.

143. The Uses of Italics. Italics serve to distinguish words in much the same way as verbal capitalization. In older usage they were often employed merely to emphasize the word or words so printed. Modern usage tends to restrict the use of italics for emphasis to cases in which emphasis contributes markedly to clearness. Italics (in manuscript indicated by underscoring with a single line) are conventionally used to distinguish certain classes of words as follows:

1. Foreign words used in an English context.

After much discussion they achieved a *modus vivendi.*
To know Italian *belles lettres* is not to know Italy, and to know English *belles lettres* is not to know England.
He had caught a new butterfly, the *Semnopsyche diana.*

2. The titles of periodicals, the names of ships, the names of characters in books and plays.

The *New York Evening Post,* the *Dial,* the *Dakota,* the *Mauretania.* In Paris he saw Rachel as *Phèdre.* In the *Post* office.

3. The titles of books, works of art, musical compositions, and important poems and essays. Many writers prefer to quote such names. Italics are more often used in books, and especially in books in which many such names appear.

Scott's *Lay of the Last Minstrel.* In 1805 appeared *The Lay of the Last Minstrel.* Milton's *Lycidas.* Rinehart's *Clyte. Aida.*

4. Words spoken of as words may be italicized. Double quotation marks, and sometimes single quotes, are used for the same purpose.

The word *knave* has an interesting history.

CHAPTER XII

USAGE IN DICTION

THE LAW OF USAGE

144. The Standard of Correctness. Good diction is diction that conforms to usage, both as to the words themselves and as to the meanings which they are used to convey. From the law of usage there is no appeal. That expression is good English which is approved by usage, no matter how low or illogical its origin; and no expression, however unimpeachable and desirable, becomes good English until it has won general acceptance. Yet there is and can be no fixed canon of good English. Our stock of words, like our social customs, tends to change, slowly and almost imperceptibly; and usage in language, like usage in manners, is a convention to be obeyed with some reservation of good taste and common sense.

The standards by which the correctness of a particular expression may be determined are fairly well summed up in these three — currency, repute, and idiom. A word is current when it is in general use at the present time, when, like a good coin, it is acceptable at face value in all parts of the country. A localism is current only in its locality; an archaism is no longer current anywhere. A word is reputable when it is available for dignified and self-respecting use in speech and writing. Many slang terms, for example, though for a time widely current, are not in good repute. An expression is idiomatic when it conforms, not only to English grammar, but also to the subtler requirements of usage which so vex the foreigner, and which are to be learned only by experience. Thus idiom and idiom alone accounts for the fact that we say *able to* but *capable of,* that we *make* remarks and suggestions, *express* sentiments, and *speak* words of welcome.

145. Violations of Usage. Expressions that violate usage are to be avoided for reasons that are obvious. Such expressions, being outside the conventional vocabulary, are liable not to be understood. Most slang, for example, however fresh and piquant, is clear only to the sophisticated, and the slang of yesterday is entirely clear to nobody. Moreover, violations of usage, because of their unusualness, are necessarily conspicuous, attracting attention that they do not deserve and bringing upon the writer the imputation of ignorance or bad taste.

Although one should seek to know and correct his errors in speech and writing, the best means of avoiding bad diction are positive rather than negative. Wide and discriminating reading and close attention to good speech wherever one is fortunate enough to hear it will give a fund of words that are above suspicion and a command of idiom that will make good English instinctive. Indeed, too great attention to details of usage and over-carefulness to avoid mistakes may lead to an affectation of correctness which, particularly in speech, is more objectionable than a modicum of robust error. The time to think most about correctness in written speech is after the first writing. Careful revision and rewriting should weed out all but the most venial offences against usage. Let your chief care be to write effectively, remembering that careless diction is ordinarily ineffective.

A complete list of even the more common errors in diction is neither possible nor desirable. Books devoted to disputed and faulty diction may be had — they grow out of date quickly — and copious lists of faulty expressions may be found in some dictionaries and text-books of rhetoric. What is attempted here is a classification of errors according to their sources, the gateways through which they creep into careless speech, a classification which one can extend from one's own reading and observation. Such errors may be divided, first of all, according to an old and entirely logical distinction, into unauthorized words, known as barbarisms, and unauthorized meanings of acceptable words, known as improprieties. One who uses a barbarism is ignorant or careless of the canon of English words. One who is guilty of an impropriety in diction violates the code according to which English words are used to express ideas.

BARBARISMS

146. Barbarisms of Illiteracy. Some wrong words are the result of a lack of the conventions of written language. Persons who make little or no use of books and newspapers may easily fall into the use of false forms or perpetuate obsolete expressions. Such errors in the speech of those whose habits are fixed are not surprising, and they do not justify the scorn of speakers who chance to be better educated. It is when they come from the lips of persons who should know better that they inflict the stigma of ignorance.

Aint, attackted, ax (ask), boughten, bursted (and busted), chaw, complected, cuss, disremember, to doctor (to go to a physician for treatment), drownded, everywheres, flustrate, froze (participle), heft, hern, het up, highfalutin, hisn, infare, illy, nohow, ornery, ourn, overly, pernickety, to red up, suspicioned, tarnal, tarnation, tastey, tuckered out, unbeknown, unbeknownst, underhanded, underminded, what-like.

147. Archaisms used for Quaintness. Words that are going out of use, or that have become restricted to poetry and to literary prose, are sometimes revived by persons who hope to give a touch of quaintness or humor to their style. A writer who can do so with skill and taste, as, for example, Charles Lamb and at times Eugene Field, may properly use such words where we should not expect them. The inexperienced writer should avoid them, for unskillful use of archaism falls flat, and archaism used with an air of smartness offends good taste.

Albeit, babe, bedecked, bedight, damsel, eld, e're, erst, erstwhile, forsooth, haply, hight, ilk, kine, maiden (noun), mayhap, methinks, meseems, morn, mid, midst, neath, o'er, oft, ofttimes, oftentimes, ope, otherwhere, otherwhiles, perchance, peradventure, prithee, proven, quoth, save (preposition), spake, swain, 'tis, 'twas, 'twixt, ween, whilst, wight, withal, yea, yore, yclept.

148. Foreign Words used for Display.
The use of foreign words to show off the writer's learning and facility is happily growing less and less common. The affectation is so obvious and so cheap that it invites ridicule. Some words that retain a foreign form and pronunciation have been found so useful in English that they are felt to be English words. *Naive, amateur, garage, chauffeur* are examples of words that need not be avoided on account of their origin. It must be admitted, too, that the occasional skillful use of a foreign word or phrase may add to the accuracy and the life and grace of English writing. But it is not easy to use such expressions with the certainty of taste that they demand. The inexperienced writer should use them rarely. There is ordinarily no place in his writing for such imported words as the following:

Ab initio, alter ego, artiste, beau monde, bêtise, chef d'oeuvre, con amore, currente calamo, distingué, éclat, en passant, entre nous, gaucherie, genus homo, hauteur, ingénue, mal de mer, métier, non est, nuance, qua, recherché, retroussé, raison d'être.

149. Clipped Words for Brevity.
Abbreviations are sometimes convenient, but they are always unsightly.

Usage is slow to accept an abbreviated form as idiomatic
— though it has accepted, for example, *cab, mob, miss,
van* — and resents unauthorized clipped words. In written
English, such words, however easily understood, seem flippant if not vulgar.

Ad, auto, bike, biz, cap, change, confab, doc, exam, grad, gym,
incog, pard, phone, photo, phiz, sport (one interested in sports),
varsity.

150. New Words Coined Carelessly. Newly coined
words, technically known as *neologisms,* are constantly being presented by their creators for admission to the canon
of English words. When such new words are the names
of new things which come into general use, the words are
likely to be accepted promptly. When they are merely
the product of careless haste and ignorance or of a desire
for novelty, the new coinages often linger halfway between
recognition and complete dismissal, until they are either
accepted by usage or wholly forgotten. They are most
often good words forced into a new part of speech or
awkwardly laden with a new affix.

Bogus, boodle, boodler, burglarize, burgle, burble, a combine, a
defy, to decease, educationalist, effectuate, enthuse, eventuate, an
expose, an invite, outclass, a steal, to suicide, a walkover, a win,
a write up.

151. Slang Coinages for Novelty. Slang is essentially
colloquial. To say that humorous and flippant barbarisms
are not to be used in serious writing, except as quoted or
at least recognized as slang, is to give sound advice. To
say that no one should use such a word, even in easy and
familiar speech, is to say too much — and to say it in
vain. For there is what may be called colloquial slang,
which when used sparingly and judiciously in speech, may
lighten the tone and even increase the accuracy of diction.
Such slang is most likely to be admissible in talk about

a subject which lies in the particular field of the talkers, and which has its own cant terms. College slang in the familiar talk of college men, racing slang among horsemen, baseball slang among players and fans is readily understood and is of some value for informality and lightness. But even such slang is to be kept out of written English or used with the apology of quotes.

Bamboozle, bootlick, flapper, flunk, frosh, grouch, a jollier, to josh, mucker, nifty, piker, plebe, renig, south-paw, sob-stuff, spoofing, think-tank, tight-wad, three-bagger, woozy.

152. Vulgarisms.

Ephemeral slang, the slang of the street-corners, has not the excuse for existence that can be made out for colloquial slang. It can serve no purpose but that of cheap humor, and it so speedily grows stale that it ceases to amuse. Any list of examples is certain to seem absurdly out of date. The following may serve as examples of the tone of vulgarism:

Bohick, beaut, dago, doc, classy, galoot, gazabo, highbrow, kibosh, loony, mazuma, nit, peacherino, rough-neck, rubber-neck, spondulicks, wop.

IMPROPRIETIES

153. Pretentious Diction.

Some improprieties arise from a desire to be impressive by using big words. The affectation of pompous diction is bad enough when the words are used correctly. When the desire to display knowledge leads the writer beyond his depth, the result is doubly bad, for it convicts him of both pretense and ignorance. Use simple words unless exactness of meaning demands large words. Avoid the overuse, or misuse to express commonplace ideas, of such words as the following:

Administer, avocation, canine, casualty, cognomen, collation, concourse, conflagration, consummated, deceased, decimated, equine, feline, gubernatorial, hymeneal, inaugurate, individual, magnificent, multitude, obsequies, officiate, palatial, partake, spectacular, splendid, strenuous, sumptuous, tumultuous.

154. Slangy Diction. Much slang consists of authorized words used in a sense not permitted by usage or in a construction not approved by idiom. What has been said of slang coinages applies here. The occasional apt use of a slangy expression in familiar speech may justify itself; the slang-habit soon becomes insufferable. The cultivation of any slang expression is unwise, for it dulls one's discrimination as to usage. Such expressions range from innocent colloquialisms to crass, and happily ephemeral, vulgarisms; for example:

To make good; to be up against; to put one over; up to one; to get by with; to get away with; to come across; to have a hunch; to be wise to; a peach; a wise guy; a swell outfit; dope, and to dope it out; to beat it.

155. The Confusion of Words Similar in Form. Careless reading and careless hearing sometimes lead to the mistaken use of words which resemble each other in sound or appearance. That two words are derived from the same root makes it important that the writer should know and remember precisely what each means. The following pairs of words are sometimes confused in meaning. If the distinction between them is not entirely clear, consult a good dictionary.

accede, cede	conscience, consciousness
accept, except	construe, construct
acceptance, acceptation	contemptible, contemptuous
accredit, credit	continual, continuous
affect, effect	convince, convict
beside, besides	council, counsel
casualty, casuality	conducive, conductive
ceremonious, ceremonial	credible, creditable
cession, cessation	decided, decisive
complimentary, complementary	definite, definitive

deprecate, depreciate
distinct, distinctive
enormity, enormousness
equable, equitable
exceptional, exceptionable
expiate, expatiate
falsity, falseness
grisly, gristly
haply, happily
healthful, healthy
human, humane
imaginary, imaginative
immigrant, emigrant
let, leave
missile, missive
most, almost
neglect, negligence
observation, observance

official, officious
practical, practicable
predict, predicate
principle, principal
prosecute, persecute
proscribe, prescribe
relative, relation
respectively, respectfully
sensible, sensitive
sewage, sewerage
signification, significance
specialty, speciality
specie, species
stationary, stationery
venial, venal
vocation, avocation
womanly, womanish

156. The Confusion of Words Akin in Meaning. Words do not fit ideas with mechanical exactness. Even a practiced and careful writer finds the nice discriminations of synonyms a difficult matter. Writers who are hasty or careless, especially those who like imposing words or technical terms, sometimes confuse words akin in meaning though dissimilar in form. Persistent use of a good dictionary is the remedy. Consult such an authority in regard to any of the following words that you are unable to use with certainty:

ability, capacity
abbreviated, abridged, brief
administer, deal
aggravate, provoke, exasperate
allude, name, mention
alternative, choice
amateur, novice
discover, invent
extensive, vast
homicide, murder

inaugurate, begin
indorse, sanction
juvenile, puerile
lend, loan, let
less, fewer
liable, likely, apt to
maintain, support, sustain
majority, plurality
apparently, evidently
balance, rest, remainder

claim, assert, insist
condign, severe
condone, repay, make up for
custom, habit
demean, debase
method, manner
party, person
points, aspects, suggestions

premature, early, false
raise, rear
talent, genius
temporary, transient, provisional
verbal, oral, literal
veritable, actual, real
vesture, attire, costume
whole, all, entire

157. Colloquialisms. Certain words have acquired in careless or ignorant speech meanings which are not approved by usage. Some of these expressions have achieved by their commonness recognition in familiar speech, especially in that easy conversation called small-talk, though they are still felt to be dubious in serious speech or in writing. Others are regarded by thoughtful speakers as inadmissible even in conversation.

Use with discretion:

Nice (agreeable or good); awfully (exceedingly); splendid (excellent); lovely (good or very good); mighty (very much); guess (suppose or be of the opinion); myself (I or me); first-rate (as an adverb); bound to (determined); fix (arrange or repair); funny (odd or surprising).

158. Singular and Plural Forms. Errors in the use of words sometimes arise from doubt whether the form is to be construed as singular or plural. Doubt is most likely to occur concerning nouns that retain the inflectional endings of a foregin language, nouns ending in *s,* and certain compound words.

1. These forms are *plurals* (of singulars in -um):

addenda
ana
Americana (and like formations)
arcana
bacteria
candelabra
curricula
data

effluvia
errata
impedimenta
incunabula
media
memoranda
paraphernalia
strata

2. Other plurals of non-English forms are:

Alumnae (alumna) and similarly formulae, larvae, nebulae, vertebrae.

Alumni (alumnus) and bacilli, genii (spirits), hippotami, loci, radii, syllabi, termini.

Automata (automaton) and criteria, phenomena.

Amanuenses (amanuensis) and analyses, antitheses, apices (apex), appendices, axes, bases, crises, ellipses, hypotheses, oases, parentheses, synopses, theses, vertices, vortices.

Beaux (beau), tableaux.

3. In the more common senses of the words, treat as *singular*:

Alms, amends, civics, economics, ethics, gallows, mathematics, measles, mechanics, mumps, news, optics, physics, the United States.

Treat as *plural*:

Assets, athletics, dice, dregs, eaves, gymnastics, nuptials, pincers, scissors, suds, tactics, wages.

Treat as *either singular or plural*:

Series, statistics, and collective words in general. Be consistent in the use of such a word throughout the sentence.

4. Use the following *plural* forms:

Aids-de-camp, brothers-in-law, courts-martial, editors-in-chief, forget-me-nots, handfuls, knights templars, lords justices, men-clerks, men-of-war, sons-in-law, spoonfuls.

159. Faulty or Doubtful Idioms.

Above. Undesirable in such use as *the above statement.* But: The shelf above was empty.

All the farther. Crude. Say *as far as.*

Alright. No such word. Use *all right.*

Anybody else's is preferable to *anybody's else.*

As. Ungrammatical in *I don't know as I do.*

Back of is colloquial only. *In back of* is a vulgarism.

Between. Absurd in *between every one.* Ordinarily use between for two, and among for more than two.

Blame on in *blame a thing on* a person is faulty. You can put the blame on him.

Claim. Do not claim that a thing is true. Claim rights or objects.

Couple. Not to be used indiscriminately as a synonym for two.

Differ from in quality; *differ with* or *from* in opinion.

Don't. Not *he don't.* Say, he, she, or it *doesn't.*

Due to is faulty in such use as: Due to the rain the exercises were postponed. Let it agree with a noun, as in The postponement was due to rain.

Either, neither. Note that the correlatives *either, or; neither, nor* require a singular verb. Pronounce them *eether, neether.*

Favor. Provincial in the sense of resemble.

Fewer and less. Use fewer of numbers; less of quantity. We had fewer admissions and less money.

Farther and further. Careful writers use *farther* of actual space, and *further* of degree.

Folks is in good use. So is *folk.*

Funny is not a good synonym for odd, curious, unusual.

Got. In *have got,* meaning possess, a distinct but well established colloquialism. Avoid it in formal speech. Prefer *got* to *gotten.*

Guess. Good when not overworked. Instead of I guess so, sometimes say *think, suppose, imagine.*

Help. Don't say *cannot help but.* Say cannot help liking, or cannot but like.

Heighth. False analogy to breadth, length, width; there is no such word. Say *height.*

Humans. Say human beings.

Hung. Reserve for objects. A criminal is *hanged.*

If. Do not use as synonymous with *whether.*

Individual. Not a synonym for person, man, woman.

In, into. Preserve the distinction between motion towards and action or state within. He jumped into (not in) the river. Come *into* contact with, not *in* contact.

Infer. Do not use as synonym of *imply* or *intend.* Infer from not by.

Kind of a. Say kind of.

Like is not a conjunction; hence it is not to be followed by a verb, as in *like they do in my town.*

Lots of. Colloquial.

Most. Not to be used for *almost.*

Mutual friend. Supported by usage.

Myself. Not to be used freely as a substitute for me. Reserve it for intensive and reflexive use, as in *I did it myself; I hurt myself*. Don't say *Mrs. Jones and myself*.

Nohow. Vulgarism.

Off of. Omit of.

One's. Do not hesitate to substitute *his* for this possessive when *one's* is over-formal.

Out loud. Prefer aloud.

Part with possessions; part from friends or places.

Peer does not mean the best of it; it means the equal of.

Plenty. Avoid such use as *plenty good enough.*

Proven. Always use *proved*. There is excellent linguistic reason for objecting to proven.

Raise. Inelegant in a *raise in salary*. Say *increase*.

Real. Ungrammatical as an adverb; e.g., real glad to see you.

Same. Not a pronoun. Very crude in I have received the goods and find same satisfactory.

Sitting hen is correct. Controversy about this form is perennial.

Some. Not a synonym for somewhat, as in *I was some tired*.

Team does not mean one horse, nor does it include the vehicle.

That far. Prefer *as far as that* or *so far as that.*

Those kind, these kind. Crude. Say *those* or *these,* or say *that kind.*

We. No longer used as a modest substitute for I. Say I or reconstruct the sentence.

Will and shall. Don't allow will to crowd shall out of your vocabulary.

  Avoid particularly the use of will in the first person when the context clearly shows that no determination or control is intended.

  Incorrect: We will probably have rain. He is gone and we will not see his like again. I will be pleased to come to your reception.

Would like. Colloquial misuse of would in the first person, particularly replying to invitations. Say I should like; e.g., I should like to accept your invitation.

Exercises in the Choice and Use of Words

I

In the following sentences the italicized words are inappropriate in everyday prose. Supply in each case a better word, and justify your choice.

1. You will find this confection a dainty gift for Christmas *morn*.
2. In ten, *nay* in even five, years you will repent of your action.
3. Men *oftentimes* forget their true interests in the enthusiasm of the moment.
4. Two *swains* from Jonesville visited in our *midst* Sunday.
5. We must protect the interests of Bucks County *ere* it *be* too late.
6. Methods appropriate to *days of yore* are out of date.

II

Correct violations of idiom:

1. The stands are full with excited spectators.
2. Let us stop at the next house and find out where we are at.
3. What is the little girl frightened of?
4. I'll be to stop at the bank and get some money.
5. Your methods have been very different to what I have been used.
6. Such things may have occurred, but I am not conversant of them.
7. I can't reconcile your statement to that of the other speakers.
8. His brother died a few months ago from the fever. He was ill also but recovered of the disease.
9. This work deals of electricity in all its branches. The author has the faculty for making technical matters clear.
10. He expressed a strong preference of stories of adventure. In that respect his taste was different than I had expected.

III

The italicized words are evidently not the words that the writers wished to use. Supply the correct word and explain the distinction involved.

1. When refused the money, the anarchist hurled the deadly *missive* at the cashier.

2. I will relate an experience every *instance* of which happened just as I tell it.

3. We were horrified to learn of the barbarities *conducted* by the Turkish troops.

4. The chairman of the committee *predicates* a sweeping victory for the whole ticket.

5. The classes of troops included in the order to mobilize *compromised* the whole of the Bulgarian army.

6. The important event to which *illusion* has been made is familiar to all.

7. It is scarcely *creditable* that the work is finished already.

8. After the child had asked three times the mother *left* him go.

9. In the periodical index I found *a surfeit* of interesting articles on Stevenson's life.

10. Special provision has been made at the almshouse for the *poor* insane.

IV

Rewrite these sentences, retaining of the words in the parenthesis the one which seems to you required by the context:

1. The (sewerage, sewage) which flows into the river pollutes the water.

2. I have already sent my (acceptance, acceptation) of the offer.

3. He was an (ingenious, ingenuous) youth when he came to the city, but he learned quickly.

4. I was merely doing what (most, almost) everybody about me did.

5. No one who knows him had any doubt of his (truth, veracity).

6. You should not have struck your little brother, even though his behavior was (aggravating, provoking, exasperating).

7. The (continuous, continued) tooting of automobile horns outside my window is annoying.

8. His (neglect, negligence) of a few simple precautions caused the accident.

9. The accident might have been much worse. The only (casualty, casuality) was a broken arm.

10. If I had not known of the (contemptible, contemptuous) treatment accorded our first messenger, I should not have thought the report of the second (credible creditable).

V

Correct such errors in the choice and use of words as you find in these sentences. Show precisely why the diction that you object to is faulty.

1. The members of my class are so enthused over the banquet that I expect everybody has subscribed.

2. I guess Biology I isn't such a cinch as most everyone seem to think.

3. The car was full in front, but in back there was plenty room enough.

4. An hour's rowing tired us, due to a strong wind, so we landed and had our lunch.

5. I would certainly like to have been there, for I hear you were all greatly effected by the speech.

6. What has transpired in the Smith Company's store? The place don't look like it used to.

7. After having been victimized by an agent for mining stocks, I have always been suspicious of them.

8. The man whose apples he stole declined to persecute him; otherwise he might have been found five dollars.

9. If I had wanted to have insisted I might of had my own way, but I would only have made a lot of trouble for nothing.

10. Your enquiry regarding my preparatory work in English received. I wish to state that I have not the data at hand for giving an exact summary of that work, but I will attempt to give a brief and somewhat inaccurate review of my work along this line.

VI

Correct or improve the following sentences:

1. I fell for his line of talk and bought the car.

2. You must convince your clientele that it is up to them to stick to a man of your caliber.

3. Two stalwart minions of the law bagged a notorious individual on Blank Street yesterday.

4. We were delayed by a bursted tire that was unusually hard to fix.

5. When we saw he was up against it, he acquiesced with our proposal.

6. Such a dicta can only brand one as presumptuous.

7. The custom of early closing in dry goods stores was inaugurated at Smith Brothers emporium this week.

8. Did you get an invite to the reception? I did, but I've got to go somewheres else that night.

9. This phenomena was so intensely interesting that each of us were riveted to the spot.

10. The assembled democratic citizenry of the state offered the gubernatorial nomination to that impeccable jurist, Judge Jones.

11. Soon the big steamer was in the channel and independent of help longer.

12. In this chapter he mentions a number of books the authors and characters of which are given.

13. The jurisdiction of the Court of Appeals is coextensive with the limitations of the State.

14. The speed, cheapness, and durability of operation of the gasoline car make it the peer of pleasure vehicles.

15. The success of the auction succeeded our most sanguinary expectations.

16. Woodworking is practicable. To some business men it acts as a useful recreation. To a boy who has some spare time it may be used as a means of earning money.

REFERENCES

A Manual of Good English by MacCracken and Sandison (Macmillan); *Text, Type, and Style* by G. B. Ives (Atlantic); *Composition and Rhetoric* by A. H. Espenshade, Chapter XVI (Heath); *The King's English* by Fowler and Fowler (Oxford).

CHAPTER XIII

USAGE IN SPELLING

SPELLING AS LITERARY HABIT

160. The Difficulty of Spelling. English spelling is undeniably difficult. It is so far from phonetic that the sound of the word is an untrustworthy guide, and it is so far from consistent that analogy is likely to be misleading. And yet it must be learned, for modern usage invests the accepted spelling with a sacredness that it hardly deserves. Bad spelling is only a little above bad manners.

Difficulty with spelling is of two kinds. Some words are misspelled because they have never been really learned. They are just as likely to be wrong as right, and the speller does not recognize his error until it is pointed out. Every teacher is familiar with the pupil who, when asked to revise *finaly,* calmly makes it *finnaly,* and is grieved to learn that the change is not an improvement. Such a bad speller usually repeats his old errors with incidental variations. Another kind of difficulty is temporary but embarrassing. The writer cannot remember at the moment how the word is to be spelled, and is distressingly conscious of his dilemma. Reflection merely increases his uncertainty. Only the dictionary or a kind friend can help him out of it.

161. The Remedy. For the chronic bad speller such extreme measures as a return to the spelling book and the methods of the elmentary grades may be necessary, yet the memorizing of rules without putting them into practice by some sort of careful drill is of little value.

Perhaps the wisest plan is to discover as many as possible of the offending words and study them until they are permanently fixed in memory. A student whose themes come back with corrections in spelling should make a list of all the words, spelling them correctly in his own handwriting, and should keep this list where it will come repeatedly under his eye. If he is conscientious in the matter, he will find that one after another of the words will begin to look odd to him when misspelled. The habit of painstaking revision will complete the work.

An occasional lapse of memory as to the correct spelling of a word is for some persons inevitable. Readiness to appeal to the dictionary is the only immediate remedy. But satisfactory spelling is, of course, instinctive, and reference to the dictionary ought to be unnecessary. If the memory can be stimulated by some convenient rule, or even by an association of some haphazard sort, it may not be necessary to consult authority. Elaborate sets of rules, with abundant exceptions, may be found in the prefatory matter of a good dictionary and in special manuals. All that is attempted here is to give a few hints which one may apply as they prove themselves useful.

162. Clues to the Spelling of Troublesome Words. Strive to master once for all, words that you have found difficult. Use these devices:

1. Fix the uncertain syllable by remembering the root or some cognate form; *e.g.*, separate (par*a*re), laboratory (lab*o*rare), athletics (Greek athlon, hence not atheletics), occurred (curro), imagine (im*a*go), exasperate (asp*e*ra), calendar (Kalends), presentiment (sent*i*re), extravagant (vag*a*re), sacrilegious (lego, not related to religion), emigrant (emigrare), immigrant, permanent (man*e*re).

2. Remember the prefix; *e.g.*, disappoint, disappear (not diss-), professor (pro, hence not proff), describe (de- not dis-), persuade (per- not pur-), amend (not ad-, hence not

ammend, cf. emendare), misspell (mis), mistake (mis- not miss), eccentric (Greek ek, hence two c's), accommodate (ad + commodum), committee (con + mitto), occasion (ob + casus), perspiration (not pre-), prejudice (not pred-), decease (de-), disease (dis-).

3. Note the suffixes, which are usually added without the dropping of a letter; *e.g.*, thinness, suddenness, soulless, woolly, baneful, singeing. Observe that argument, abridgment, acknowledgment, and a few others are exceptions. Words ending in y usually change y to i before a suffix; e.g., beauty, beautiful; bounty, bountiful; duty, dutiful.

4. Observe the pronunciations; *e.g.*, villain (not pronounced villyun, hence not -ian); amateur (not -tu-er), column (not rimed with volume, cf. columnar), similar (not rimed with familiar), grievous (not grievyous).

5. Recall associated words; *e.g.*, ridiculous (when tempted to write rediculous, remember ridicule), tyranny (one r in tyrant), parallel (parallax), definite (finite).

6. For remembering the order of e and i in such words as receive and believe, various rules have been suggested. Such key words as Alice or Celia, in which i follows l and e follows c, give a helpful hint. A broader rule is the fact that after s-sounds the form is ei (when pronounced e) except in siege. After all, the only safe way is to learn to spell each word. Here are the more familiar of them:

Conceive, receive, deceive, perceive, leisure, seize, sheik, sleight, weird.

Relieve, believe, frieze, niece, siege, liege, lief, lien, wield, yield, conscience, grief, ancient.

7. The plurals of nouns ending in o are not uniform. A number of such words add es; *e.g.*, buffaloes, calicoes, cargoes, desperadoes, dominoes, fiascoes, heroes, indigoes, innuendoes, jingoes, manifestoes, mosquitoes, mottoes,

mulattoes, negroes, (but negritos), noes, potatoes, tomatoes, tornadoes, torpedoes, viragoes, volcanoes. Most other words ending in o add s. A few form the plural either way.

CONVENTIONS IN SPELLING

163. Compound and Divided Words. The hyphen serves as a mark both of compounding and of division. It is used (*a*) to join into a compound words which are to be thought of as making one idea, and (*b*) to join the parts of words that are for any reason broken into syllables or letters. It is not possible to give definite rules for the compounding of words for the reason that many compounds are transition forms. When two words come to be much used together, they are likely to be treated for a time as independent forms, then hyphened, and later, perhaps, merged into a simple word. Thus the game that was once called foot ball (like medicine ball), is now sometimes written foot-ball and more commonly football. It is well to reduce the use of the hyphen so far as usage permits; that is, to write as one word the compound that may be given either the hyphened or the solid form and to write as separate words those couplets that are not clearly established as compounds. The later dictionaries are more explicit in such matters (though they are not always consistent), and they should be consulted in specific cases. General principles are so open to exceptions that it is scarcely worth while to study them. The following hints may be helpful:

1. Use the hyphen regularly in compound numerals: twenty-five, forty-one. But: two fifths, when the fifths are thought of as distinct, and two-fifths if the fraction is felt as a unit. But, fifteen, fourfold.

2. Use the hyphen ordinarily in adjective combinations that precede their noun: A two-fifths share; a four-fold

mystery; an over-zealous servant; the so-called guardian. But, falsely so called. Be not over zealous.

3. Usage is uncertain as to to-day, to-morrow, to-night. The hyphened form is the more conservative and at present the more general. Some writers prefer today, tomorrow, tonight.

4. The following lists of words may prove helpful as suggesting the tendency of usage as to compound words.

Written Solid	Hyphened	Written Separate
already	able-bodied	all right
altogether	boarding-house	any one
anybody	brother-in-law	a while
anyhow	by-law	bee line
anything	cut-out (noun)	blue jacket
baseball	forget-me-not	black list
busybody	good-by	building site
bystander	great-grandfather	cartridge belt
cannot	half-hearted	card index
deathbed	hanger-on	college life
everybody	mother-tongue	dairy farm
forever	non-partisan	day laborer
halfway	office-holder	every one
inasmuch	old-fashioned	half brother
moreover	quarter-mile	hand bag
nevertheless	rear-admiral	night latch
nowadays	self-respect	one's self
nowhere	six-foot	printing press
rainbow	starting-point	real estate
taxpayer	touch-down	street car
typewritten	trade-mark	some one
warehouse	twenty-five	time limit
whenever	two-step	verbal noun
wherever	well-bred	waste product
whoever	wonder-worker	water color

164. Abbreviations. Before using an abbreviation a writer should be certain of two things: (1) that the abbreviated form will not be obscure; (2) that the use of the abbreviation will not be inelegant. A few recognized abbreviations are no more obscure than the words for which they stand. Others should be explained either in a footnote when they are used for the first time or in a preliminary list. The second requirement may be met by restricting the use of abbreviations, except a few well-established forms, to alphabetic lists, formulas, tabulations, and to such half-detached prose as notes and references. Some use of abbreviations is permissible also in business letters and in technical or scientific descriptions. In ordinary connected discourse, however, few abbreviated forms should be used. Remember that an abbreviation (not a contraction) is always followed by a period.

Use regularly as a part of the name of a person: Mr., Mrs., Messrs., Dr., M. D., D. D., LL. D., D. C. L., F. R. S., R. A., Ph. D., Ph. B., A. B., A. M., Jr., Sr., St., Esq., U. S. A., U. S. N.

Note that Miss is not an abbreviation.

1. Use sparingly, as for example in the address of a business letter, the following when prefixed to the name including initials or written in full: Capt., Lieut., Rev., Rt. Rev., Prof., Hon., Rt. Hon., Gen., Col. Spell out all of these when the initials are lacking. Many writers spell them in any case.

Capt. A. B. Smith, U. S. N.; The Rev. Dr. Ralph Johnson; Professor Bloomfield; Captain Brown; Colonel Goethals. The Reverend Dr. Johnson.

Avoid the vulgarism of Reverend Johnson.

2. Use in dates and times of day: A. D., B. C., A. M., P. M., (a. m. and p. m. are permissible), M. (meridian). Ordinarily spell out the names of days and months. Inst., prox., and ult., as applied to months are obsolescent and awkward. Give the name of the month.

3. Use sparingly (in literary composition, not at all)

i. e., e. g., cf., q. v., viz. (read as *namely*), vs., loc. cit., etc.,
N., E., S., W., C. O. D., p. or pp., f. or ff., N. B., P. S.

4. Per cent. is almost universally used for per centum.
Many publications omit the period. Do not use *etc.* as an
easy refuge from the mental effort of making a series complete. If necessary, say " and the like," " and others," or
some such expression.

165. Numerals. Whether numbers are to be represented
by words or by figures is determined partly by the context
and partly by the immediate effect. Thus a piece of
writing in which numbers are much used will prefer figures,
and a series of numbers in the same sentence will be made
consistent; whereas an isolated number is given the form
that seems more convenient and sightly.

1. Use Arabic figures regularly for the names of years,
numbers of houses, pages or sections of books, divisions
of land, persons or things in a numerical series.

The year 55 B.C., 1910, 25 Bank Street, pp. 5–6, Section 5 of
Article II, Ward 12, Conductor Number 2543, Shelf 46.

2. Use Arabic figures for the days of the month when
the date is given in full.

May 5, 1910. The fair will be held October 5, 6, 7, and 8.
Note. — The form May 5th, 1910, is undesirable. The form
5/5/10 is unsightly and inconvenient. *May the fifth* may be
written in formal notes.

3. Use words for the clipped forms of years and the
names of decades.

In eighty-five, the spirit of seventy-six, the nineties. But, the
class of '99.

4. Use Arabic figures for all numbers the expression of
which in words would be long or awkward. Ordinarily,
such numbers, both cardinal and ordinal, as would require

three or more words and sums of money which include dollars and cents should be expressed in figures.

J. E. Morford took from 155 pear trees 755 boxes which sold at $2 a box, net, thus making a profit of $1510 an acre. — *Review of Reviews.*

$1.75 a year; $20.18 in the treasury; $375; write $375.00 only when the figures are arranged in columns.

5. In ordinary discourse, where the matter is not technical and numbers do not occur frequently, prefer words to figures, except in such cases as have been noted above.

One dollar a year; twenty cents a dozen. He gave the boy a quarter. A two-cent stamp and twenty-three cents in change. West Thirty-third Street; ten years old; eighty-five years; his eighty-fifth birthday.

6. Use Roman numerals (without period) for the names of rulers, the chapters of books, the articles of documents.

George V succeeded Edward VII as king. Leo XIII; Chapter IV, Article X, Section 5 of the Constitution.

7. In ordinary discourse do not use the signs %, °, @, □ ft., 6′ 10″. Reserve them for tables and for technical or scientific writings in which such symbols are specially needed. Do not write # 25 for Number 25.

REFERENCES

Learn to Spell by L. W. Payne (Rand, McNally); *Essentials of Spelling* by Pearson and Suzzallo (American Book Co.); *A College Handbook of Writing* by G. B. Woods, Chapter V. (Doubleday, Page); *The Mechanics of Writing* by R. W. Pence (Macmillan).

CHAPTER XIV

USAGE IN LETTERS AND MANUSCRIPTS

THE FORMS OF LETTERS

166. The Letter. Of all the literary types, the letter alone deserves discussion here, for it differs notably from every other form of writing. The author of a letter is his own publisher. Consequently, he is responsible, not only for the matter of his writings, but also for those details which a writer for the press leaves to editors and proofreaders. The selection of the paper, the arrangement of margins and spaces, as well as spelling and punctuation, are all to be determined by the knowledge and taste of the writer. Writing intended for the printer is made impersonal by the fact that it is addressed to a considerable number of readers. It is in most cases to be read by " all to whom these presents come,' as the old legal phrase has it. A letter, however, is a personal communication to a specific reader. It is in our personal relations that we are most careful to observe the laws of courtesy. Letters are also usually designed to serve a practical purpose, and practical ends must be accomplished as conveniently as possible. The two principles which determine the form of a letter are therefore, courtesy and convenience.

According to their varied observance of these principles letters may be regarded as of three types — the business letter, the formal note, and the friendly letter. The business letter is first of all convenient — for writing, reading, filing, and answering. Courtesy, though essential, is less significant. The formal note, on the other hand, strictly observes every requirement of courtesy, and avoids all convenient short cuts and abbreviations. In the friendly letter the rigidness of both principles is relaxed; for such a letter, being between friends, may approach the informality of conversation, and may forego the exactness of detail demanded by business.

167. The Business Letter. The distinguishing characteristic of a business letter is its completeness. All the information needed for using it appears at the beginning of the first page. The date and place of writing, known technically as the heading, the name and address of the person written to, known as the address, and the name of the writer, known as the signature, written last to authenticate the body of the letter, are three parts of a business letter essential to its convenience. Two other parts, the formal salutation and the complimentary close, are required by courtesy. Printed letter heads often expand the heading so as to give further information, such as the names and positions of the officers of the company, or the location of factories or branches. Whether written or printed, the heading should be sufficiently exact to serve when combined with the signature as an address for the reply.

In a correctly ordered business letter the essential parts are not only present, but they are arranged on the page so as to balance each other and produce a neat appearance. The body of the letter should be as nearly as possible in the middle of the page. If the letter is to be brief, leave a wide margin at the top. If it is to be long, begin well up so that the top and bottom spaces will be nearly equal. The heading should be above and to the right, ending at the right margin, symmetrical with regard to the address, which is to the left, beginning at the left hand margin. The salutation begins also at the left margin, and the signature ends at the right margin.

In general, symmetry is obtained in handwriting by indenting successive short lines about an inch at a step. This not only makes the effect more pleasing; it has the advantage of making essential parts of the letter stand out where they easily catch the eye. In typewritten letters the indentions are sometimes omitted for mechanical convenience.

168. The Text of the Business Letter. In the phrasing and punctuation of the business letter, convenience is similarly recognized. The usually admitted abbreviations, such as may be found listed in a good dictionary, are appropriate in a business letter. Terminal punctuation of the heading, address, and complimentary close may be omitted except as required by abbreviation. The formal salutation may be punctuated with a colon or a colon and a dash. Do not use a comma, which is for informal salutation. The use of a dash, either alone or in combination with a comma, is undesirable. In form the salutation may be *Dear Sir, Dear Sirs,* or *Gentlemen.* The usual complimentary close is *Yours truly.* That form should be used regularly in business communications. Courtesy no longer requires a heavily formal close. " I am, my dear Sir, with highest regards, Your most obedient servant " was once thought suitable in a business letter. Today it is better usage, certainly, though not prevailing usage, to omit all forms of hanging close, such as " Hoping to hear favorably from you, we remain, Yours truly." End your letter with a complete sentence, say *Yours truly,* and sign your name.

The phrasing of the body of the letter should be that of any other simple and direct prose. Convenience does not demand clumsy abbreviations. Do not say " Y'rs of the 10th rec'd." Do not use dubious or awkward English, such as " In reply *would say.*" " Have sent goods." " Your favor to hand."

The abbreviation *inst.* for the present month, *prox.* for

the coming month, and *ult.* for the past month are clumsy and antiquated. If the letter you are replying to was dated September 12, say September 12, no matter when you are writing. Courtesy to your correspondent does require complete sentences, direct and exact expression, which will imply that though you have no time to waste you have time enough to deal properly with the business in hand. The opening sentence of a business letter is often difficult, partly because of a somewhat foolish prejudice against beginning with the pronoun I. If I is the natural opening for what you want to say, there is no reason for avoiding it. If it is desirable to allude to the date of the letter which you reply to, say simply " Your letter of September 12 has been received. In reply let me say that . . ." or " In reply to your letter of September 12, I wish to say that . . ." Do not call it a favor as in " Your favor of the 12th inst. at hand. In reply would say. . . ."

The paragraphing of the business letter should adjust itself to the separate items of business. Each separate matter will have its own paragraph, even if some paragraphs are as short as one sentence, and the usual rules for paragraphing will not apply.

It sometimes happens that a business letter is addressed to a correspondent whom one knows personally and toward whom one wishes to lessen the formality of the business form. In such a case a compromise between the business and the informal salutation is often used, as follows:

Mr. John Doe,
   Tarrytown, N.Y.
My dear Mr. Doe:

A woman signs a business letter with her name and adds in parentheses the information that will enable her correspondent to address her properly. Thus a Miss Jones will sign (Miss) Mary E. Jones; and Mrs. Jones will sign Lucy A. Jones. and will write below (Mrs. John J. Jones).

Neither will ever sign a commuication with the titles Miss or Mrs., nor will a man sign himself Mr., Dr., or Capt., though, if the circumstances require it, he may add the name of his official position in parentheses.

169. The Formal Note. Social usage makes the formal note rigidly conventional. It should be free from any sign of haste, carelessness, or whim. Courtesy to one's correspondent requires that one take whatever pains may be needed to conform to usage and at the same time to make the note a neat and careful expression of one's self. Such a note is usually phrased in the third person and preferably in the most commonly used terms. Do not try to express sincerity or warmth of feeling by variations from the usual. If such an expression is desirable and appropriate, the note should not be formal, but should be in the first person.

Formal notes are most commonly used to give, accept, or decline invitations and to acknowledge formal messages of congratulation or condolence. The following forms are well established by usage:

Mrs. John Brown requests the pleasure of Mr. and Mrs. John Smith's company at dinner on Monday, April the tenth, at seven o'clock.
205 Blank Street,
April first.

Mr. and Mrs. John Smith accept with pleasure Mrs. John Brown's kind invitation to dinner on Monday, April the tenth, at seven o'clock.
2906 Main Street,
April the second.

Mr. and Mrs. John Smith regret that on account of a previous engagement they are unable to accept Mrs. John Brown's kind invitation to dinner on April the tenth, at seven o'clock.
2906 Main Street,
April the second.

Mrs. Henry Brown gratefully acknowledges Mr. and Mrs. John Smith's kind expression of sympathy.
2215 Market Street,
May the fifteenth.

Mr. James Madison requests the honor of your company at a luncheon at the Hotel Savoy on Friday, the twelfth of June, to meet Miss Margaret Brown.
The Country Club,
June second.

The following general rules may be offered:

In the formal note avoid all abbreviations except Mr. and Mrs. Write out numerals except such as require more than two words. In general write out days of the month and use Arabic figures for numbers of houses. It is not necessary to space a written note like an engraved one. Use unruled note paper, white or cream, not tinted; and put the written message evenly in the middle of the sheet, leaving about the same margin on all sides. Young persons not yet burdened with many social responsibilities are likely to use the formal note chiefly in replying to invitations. They should observe that the reply always takes the degree of formality used in the invitation. If you are invited informally, reply informally. In any case always use the same form throughout. In the phrasing of the note avoid " will be unable to accept "; the acceptance is in present time. The expression " invitation for dinner," though sometimes used, is less desirable than " to dinner."

170. The Friendly Letter. A letter between correspondents who know each other personally, or who though unacquainted stand upon common ground, may, of course, take the form of the business letter, or if the situation demands it, of the formal note. In many cases, however, neither the completeness of the business letter nor the conventional courtesy of the note is desirable. In such a case the business form is modified. The heading is simplified or dropped altogether. The address is unnecessary, and the salutation may be varied to suit the degree of intimacy expressed by the letter. The following is a good form:

1112 Hathaway Road

Dear Mr. Jones,

You will remember that at the Club yesterday evening you expressed a desire to know Bob Smith's address. I have just come upon it among some papers and am happy to send it to you. It is 235 Morton Street, Denver, Colorado.

Yours very truly,
JAMES W. BROWN.

May 14, 1915.

If the heading is embossed or printed on the stationery, nothing at all need be written above the salutation. If it is desirable to let your correspondent know your exact address, make the heading complete. If your permanent address is well known to him, omit all details except such as will show where you are writing. The salutation admits of wide variation, and may be followed by a comma or by a colon. *My dear Mr. Jones* is regarded as more formal than *Dear Mr. Jones*. These are the usual forms. When close intimacy warrants, *Dear Jack, Dear Uncle Bob, Dearest Mary*, and similar variants are appropriate. The complimentary close also reflects the degree of friendship. *Yours very truly* is perhaps the most common. *Yours sincerely* and *yours faithfully* between friends, *Yours cordially* in an invitation, *Yours affectionately* or *Yours lovingly* between members of the same family, are common enough.

A few forms are frowned upon by usage. Do not write:

Mr. Jones,
Dear Friend:

Do not use the name only without any salutation. Never omit the *Dear* from the salutation. It is purely conventional and implies neither intimacy nor affection; it does not even imply social equality. Do not drop *Yours* from the complimentary close. That is, do not sign yourself *Sincerely* or *Faithfully* but always *Yours sincerely* or *Sincerely yours*. It is perhaps better, in order to relieve the friendly letter of formality, to put the date at the close, in the lower left hand corner.

171. Paper and Envelopes. For business correspondence white unruled paper of letter size, $8\frac{1}{2}$ x 11 inches, is most commonly used, and is most convenient for filing. For the business letters of one who writes such letters only occasionally, and has no letter-heads and no typist, single sheets, note size, 5 or $5\frac{1}{2}$ x 8 inches, are often more convenient. Only one side is used for writing. The envelope for either size of paper will be about $6\frac{1}{4}$ x $3\frac{1}{2}$ inches. Letter paper is folded first horizontally across the middle so as to fold the writing in. This doubled sheet is then folded vertically in from the sides so as to make two creases which divide the paper into thirds. So folded the letter will slip easily into a commercial envelope. Care should be taken to fold neatly, so that the edges will be even. Note paper in single sheets is folded in three thicknesses horizontally. The envelope should be addressed legibly, the lines indented as in the address in the letter. Terminal punctuation except after abbreviations is unnecessary. Many careful writers prefer not to abbreviate the names of states in handwriting. No word or symbol need be prefixed to the street number.

Paper for social and friendly correspondence should be rigidly conventional. It is usually heavy enough so that if need be both sides may be used. The order of pages in a book should be followed, and the writing should be kept within margins. The effect of neatness and certainty in the form of such letters is well worth striving for. The sheets are folded once, horizontally, and slipped, fold downward, the top of the first page facing out, into envelopes which match them exactly in size and quality.

THE PREPARATION OF MANUSCRIPTS

172. Copy for the Printer. The importance of neatness and accuracy in manuscript intended for the printer is obvious. The typesetter expects to " follow copy." It is not his business to supply omissions or to correct the author's mistakes. If possible the manuscript should be typewrittten, with a black ribbon. In any case it should be written on one side only of sheets of white paper, of uniform size, preferably about 8½ x 11 inches. A margin of an inch or more should be kept on the left, and paragraphs should be indented about an inch. Be sure that no unevenness in either margin could mislead the compositor into thinking that a paragraph break is intended elsewhere. If you wish to make a paragraph where you failed to indent put the paragraph sign in the margin, and indicate by a bent line the point in the text where the break is to occur.

Pages should be numbered consecutively in Arabic numerals, preferably at the top of the sheet, either in the middle or at the right hand corner. If new pages are to be inserted, designate them by letters. That is, if three pages are to go in between 17 and 18, the numbering will be 17, 17a, 17b, 17c, 18. If the pages are taken out, note the fact at the end of the page preceding the gap. If two pieces of paper are put together to make a page, use paste rather than pins or clips. Directions to the printer as to size of type or other matters may be written in the margin, encircled by a line to show that they are distinct from the text.

The finished manuscript should be kept flat, not rolled or folded. It is not necessary to fasten the pages together with pins or clips. If such fastenings are used they should not be relied on to fix the order of the sheets. This should be made entirely clear by the page numbers, helped out in a case of a long work by a table of contents. Since different parts of the same manuscript may be given to several different compositors to set up, these directions are important. The manuscript should bear all necessary information for its use, such as the name of the author and the purpose for which it is intended. A careful final reading to catch up errors and to make sure that details of spelling, punctuation, and the like are consistent will save trouble and expense later. Students who have opportunities to act as correspondents for newspapers will find that " clean copy," that is, copy that requires little editing, is appreciated.

173. Themes and Essays. Writing undertaken for practice in English composition or as part of the work in other school or college subjects should have the same care as writing for the press. The habit of making the written text complete and correct in details is invaluable. Even the rough copy should be accurate as far as it goes. Ability to use a typewriter is of advantage, because the legibility and compactness of type make errors and faults of style easier to detect.

Manuscript to be offered to a teacher should have ample space for corrections and comments. Use only the paper prescribed in the course. Drop the title two inches from the top of the page and leave one or two lines blank between the title and the first line of the text. Leave a generous, even margin on the left broken only by indention to mark paragraphs. Keep the right edge more or less even, leaving only a narrow margin. It is best in handwriting not to divide many words at the end of the line Never leave blank so much of a line as to make the reader expect a paragraph break where none is intended. Number the pages at the top in Arabic numerals, omitting if you like the number on the title page.

Cultivate an even, legible handwriting, linking all the letters of a word, and avoiding back-hand or very slanting script. Don't erase unless you can do so neatly. Draw a line through words that are to be stricken out. Use the caret to indicate the place of insertion for words to be added, and write the words neatly above the line, centering them over the caret. If many such changes are needed, rewrite the page. You will probably find it possible to make other improvements as you do so. The writing should not be so large as to sprawl, nor so microscopic as to be difficult to read. Do not let the long letters of one line reach up or down into the letters of adjoining lines.

Do not expect to practice good craftmanship in writing without adequate tools. Have a good supply of paper of two kinds — a cheaper quality to be used for rough drafts and tentative outlines, and plenty of the kind required by your instructors for the finished work. Have pens and pencils with which you can write comfortably. Adopt early some convenient system of taking — and keeping — notes in the class-rooms and in the library. Above all, supply your desk with a trustworthy dictionary and learn to use it readily and easily.

REFERENCES

Letters that Live by Lockwood and Kelly (Holt); *Letters and Letter-Writing* by Charity Dye (Bobbs, Merrill); *Business English and Correspondence* by Davis and Lingham (Ginn); " The Practical Side of Writing " by R. C. Holliday, No. V., *The Bookman*, July, 1922; *A Manual for Writers* by Manly and Powell (Chicago).

APPENDIX

I

The explanation (in from 600 to 1500 words) of a hobby or a handicraft that you know about from experience. Tell what it is, how it is practiced, and what makes it interesting or valuable. Be sure that you really know your subject. Shun printed information. Rely wholly upon yourself or upon original sources of material. Choose your own subject and submit it to the instructor for approval. Here are some specimen topics. Adapt them to your purpose and phrase your own title:

1. Stamp collecting	21. Insect study
2. Bird study	22. A vegetable garden
3. Pigeon raising	23. The hay harvest
4. Walking tours	24. Army and navy signals
5. Canoe trips	25. Electric bells
6. Camping	26. Carpentry
7. Camp cookery	27. Blacksmithing
8. Amateur publishing	28. Trout fishing
9. Bicycle tours	29. Toy aeroplanes and gliders
10. Amateur wireless sets	30. Kites
11. Snap-shot photography	31. Sail-boats
12. Home cement work	32. Swimming
13. Picture framing	33. Deep-sea fishing
14. Chicken raising	34. Trapping
15. China painting	35. Wrestling
16. Flower gardening	36. Amateur printing
17. Amateur astronomy	37. Taxidermy
18. Belgian hares	38. An herbarium
19. Cake baking	39. Bookbinding
20. The care of a motorcycle	40. Stenciling

II

How some industry or public utility is carried on. Avoid making this a mere generalized narrative, following an article through a process. Analyze the industry into three or four main parts: for example, (1) the plant, (2) the raw material, (3) the process, (4) the finished or delivered product. Before writing, visit the plant, ask questions, and take notes. Learn all that you can about the industry. Read advertising matter and printed reports, if they are available. Do not read encyclopedia or magazine articles. Choose a subject that you can personally learn about:

1. City dairy
2. Ice cream factory
3. Steam laundry
4. The manufacture of gas
5. Telephone exchange
6. Hydro-electric plant
7. Candy factory
8. The manufacture of ice
9. Job-printing plant
10. Brick-yard
11. City water-supply
12. Cannery
13. Iron foundry
14. Bakery
15. Cold-storage plant
16. Street railways
17. Railway switch tower
18. Ship-yards
19. Wagon factory
20. Fish hatchery
21. Rope walk
22. Cooper shop
23. Automobile garage
24. Sewage disposal plant
25. Filtration plant
26. Piano factory
27. Fire-engine house
28. Dry dock
29. Soap factory
30. Daily newspaper
31. Cement works
32. Coal mine
33. Coke furnaces
34. Portrait photography
35. Box factory
36. Grain elevator
37. Creamery
38. A carpet-cleaning establishment
39. A saw mill
40. Glass works

III

A public or semi-public institution. Write only after a personal visit. Use a printed report if it is available, but

rely chiefly on observation and questions. A typical plan
might run as follows: (1) What it is — its origin, government, means of support, organization. (2) What it does
— its agencies and its works. (3) What it signifies — its
service to the public.

1. City Y.M.C.A.
2. Organized charities
3. Hospital
4. Almshouse
5. County jail
6. Public library
7. Orphanage
8. Private school
9. Public education in . . .
10. Museum
11. Institutional church
12. Social settlement
13. The Tax department
14. High school
15. Soldiers' home
16. Health department
17. S.P.C.A.
18. Fresh Air Society
19. Neighborhood improvement
    association
20. Country club

IV

An exercise in constructive imagination. Assuming certain resources, tell how you would use them under imagined
conditions. The explanation may be put into narrative
form, it may be the description of a finished work, or it
may take the form of preliminary plans; but the purpose
is to explain. Be specific.

1. You — a bachelor of thirty — find yourself appointed guardian
to a boy of thirteen, with eight hundred dollars a year for his
expenses. Plan his life for the next four years, until he is ready
to enter college. Characterize the boy and yourself and be
specific. Use narrative form if you choose.

2. Your friend Miss Jones has invited her nephew and his chum,
who are to enter college next fall, to live at her house. Not being
familiar with the needs and tastes of college students, she asks you
to fit up for them two rooms, now unfurnished, to serve as bedroom and study. She allows you three hundred dollars for the
purpose. Assume exact dimensions and be specific.

3. A wealthy man, formerly a resident of your city, has left a
fund of five million dollars to be used for the benefit of the city.

He has appointed you executor with full powers. You give to the reporter of a daily paper an interview explaining the uses to which you expect to devote the trust fund.

4. You are one of four boys who have received from a relative a gift of one thousand dollars, to be used for a permanent camp on the shore of a lake. Tell in detail how you used the money. If you choose, write from the point of view of the generous relative, who goes to visit the completed camp.

5. The Oriental Steel Company employs four hundred boys. Wishing to provide an athletic field for their employes, they set aside six acres of level ground on the water front, and give you ten thousand dollars to use in equipping the field. Tell what you would do with the money.

6. A college literary society has received from the college a suitable room as a meeting place and from three alumni a fund of fifteen hundred dollars for furnishing the room. You are chairman of the committee appointed to expend the fund.

7. You and an intimate friend of your own age have four hundred dollars each to be spent in travel in America during a vacation of two months. Plan the best possible use of the time and money.

8. A friend of yours who is building a new house commissions you to design and make for him a flower garden of one acre. He gives you a fairly level tract, a credit of five hundred dollars for supplies, and the labor of a gardener and an assistant for two spring months.

9. You were invited by your aunt, who lives in the country, to plan a house party for the entertainment of a group of young people three or four days during the Christmas holidays. All the resources of a large farm were at your disposal, and the guests were congenial. The novel and delightful program which you devised was entirely successful. You describe it to a friend in the city who knows your aunt's home.

10. A very busy lawyer has decided to buy an automobile. His mother, his widowed sister, and his little niece live with him. He leaves to you the selection of the car best suited to his needs, and the building of a garage on his lawn. When your plans are all made, you explain them to him in detail, giving approximate cost and showing why you regard your suggestions as wise.

V

" An institution is the lengthened shadow of one man."
Write about such a man in his relation to the institution
with which he is identified. Don't give a " sketch of his
life "; tell only so much as is necessary to make clear
that part of his life in which we are particularly interested.
Use not less than three authorities; for example, the standard biography, a slighter biography, and an encyclopedia
article, with such history references as you find. If your
sources are not adequate, choose another topic. Append
to your theme a list of your authorities, and be careful
to give credit when you use an author's exact words.

1. Fulton and the steamboat
2. Bismarck and the German Empire
3. Lincoln and Emancipation
4. John Paul Jones and American Naval Power
5. Knox and the Scotch Reformation
6. Livingstone and African Missions
7. Franklin and French Intervention in the American Revolution
8. Morse and the Electric Telegraph
9. Field and the Atlantic Cable
10. General Goethals and the Panama Canal

VI

Biographical Studies. The writing of a condensed " life "
of somebody whom you know about only by means of
biographies is hardly a profitable exercise. Choose rather
a single aspect of your character's career or a definite part
of his life. Find several sources, so that you can do more
than merely condense or rephrase the text of your authority. Write about somebody that interests you.

1. Washington as a young man
2. Washington's life at Mt. Vernon
3. Franklin in France

4. Franklin as a citizen of Philadelphia
5. How Lincoln became President
6. The Lincoln-Douglas debates
7. Robert E. Lee before the Civil War
8. Jefferson and the University of Virginia
9. Thomas Paine and the American Revolution
10. Dr. Johnson and his Dictionary
11. Scott at Abbotsford
12. Dickens visits America
13. Longfellow abroad
14. Irving in Old New York
15. Macaulay as a literary worker
16. Hawthorne at Brook Farm
17. George Eliot's girlhood and education
18. Gladstone and the American Civil War
19. Parkman's life among the Indians
20. Stevenson and the outdoor life

VII

My home town. The town or city in which or near which you live may be discussed briefly from a single point of view. The larger the city, the greater the need for limitation of the topic. Tell about its:

1. History
2. Geographical situation
3. Commercial situation
4. General plan
5. Streets
6. Lighting system
7. Sewerage
8. Police
9. School system
10. Form of Government
11. Public spirit
12. Social life
13. Clubs
14. Churches
15. Growth in population
16. Manufactures
17. Natural resources
18. Advantages as a boy's place of residence
19. Parks
20. Library or libraries

VIII

My preparatory school. Write about the school in which you prepared for college, choosing a single and definite point of view. Don't boast or make sweeping comparisons. Avoid weak generalizations. Give the facts, as if to a reader who had asked you questions. Tell, concerning the school, its:

1. History
2. Financial support
3. Government or control
4. Teaching staff
5. Building or buildings
6. Grounds or campus
7. Equipment
8. Heating and ventilation
9. School library
10. Societies
11. Athletic sports
12. Methods of discipline
13. Local customs
14. Plays and entertainments
15. Commencement exercises
16. School paper
17. The most interesting course
18. The hardest course
19. Holidays and public meetings
20. Service to the community

IX

My reading. A theme giving an account of your tastes and habits in reading or growing out of an examination of a book or paper. Limit the subject.

1. My daily newspaper
2. How I read the newspaper
3. The classified advertising
4. The editorial page
5. Special departments in a city daily
6. My reading of periodicals
7. The juvenile periodicals that I liked
8. A comparison of *The Outlook* and *The Independent*
9. *Collier's Weekly* and *The Saturday Evening Post*
10. *The Century Magazine* and *Harper's Magazine*
11. Contrast *Scribner's Magazine* and *The Atlantic Monthly*
12. A periodical that was new to me
13. My own books

14. Books that I would buy with a gift of ten dollars
15. My vacation reading
16. A novel that repaid the reading
17. A character in fiction desirable as a comrade
    Cf. Alan and David Balfour
18. My likes in fiction
19. The most detestable character; e.g., Miss Murdstone
20. Five books for an exploring journey for six months

X

Turning points in history. There are events which, though stirring and significant in themselves, are memorable chiefly for their influence upon history. They are to be written about not as narratives but as facts to be explained. Your outline will include, for example: (1) Briefly, what led up to the event, (2) What happened, (3) What is signified and why:

1. The Signing of the Magna Charta
2. The Defeat of the Armada
3. The Fall of Quebec
4. The Battle of Concord
5. The Signing of the Declaration of Independence
6. The Surrender of Cornwallis
7. The Completion of the Union Pacific Railroad
8. The Attack on Fort Sumter
9. The Monitor and the Merrimac
10. Pickett's Charge

INDEX

References are to pages. Words and phrases cited as examples of faulty or disputed diction are not included in the index; they are listed alphabetically in the text.